Getting Rid *of* Ian

A Memoir of Poison, Pills, and Mortal Sins

Penelope James

Carlyon Books
San Diego

Getting Rid of Ian
A Memoir of Poison, Pills, and Mortal Sins

Author: Penelope James
Cover and Book Design: Marty Safir, Double M Graphics

All the characters, incidents, events, and information in this book are based on actual people, happenings, and conversations. To protect identities, some names have been changed. Both English and American spelling are used according to where events took place or used interchangeably to indicate transition from English to American spelling.

Events and conversations are based on letters, accounts, and journals kept by the author from age 8 to 17. Four chapters have been published as short stories: *Much Ado about a Box* as *A Present from Me to Me* in *Commonties.com* in 2008; *Lord of the Ocean* as *Farewell to England* in *The Mexico City News* in April, 1960; *When Is Murder Not a Mortal Sin?* in *A Year in Ink Anthology #8*; *Salting Ian* as *Witchcraft in Memoirabilia Magazine #5*.

ISBN: 978-0-9967538-0-7

Published by
Carlyon Books
San Diego
www.carlyonbooks.com

To Charles
With thanks
Penelope James

In memory of my inimitable parents, Tita and Jimmy.

For my sister and co-conspirator, Anne,
and for Christopher who made this possible.

Contents

1

LEAVE IT UP TO GOD
Mexico City, 1955

"We must get rid of him," I tell my younger sister Anne. We're in my bedroom with the door closed, but I'm whispering. Ian might hear us—he has ears everywhere. "Let's pray for him to die."

"That's a mortal sin," Anne says with horror in her voice.

"No, it isn't. All we'll do is ask God to make it happen sooner rather than later."

"We can't ask God for things like that," Anne says.

I'd like to shake her—she's so stubborn. Drive some sense into her head. She's ten. I'm almost two years older, and I know what's best. "If Ian dies, Mummy won't be in a state of sin anymore, and Ian's family will probably forgive him for marrying Mummy. And he won't go to hell because his daughter's a nun."

"It still doesn't seem right," she says.

"Come on, Anne," I say, like Daddy did when he wanted her to understand something. "Think of what happened in the war. Both sides prayed to God for victory. We won because the Americans joined us, and there were more people praying on our side. Why don't we leave it up to God?"

Anne gives in.

We go to the church and light candles and kneel, but I'm

1

not comfortable praying for Ian to die. It isn't as easy as talking about it. So, all I ask is, "Please, dear God, just get rid of Ian."

Three days later, Ian has a coronary thrombosis.

"See," I tell Anne. "God is on our side."

2

BLAME IT ON THE WAR
England, 1950

Who knows what got into Mummy and Daddy when they met in New York City during the Second World War? Mummy fell for Daddy, a Commander in the Royal Navy, because he looked so distinguished in his uniform. Daddy thought Mummy was the most attractive girl he'd seen in a long time—and he was fussy—and he found her very funny. They liked each other enough to get married three weeks later.

"We did things in wartime that we wouldn't dream of doing in peacetime," Mummy tells me. "Like marrying someone you hardly knew."

When Daddy took off his Royal Navy uniform, Mummy didn't like him half as much as before. And when he brought Mummy to England, he didn't find her as funny as before.

So far, that's what Mummy has told me.

I'm with her in her bedroom, watching her put on her face before we go out to buy my school uniforms. Most of the time, she sits at her dressing table; it has a skirt with pink taffeta flounces, and the top is covered with perfume bottles, her grandmother's silver hair set, and a three-sided mirror so she can take a jolly good look at herself.

"You see, I married a stranger," she says. "A man eighteen years older who came from a very different background."

Mummy is American, but she's also half-Mexican. A long time ago, her American father went to Mexico as a foreign correspondent and met her mother there. Mummy was born in New York and grew up in Mexico City. Her name is Carlota, but everyone calls her Tita. She's not like other mummies because of her Bad Leg from a plane crash when she was twenty-one. That's why she has to take care of herself and can't hurry in the morning. She keeps the pieces of the crucifix she was holding when the plane crashed inside a case under her pillow because she's sure it saved her life.

She smiles at me. "Your daddy was in a hurry to be married before he was ordered back to England. So he didn't give me time to think about what I was getting into. I spent my wedding night crying my eyes out."

"Did Daddy make you cry?"

"No, your daddy tried to console me and he was so kind, I decided to make the best of it."

Mummy tilts her head and looks at her cheek in the side mirror. "But I really blame my mother. She wouldn't let me postpone the wedding."

"Granny-in-Mexico?" That's what Anne and I call her because we also have Granny-in-England.

"She told me, 'You're twenty-six and you'd better not waste this chance to marry a Royal Navy officer. And she hadn't taken three airplanes and a train to travel from Mexico to New York City for nothing."

She puts her elbow on her dressing table and rests her chin on her hand, as if she's thinking. "Though looking back, I needed someone like your daddy who understood me. He's the one man, apart from my father, who appreciates my mind."

Mummy's mind is very important to her. She's always talking about how she has a lot on her mind, and she will go out of her mind if Daddy doesn't do something to make money, and how she needs to stimulate her mind, which is why she goes up to London whenever she can.

Mummy studies her face in the mirror as if she doesn't like what she sees. "You have to suffer to be beautiful," she says and picks up her tweezers and plucks her eyebrow.

I go "Ouch!" inside. I don't want to be beautiful and have to suffer like she does.

Mummy suffers a lot. Because Daddy goes around with his head in the clouds. And because she can't see her parents in Mexico as often as she'd like. And because the plane crash ruined her life and gave her a Bad Leg.

She picks up a pencil and draws her eyebrows where she likes them to be. "Our love had to grow after we were married because there wasn't time before. And, of course, your daddy gave me my two lovely daughters."

I'm seven, with long fair hair and dreamy blue eyes like Daddy's. My name is Penelope, Penny for short. My parents named me after the HMS Penelope because they met at a cocktail party on board that ship. I was born right here in Rustington after they arrived in a convoy.

My sister Anne was born up north. Mummy calls her a "Lancashire lassie." She's five, and pretty, with a round face and golden curls. But when she doesn't get her own way, she throws a tantrum. Grace, our help, says, "Who would believe a little angel like her would be such a handful?"

Most of the time, I try to behave myself, but I have a big imagination. That's where a younger sister comes in useful. Anne will do anything I ask her to do. Like dumping water on Grace after she tells me off. Or picking a fight with a boy who was mean to me. Or helping me build a prison behind the hedge where we're going to hold him captive along with the slugs and snails and worms. But I'm glad when Anne's not around because then I have all the attention for myself.

I'm hoping Mummy will hurry up and not chat for hours the way she does with friends. Once when I was on holiday, Aunty Vera came to call when Mummy was in the tub. She went right in even though the bathroom was all steamed up and Mummy was lying there naked. Aunty Vera sat on the laundry basket and they talked for an hour.

The phone rings. Oh, no. Mummy can spend forever on it. She says, "Hello," and then "Yes, this is Mrs. James," and listens a minute and says, "I'm very sorry. My husband didn't tell me," and "I'll resolve this without delay."

She hangs up and gives me one of her looks. Her eyes are like two dark coals in the fireplace. "Can't Jimmy do anything right?" When she calls Daddy "Jimmy" or "your father" to me, I know something is wrong.

"What's the matter, Mummy?"

"Your father hasn't paid the grocer in over a month, and they refuse to deliver any more groceries until we pay them twenty-five pounds. Where are we going to find that amount? The problem is, the grocer wants what we owe him right now." She goes on, working herself up, until at last she says, "I have an idea. Those silver goblets that your father's commanding officer gave us when we were married, I'm going to sell them. Jimmy won't like it, but what else can I do? Now, where was I before that call?"

"As soon as you're ready, we're going to buy my uniforms."

She takes a cigarette out of her silver cigarette case and lights it. "I need to calm down and clear my mind. Jimmy offered me security, and I believed him. I thought he'd bring me here to England, and we'd live in comfort, instead of wondering where our next meal is coming from." She blows out smoke and flicks her cigarette in an ashtray.

Hurry up, Mummy. Instead she glances around her bedroom, which has everything to make her comfortable,

6

including a chaise longue. Daddy has his own room where he can get some sleep if Mummy wants the bed to herself. Or when she cuddles with us and tells us stories that go on and on. Every time she's at the end, Anne says, "I want more," and Mummy starts another.

"I've come to love this house, but you should have seen it when the GIs left. I had to scrape the bathtub with a knife—it was covered with chewing gum. And they dug a trench in the back lawn and ruined it forever." She picks up her powder puff and dabs on Elizabeth Arden powder. "I love this country as well, but not what's happening here. We gladly made sacrifices in the war, but it's 1950. Why should we still be going without, years after it ended? As Shakespeare says, 'Life is as tedious as a twice-told tale.'" When Mummy went to Sarah Lawrence College, she fell in love with Mr. William Shakespeare, and she recites things he wrote all the time.

Then she says, "I must get a move on, or we'll never do anything," and stops talking. What will she wear? In Rustington nobody dresses up much—except for Mummy. She pulls out a summer dress and holds it against her while she looks in the mirror. "No, this isn't right for today." She takes out another dress, studies it, and puts it away. "What a pity, all my lovely clothes going to waste here." With a sigh she chooses a skirt with red flowers on it and a white blouse. I help her dress as Mummy finds it hard to do it on her own, and I make sure the lines on the backs of her stockings are straight.

"How do I look, Penny?"

I tell her, "Very pretty." She beams at me. Mummy always wants to hear nice things about the way she looks.

Downstairs, she collects the goblets and puts them into a bag, which she hands to me to carry. "I hope they give me a good price for them," she says.

It's two blocks to the bus stop, but Mummy has a hard

time walking there because of her Bad Leg. After her plane crash, when the doctors stuck it together again, they left it shorter than the other. Her Bad Leg has long scars all the way down the front, criss-crossed with other scars from all the operations on it, and it's very thin with a bump near the bottom. "It's a miracle I can walk as well as I do," she says, "and that's thanks to your daddy; he took me on long walks when we were first married."

We get onto the bus, and all the seats are taken. She acts like she's losing her balance, and cries out, "I'm a cripple. I have to sit down." Three people stand and offer her their seats, and she limps over to one in the front row, gasping as if she can hardly breathe, sinks into it, and sighs, "Oh, oh, OH," sounding like she's in pain. People turn around and stare at her. She pats the seat next to her that someone else gave up for me to sit there.

My face must be bright red. Everyone else is quiet and minding their own business, the way English people behave, but they can't help hearing what Mummy has to say in her loud American voice. English people don't raise their voices or draw attention to themselves, but she always does wherever she goes. She tells me how she wants to go to Mexico and have her Bad Leg seen to because pieces of metal from her plane crash are coming out. I glance around and people are listening, though when they see my eyes on them, they look up at the ceiling or down at their feet.

We get off the bus on the main street in Worthing, a town much bigger than Rustington. It has department stores and a pier and hotels on the beach for holidaymakers.

We go into Letts Antiques, and Mummy walks to the counter and asks the man there if he will buy her goblets. She pulls them out, and he examines them and says they have nicks in them and they're not perfect. "I can give you five shillings for each one."

She's says, "No, they're worth a lot more than that," and we walk out. It's a hot summer day, and I'd love to sit on the beach and have an ice cream, but Mummy says we have business to attend to. We go to another store that says Pier Pawnshop. The man there offers Mummy three pounds for the six goblets. By now, I can see she's beside herself, and hot and tired from walking around. "These goblets are worth at least two pounds each," she says.

"Perhaps, but not if you pawn them. The good thing is that you have three months to redeem them," he tells her.

She's thoughtful. "My godfather should be in London next month. I can redeem them then." Every six months or so, Mr. Waswick comes and stays at Claridge's Hotel in London. She goes up to see him, and he gives her a check to pay off bills and buy new clothes and toys for Anne and me.

"Right now I need more than what you're offering for the goblets." She taps her long red fingernails on the counter, then looks up as if searching for an answer. "Dear God, enlighten me." Suddenly, she holds out her hand, palm down with fingers stretched out towards the man. "How much will you give me for my engagement ring?"

He stares at it. "I need to take a look."

She pulls it off and hands it to him. He uses a magnifying glass. "One carat," he says, "but it's not a perfect diamond."

"Oh, yes, it is."

"It has a flaw. Thirty pounds."

"It's worth much more than that."

"Madam, this is a pawnshop, not a jewelry store."

She frowns, stares at the ring, puts it back on her finger, and takes it off again. "All right," she says. "I'll redeem it, of course."

The man nods and puts it in an envelope. He gives Mummy a bunch of five-pound notes for the ring and three one-pound notes for the goblets.

We leave the store and Mummy says, "Now I can pay the grocer. And we'll have lunch and buy your uniforms." We walk over to Bentall's. She stops outside the window. "I like those dresses," she says. "What do you think?"

"They're lovely, but Mummy, can we afford them?"

She turns fierce eyes on me.

"I hocked my engagement ring to pay for the food on our table, so if I want to buy new dresses for you and your sister, that's my prerogative." She points at the window. "Would you like that one, Penny?"

I stare at the blue dress with the flouncy skirt and the sash at the back, and imagine myself in it.

"I will feel like a princess," I tell her.

3

THE MAN WHO INVENTED THINGS

Daddy thinks. It's what he does. Most daddies go out to work, but Daddy thinks instead. Thinking isn't easy, and there aren't many people who can do it. Daddy is an inventor, and that's why it's important for him to think a lot. If his inventions catch on, he'll become rich and famous. Then he won't have to sell his shares, and we can pay off our bills, and Mummy won't nag him anymore or say that he goes around with his head in the clouds.

When he's thinking, his eyebrows come together and nearly join over his long nose, and his eyes lose their dreamy expression. You'd swear he'd swallowed a whole bag of toffees. Say something to him, and he doesn't answer. He's too busy thinking.

Mummy tells us not to interrupt him, and then she does just that. "Jimmy, you didn't wash the dishes," or, "Don't forget the greengrocer's." She can't understand how busy he is inside his head. She keeps after him until he walks to the beach where he can think in peace.

Most of the time Daddy invents in his head—things he's going to invent once he's sold the ones he's working on. He has a workshop where he paints everything bright blue, and because he's always gluing things, his crumpled old clothes smell of paint and glue.

Mummy asks, "Whatever happened to the distinguished commander I married?"

He has a helper, Jock, in his workshop. Jock isn't all there in the head because he was blown up during the War. He's quite harmless, not like the dirty old men from the veterans' home who go around scaring little girls. Jock's head is lopsided, so his smile comes out on one side of his face. Most of his fingers are gone, but he's handy with what is left.

Daddy buys patents to stop people from stealing his inventions. Mummy is cross because he's throwing away money on them. Daddy always answers that we'll have plenty of money once he sells his inventions, but he needs the patents. "In the meantime please, Tita, children, don't tell anyone what I invent."

That's hard because people keep asking, "What does your daddy invent?"

All we can say is, "Things."

"What kind of things?"

"Just things."

That makes people even more curious.

Daddy says, "Tell them I invent atom bombs." He means it as a joke, but Anne takes it seriously and so do some people. They say how exciting to have an atom-bomb inventor living down the lane, but others, led by Mrs. Snook, who Mummy calls a busybody, come to the door to tell him they can't have someone inventing dangerous things like bombs in our village. What would happen if one blew up accidentally?

"Don't worry," he says," that's a silly story I told the children," but I don't think they believe him because I hear Mrs. Snook saying, "That man is up to no good."

Then Anne, who can't keep a secret, tells everybody that Daddy invents doors and boats and beach huts. So now they're saying that's odd—why would Daddy want to invent things that have been around for years?

Mummy keeps at him to stop wasting his time and find a job so we can pay our bills. Since his mother is too tight to help us out, her parents in Mexico have been sending us money.

"There aren't any jobs for men my age," he says. "Not with a million men out of work in Britain."

One afternoon Daddy and I bump into Hoare who used to be our odd-job man when we were well-off. Hoare tells Daddy the government is giving away money to people who need it, and why doesn't Daddy go to the Assistance Office to fill out a form?

Daddy stands as straight as if he was on parade and listens without smiling. I can see he's annoyed and doesn't want to ask the government for money, but we could do with it so I tell Mummy what Hoare told us. It makes her angry. Who does Daddy think he is not to accept money from the government?

He says he can't because if the government finds out about his inventing things, they won't let him go on doing it. Besides, we don't need their help.

That night, they have a row and Mummy's voice is so loud, it wakes me up. "Jimmy, if you go on like this, we'll lose this house." Where do people with no homes live? I fall asleep and dream I'm Little Nell in a story by Charles Dickens, dancing to death to earn money to stay alive.

Daddy invents our beach hut; it's made of plywood, with a curved roof and is painted creamy white, not at all like the grey sheds of weather-beaten planks along the beach. What's more, Daddy stands our hut on the bluff on its own instead of down on the shingle with all the other beach huts. I'm not sure I like being different from everyone else.

Most of all, Mummy dislikes his model catamarans. We come back from visiting friends in London to find the whole house stinking of glue. Daddy's been cooking his boats in her oven.

"It's the fastest way to dry the glue," he says. The models don't look like much: two blue plywood shafts, each about a foot long and crossed by what Daddy calls a rectangular aluminum mast. Daddy takes Anne and me to sail them on public ponds. They whiz along like blue streaks and make people mad because they're in the way or crash into other people's sailboats.

Each catamaran has a sticker with Daddy's name and address on its metal sail. We carry a bunch of them down to the sea, and he tells us to put them in the water and let them sail away to who knows where? Everyone on the beach watches as they speed off down the coast, a dozen blue specks on the sea.

I hear Mrs. Snook say, "That man must be daft."

Letters arrive. People are picking up the catamarans all down the South Coast. A postcard comes from a man in France and a story comes out in the local paper, *The Littlehampton Gazette*. People stop Daddy on the street. "Who would believe it of a tiny little thing like that?"

Ripley's Believe-It-Or-Not gets hold of the story of the toy catamaran that crossed the Channel.

Daddy is famous.

He isn't happy about *Ripley's* calling his model catamaran a "toy" because people want to buy them to play with. He wants to build full-scale catamarans and not waste his time making toys. "I still have to iron out a few details," he says.

Someone talks to Mummy on the phone. They want five hundred toy catamarans for the Olympia Boat Show, the biggest, most important in the world. Mummy says yes, of course, and she takes the order, but Daddy doesn't think he can make that many in six weeks.

She urges him on. "For God's sakes, Jimmy, do something. I'm sure they will take as many as you can send them." Daddy gives in and gets cracking with the help of Jock and some of the older orphans who live at the orphanage but are on summer holiday. It's no good. He can't fill the order in time for the show, so he's left with a lot of little catamarans. He sells some to toy shops and uses the money to pay the grocer and the butcher's bills.

Daddy builds a big catamaran that he goes sailing in instead of his old sailboat. He's practically the only person in England who has one because catamarans come from the South Seas, and the Channel is too rough for them. He wants to prove that catamarans do work here and then everyone will want one. It's in the experimental stages, so he won't let anyone else go out in it. The two six-foot-long shafts are bright blue, and it has four red crosswise sails. The catamaran rides so low on the water that we can just about see it from the beach.

Mummy has nothing nice to say about it. "It looks like something rigged up by a castaway," and, "Jimmy, you love your catamaran more than your family," and, "The only way I know you're still alive is when I see the red sail bobbing on the horizon."

Sometimes he sails out so far we can't see him at all.

When she keeps at him, he tells her, "Tita, if you go on like that, I might do a Mr. Ball on you." I know he's joking but I can't help worrying. One day last fall, Mr. Ball went off to the air show at Bigham Hill with two quid in his pocket and didn't come home. The police went looking for him. It turned out he'd run off with a blonde bombshell from Brighton and he never came back.

*

Good news, Daddy's found an investor to put up money: a Mr. Pinkerton who believes that big catamarans have a future on the South Coast. Mr. P. comes to tea and has to sit on the sofa because he doesn't fit into an armchair. He's one person

15

who hasn't felt the post-war pinch. He finishes most of the cucumber sandwiches and tea cakes and three slices of Victoria sponge cake.

"That man eats like Henry the Eighth," Mummy says after he leaves. "Don't ever invite him for a meal."

Daddy tells Mr. P. the catamaran is still in the experimental stage, but Mr. P. says if he's investing his money, he wants to go sailing in it. So Daddy takes him out, and Mr. P. likes it so much he says yes, he will invest. He starts coming down every weekend so he can keep on going out in Daddy's catamaran.

There is nothing better than a good summer's day at the beach. A nice hot sun, a spotting of clouds in the blue sky, the wind a light breeze, and the water swaying lazily on a Sunday afternoon. People lie on blankets on the shingle* or outside their huts and have their teas. There are some sailboats out towards Littlehampton, two miles away, but except for a couple of dinghies, Daddy's catamaran with its red sail is all we can see on the water.

We have a picnic hamper with cheddar cheese and Marmite sandwiches, and Cadbury's chocolate biscuits, and a bottle of orangeade, and a thermos of hot tea. Daddy has rigged up a windscreen and an awning, and Mummy is quite comfortable in a beach chair reading her *Ladies' Home Journal* from America. Anne and I play on the breakwaters—wooden stumps like ragged soldiers—while they are still dry, before the water makes them slimy and slippery. They're as much a part of our beach as the sand. Anne gets up and down them in no time at all. She follows me all over the place. Mummy tells me I have to look after her, even when I don't want to.

Anne and I go in to bathe where the sea forms a cove between the breakwaters. All of a sudden she starts howling.

---

* shingle, a mound of rocks and stones and shells stretching along the seashore.

16

I think she's hurt her foot on a sharp shell, but she's pointing out to sea and screaming, "Daddy's gone down!"

Where moments before there was a red sail, now there is nothing. But catamarans aren't supposed to capsize. Daddy told me that.

I try to shut her up. "Daddy will be all right, I know he will," because it's the only way of telling myself he can't have drowned. Anne runs up the shingle crying, "Daddy's gone down!" all the way to the hut. I'm sure everyone on the beach hears her.

Mummy jumps up, and when she can't see anything, calls, "Help! Help! My husband's capsized!"

Other people stand to take a look and point out to sea. A man comes running over with some field glasses. "Here, see for yourself. Your husband's boat turned over, that's all."

"Thank God, my Jimmy's alive!" she shrieks. We take turns peering through the field glasses. Daddy and Mr. P. are swimming around the upside-down catamaran.

Somebody says a man has gone to phone for help, but who knows how long it will take. Somebody else says they will look for a man who owns a motor boat. Mummy asks our neighbour, Mr. Tilston, if he can go out in his boat and pick up Daddy. But Mrs. Tilston makes a face. "We're having our tea."

"Don't worry," Mr. Tilston says. "They have something to hang onto and a boating accident on a calm day isn't much of a problem. They'll have it right side up in no time."

He's trying to be kind, I know, but Mummy's angry. "Don't tell me not to worry. Why do you British have to be so stiff-upper-lip about everything? Can't you go out in your rowboat?"

Mr. Tilston glances at Mrs. Tilston's set face. "I'll go as soon as I've finished my tea."

We go back to our hut. Mummy is trembling. "I can't

17

believe these cold-blooded Englishmen would rather finish their tea than go to the rescue of their fellow men. What if your daddy drowns in the meantime?"

After what Mr. Tilston said, I'm not worried anymore. Daddy isn't going to drown, not on a day like today, and Mummy is all worked up as usual. So is Anne, who's crying.

The whole beach is watching Daddy and Mr. P. Some people stand on the higher part of the shingle to have a better view. Out come more field glasses and telescopes. They point at us, and a few come over to ask if there's anything they can do. We're the most important people on the beach. So why isn't someone doing something to rescue Daddy and Mr. P.?

Mummy is sobbing. "I'll be left a widow because the entire beach sat and watched two men drown."

Anne, the show-off, tells everybody that it's her daddy out there, and people give her sweets and biscuits so she will be brave. I stay with Mummy. I have to stop her from behaving as if Daddy has drowned and gone to heaven.

"Boats like that catsaman thing ought to be banned," Mrs. Snook says in a loud voice so we can hear her. "I knew the Commander would come a-cropper fiddling with those things."

"That woman sounds like a fishwife," Mummy says to me. Then, raising her voice, she tells Mrs. Snook, "The correct name is catamaran." Mrs. Snook's face twists and she turns away.

A man comes over and says he works for *The Littlehampton Gazette*. Does Mummy mind answering a few questions? "Don't you think it might be a bit risky to sail this kind of craft in the Channel?" he asks.

"To tell the truth," Mummy says, "I worry all the time about my husband's safety."

The man takes notes of everything. Why is she telling this to him? She does have a way of sticking her foot into it.

At long last Mr. Tilston and another man carry a boat

down the shingle. It takes ages for them to row out to where Daddy and Mr. P. are hanging on. We watch through the field glasses as Daddy seems to be arguing with them. Then he ties the catamaran to the rowboat and climbs in. Mr. P. can't. I suppose it's because he's so fat. He has to be towed in along with the catamaran. When he comes out of the water, he looks like a washed-up whale. Daddy is drenched, but from what I can see, none the worse off.

Mummy and Anne run down the shingle to greet him, both shouting at the top of their lungs. Mummy cries, "Jimmy, I thought we had lost you."

"I'm all right, Tita," Daddy says in an impatient voice.

The man from the *Gazette* asks if he still thinks it's safe to sail this craft in the Channel.

"This catamaran is in an experimental stage," Daddy says. "It's not ready for the general public." His face is stern, not his usual nice one. Maybe because he's wet and tired.

Mr. P. is in a bad mood. He sits in Mummy's beach chair and doesn't say anything. He's angry because the catamaran turned over, but it was really his fault because of his weight. Next weekend, he sends Daddy a letter saying he isn't interested in catamarans anymore.

The story comes out on the front page of *The Littlehampton Gazette.*

"South Sea Craft No Match For Channel Waters."

Daddy is famous again.

4

WHEN LIFE WAS SO TENDER

On Sunday, Mummy cooks breakfast. A proper breakfast, not the porridge or cereal Daddy gives us every day. She makes baked eggs, one each in its little glass bowl with butter and cream from the top of the milk. Then we go with Mummy to half-past-ten mass at Saint Joseph's. It's the one day that she has to hurry. "Mass is much too early, and I haven't put my face on. The good Lord will understand." Quite often, she wears a hat with a veil. "It covers a multitude of sins," she says.

I try to follow the Mass, using the prayer book Granny-in-Mexico gave me, but it's rather boring, and I daydream until Anne pulls my arm to kneel.

At home, we find Daddy singing in the kitchen while he packs a picnic lunch. As he's busy, I look at the paper, but the part I want isn't there. Daddy must have hidden it. He says I'm too young to read about Peter the Great of Russia who fell in love with Catherine, a tavern maid in Lithuania. I find it, behind the cushions on his armchair, and take a quick look. This week it's about how Peter the Great imprisoned his son in a dungeon, and as if that wasn't enough, murdered him. Even worse, he impaled—I don't know what "impaled" means but I guess—thousands of his enemies on spikes. I wouldn't have missed reading this for the world.

I go into the living room and pick Mummy's *Metropolitan Book of the Opera* from the bookcases there. I like the stories, though most of them end in people dying. One is about Jason who went off in search of the Golden Fleece and left his wife, Medea. When he married someone else, Medea murdered his bride. Then she killed her own children and went crazy with grief. Almost everyone in operas dies. I bet you they just keep on singing at the top of their lungs to the very end.

Down at the beach, we can't go in swimming because the tide's way out and left a long line of rocks. Anne and I don't like clambering over them and getting cuts on our feet or crabs pinching our toes. The poor little boys from the orphanage are paddling in the shallow water past the rocks. I know it's them because they don't wear bathing suits and I can see their pink bottoms. Riders canter by on horseback. People are flying kites, building sandcastles, playing with balls, having races, and digging in the sand.

We eat cold roast lamb sandwiches and potato salad, and Daddy slices up a Mars bar. We have to share it because sweets are rationed, even though the War ended six years ago.

"It's such a lovely day," Mummy says, "I wish we weren't expected at your mother's."

When Mummy and Daddy arrived in Rustington, Granny, Grandpa who died last year, and Aunty Rena met them at the railway station. Mummy had taken special care to look nice. She didn't know that Granny didn't like Americans much because the Duchess of Windsor made King Edward VII abdicate and marry her. The way Mummy tells it, "Your granny walked towards us as if she had a ramrod up her back, and she held out her hand and said, 'How do you do?' I felt like I'd been doused in cold water. Your Aunty Rena gave me a hug and said she'd help me settle in. She was jolly and frumpy in her knitted clothes. She promised to look after me, and she did, in her way."

Granny won't come to our house. Years ago she moved the furniture around when Mummy was out. Mummy came back and didn't like what Granny had done and said some nasty things to her. Though Mummy sent an apology note asking her forgiveness, Granny swore she'd never set foot in our house again, and she's been as good as her word. Anyway, she doesn't leave her house much anymore. Not even for a walk.

Mummy calls Daddy "Jimmy," short for James, because she feels his name "Randolph" sounds too formal and she doesn't like "Dolph," which is what Granny and Aunty call him. Maybe she just wants to be different.

Daddy sees Granny almost every afternoon, which annoys Mummy. She tells him he has an Edipus complex. I look up Edipus in the Bible. He's not there. Then I look for him in the *Metropolitan Book of the Opera* and he's there spelled with an O before the E. He was a Greek king who married his own mother because he didn't know who she was. Since Daddy didn't marry his mother, why does Mummy tell him that?

We'd love to stay at the beach all afternoon but at half-past-three, Daddy tells us to hurry. We have to be at Granny's at four on the dot.

Granny has a scent like old flowers. It fills the house no matter where she is. She's prettier than other old ladies. Mummy says Granny's kept her looks because she takes very good care of herself, spends every Saturday in bed, and lets Aunty do all the housework.

Granny's lips hardly move as she says, "Did you have a nice day at the beach?" She speaks slowly, as if it's hard for her to move her mouth. Everyone is afraid of her.

I'm not sure I love Granny, and I'm not sure she loves me. Daddy says, "Granny is very affectionate. She just doesn't know how to show it."

Aunty Rena is the opposite of Granny, always smiling and bouncing around, though Mummy says she has a chip on her shoulder because she lost out in life and never married. She doesn't seem to mind about losing out in life, except she's very bossy and likes to tell everybody off, even Daddy who's her younger brother.

For tea Aunty has made a fruitcake and a lemon cake with hard, white icing. "Have you been good little girls this week?" Granny asks, and we say "Yes, please," and we have a slice of each.

They like to talk about the War. They were glad when it ended, but nobody likes the way things are now, with all the shortages and rationing and unemployment. Daddy says a man his age doesn't stand a chance. Not with so many young men out of work.

It's still daylight when we leave. Anne and I are in front on the tricycle. She's on the handlebars and I'm peddling for all I'm worth, and Mummy and Daddy walk behind.

"You'd think she'd do more to help us out," Mummy says, "since Penny and Anne are her only grandchildren."

"Mother doesn't look at it that way. She still believes I have most of my shares."

"She will find out you sold them and then what will you tell her? We need her to help us out now."

"I don't want to ask her, not yet."

"Not until we're all dying of hunger."

"Tita, do you have to be so dramatic about everything?"

Mummy says, "Tell your mother the quality of mercy is not strained."

"I doubt very much if my mother would appreciate having Shakespeare quoted at her," Daddy says.

*

Mummy doesn't like to be reminded of her plane crash.

23

Then she talks about it all the time. "It's a miracle I'm alive," she says, "and I can walk. Thanks to Dr. Philip Wilson in New York who saved my leg when the other doctors wanted to cut it off. I told them no, I was going to dance again."

She tells us about her plane crash in bits and pieces. "We were struck by lightning at twelve thousand feet and crashed into *El Cofre de Perote*." Which I think means Perote's Coffin or mountaintop. She calls her plane crash "the dark shadow that stole my youth." She was twenty-one when it happened. An Indian saw the plane fall out of the skies and he ran towards it thinking it was an angel from Heaven. Then he heard Mummy scream and pulled her out of the flames. But he couldn't save the two young men. She thinks one of them, Peter, died when they crashed, but the other one, Danny, was too tall to get out of the plane, and he may have burned to death.

The crash made headlines because Danny was the American President Roosevelt's nephew and Peter came from a well-known American family, the Harrimans. The story came out in all the newspapers and *Time* magazine and Mummy was famous for being in the crash with them.

Afterwards, Mummy had lots of operations, as many as eighteen. That's why she loves going to the doctor and taking medicines and talking about how her leg or her back aches and how she suffers all the time being sick. She likes us to be sick, as well, because she can look after us. Sometimes if we don't want to go to school, we say we're not feeling well. Anne's very good at pretending, but I have to be really sick to stay at home. Like today, I have a bad cold and I'm lying in Mummy's chaise longue when Daddy comes to say he's off to his workshop and Grace called to say she'll try to come in.

"I wish Mr. Waswick would come to town," Mummy says. "I sorely miss my godfather."

I miss him as well. Whenever he's in London, he helps

us out and gives Mummy a nice present. Two years before, he paid a famous artist, William Longstaff, to paint her portrait in her wedding dress. In it, Mummy has a lovely face, but it isn't her. When Daddy saw it, he said, "I like the backdrop." Mr. Longstaff hung it in his exhibition at the Royal Academy, and now it's downstairs in the living room.

There's a knock on the door. Mummy says, "Come in."

"Good morning, madam." It's pretty, plump Grace with her yellow hair and bright red lipstick. She gives Mummy a kiss on her cheek.

"Oh, Grace, I'm so glad you came. I have a sick child on my hands. Sit down a moment."

Grace sits and they talk about the weather, and which princess is prettier: Mummy says Princess Elizabeth, and Grace and I say Princess Margaret.

The next you know, in barges Aunty Vera. "So here you are," she says. "When nobody answered, I let myself in the back."

Aunty Vera isn't a real aunt, just a friend. She looks like pictures of Queen Elizabeth I, with curly red hair poking out under her round hat and hairnet. She's wearing a purple jacket, a flaring black skirt, a long strand of pearls, and white gloves. And no knickers. I know she doesn't wear any because Mummy told me one day they went to a concert, and Aunty Vera had to climb over some chairs to reach her seat. Mummy and everybody else who was looking could see her hair down there was also red.

She says, "I'll sit next to Penny and keep you company. How old are you now, Penny?"

"I was eight last August."

"I say! You're a big girl." She turns to Mummy. "I'm going up to London. Our flat there has been empty too long, and I want to go to the theatre. Why don't you come too?"

"I don't know if we can afford it," Mummy says.

25

"Then I'll invite you," Aunty Vera tells her. So Mummy goes to London and stays five days. She borrows money for shopping and buys herself, and us, winter coats.

Daddy isn't pleased. "The girls already have their school coats. They won't wear these much."

"They are like the ones the princesses used to wear," Mummy says, "and they'll last forever."

"I'm afraid they won't," Daddy says. "The girls will grow out of them in a year."

*

In early October, Mummy says, "Jimmy, children, I'm going to have a spinal fusion. I'll spend several months in the Royal Orthopaedic Hospital in London."

"What's a spinal fusion?" Anne asks.

"It's an operation to heal my back so it won't hurt anymore," Mummy says. "It was injured in the plane crash, but the doctors didn't realize because they were so busy trying to save my leg. The problem's at my fifth vertebra. If it's not attended to, I'll be paralyzed for life."

Daddy and Anne have the same look of shock that I must have. We're tired of listening to Mummy complain about how much her back hurts, but it's true and it sounds awful. Months in hospital. Over Christmas. She tells us, "Your daddy will look after you while I'm away. I suppose you will eat at Granny's on weekends."

Anne and I make faces. That is not good news.

Before Mummy leaves, she makes a Victoria sponge cake and little biscuits that she calls cookies and lets us help beat the mixture and we lick the spoons. We're all so happy, and the kitchen smells so good, and Mummy is smiling that we forget this is her last day and in a while she will have a dreadful operation and not be here for months.

*

26

Aunty Rena serves us each a big slice of meat pie with a thick, salty crust and gravy. I'd give anything to wash it down with water, but Granny doesn't let us drink any with our meals. She eats very slowly, clacking her cutlery on her plate, and expects us to follow her example.

"Eating fast is bad for your digestion," she says.

Aunty comes in from the kitchen and plunks her plate on the table.

"So you're going up to London to see your mother?" she asks. "My word, that spinal fusion is taking a long time. What's it been? Three months." She stops to chew and swallow her food and then says, "Who would have thought that was the matter? She kept saying her back was hurting. Those Mexican doctors must have been blind not to notice her back was broken."

"They were trying to save her leg," Daddy says, but Aunty doesn't pay attention and goes on. "She's very fortunate we have the National Health. In any other country she'd have to pay a fortune for that operation."

Today's sweet is gooseberry pie. With custard.

"Penny's allergic to custard," Anne says.

"What does that mean?" Aunty asks.

Daddy says, "People get tummy upsets from eating things that don't agree with them."

Aunty sniffs. "Well, I never. What will they dream up next?"

Poor Aunty. From what I've heard, being a spinster is the worst thing that can happen to a woman. Mummy says spinsters are hot-tempered like Aunty or frustrated because they never found fulfilment. It's a pity because there are a lot of spinsters in England who were left behind when their young men were killed in the First World War. Although Aunty doesn't seem to mind being a spinster. I suppose she got used to it.

After we finish Granny makes us stay sitting down for

half an hour to finish digesting our food while the grown-ups talk about shares that Mummy calls stocks. The way Granny and Daddy talk about them sounds like a game. I know Daddy doesn't want Granny to find out he's sold most of his shares because she will tell him off.

While Mummy's away, Daddy prepares our teas of toasted cheese sandwiches or baked beans or sardines on toast, and sometimes we have scones and honey. He lets us stay up late to listen to light comedies on the wireless. One of our favourites, *Life With the Lyons,* is about an American family living in England. Bebe Daniels Lyons has such a slur it can't be real. The other is *Take It From Here* with Dick Bentley and Jimmy Edwards. Daddy goes around the house singing, "Take it from here, you can take it from here," at the top of his lungs.

At half-term, we go up to London to see Mummy at the Royal Orthopaedic Hospital. Mummy is in King's Ward with five other ladies. She cries when she sees us. Anne cries as well.

"Have you missed me?" Mummy asks.

Anne says yes.

"I miss your cooking," I tell her.

"The operation was worse than I expected. You almost lost your mother," Mummy says.

Daddy tells her, "But Tita, you came through it all right, and now you're getting better."

"It was very painful," she says, "and I'm still weak. At first I could hardly move my arms and had to be fed like a baby. This plaster cast is very uncomfortable. Do you want to see it?"

The cast is a chunky, white thing like a shell that covers her body from below her breasts to the top of her legs.

"How do you go to the toilet?" Anne asks.

"I use a bedpan, and a nurse comes to help me." Mummy talks about how hard it is to endure the plaster cast day and night, especially when her skin is itchy. The only thing that makes her life bearable is the company of the other ladies in the ward. They have all made friends and told each other their life stories. Someday she wants to write a book called *King's Ward*.

"It sounds too much like *King's Row*," Daddy says.

"Oh Jimmy, you would say that. To think I won't be able to do anything or go anywhere. I'll be good for nothing." She starts crying again. "I'm useless. I'd be better off dead."

"You're lucky to be alive," Daddy says. "Now children, tell your mother what you've been doing. Try to cheer her up."

Perhaps we do cheer her up a little. She asks us to write on her plaster cast. Anne writes, "I hope you feel better soon," and I write, "I miss you very much."

Afterwards, Daddy takes us to Lyons for strong black tea, with lots of milk and sugar, and raisin buns with icing. Anne and I had a good time on this visit to London, except for going to the hospital.

*

Mummy comes home in February after four months in the hospital. She has to wear a heavy corset that she calls her "suit of armour." It's almost as bad as the plaster cast, but at least she can take it off for a while and let her skin breathe. A lady comes to give her sponge baths. Daddy takes up her trays. Grace does the cooking and cleaning, though she spends a lot of time keeping Mummy company.

It's our spring holiday, but Mummy doesn't want us to leave her all by herself. Daddy brings the wireless upstairs and puts it in Mummy's bedroom so we can listen to the news and comedies together.

"Can you believe the nurses left me upside down on a table for hours in the dead of winter? They forgot about me. When they found me I was blue with cold." She asks Daddy to write a letter about it to their MP, who's bound to pay attention to a retired Royal Navy Commander. Daddy says he'll do it, but

I can tell from his voice that he won't. He doesn't like doing things that will draw attention.

During the time Mummy was in the hospital, Anne never threw one tantrum, but since Mummy came home, Anne's throwing them again. Daddy says all she wants is attention, and if we ignore her, she'll shut up. But Mummy always begs her, "Please, Anne, be a good little girl." So Anne keeps on howling, like a train's horn, until she's too tired to go on.

By March the doctor tells Mummy she can lead a normal life. She has to wear an orthopaedic corset for a month or so. The new one isn't as heavy as the old one, and she can take it off at night. She can have proper baths. Mummy still spends a lot of time in bed. Daddy keeps saying she should move around more. He wants her to stop taking so many pills, but she says she got used to them in the hospital, and she needs them for her nerves.

I hope she keeps on taking her pills. When she doesn't, she tells Daddy his mother has alienated our affection. And how he hasn't cut the "umbilical cord." I ask her what that is.

"A cord that attaches an unborn child to its mother," she says.

"So why do you say Daddy's attached to Granny with an umbilical cord?"

She gives a start. "Oh, that's symbolic. They cut it when a child is born. If they don't, a child is still attached to its mother."

5

DEAREST JIMMY, I MISSED YOU SO MUCH

"There's no getting out of it, Jimmy," Mummy says. "I have to go to Mexico for another operation. If I don't, my leg may have to be amputated."

"Isn't that excessive?" Daddy asks.

Mummy gives him one of her looks, closing her eyes a bit and pulling in her nose. "You're like all of your countrymen—inured to the pain of others. I can feel pieces of metal from my plane crash like bumps under my skin."

"Can't you have it done in England? I don't think we can afford another trip."

Mummy glares at him as if she'd bite off his head. "After my spinal fusion I don't ever want to go under the knife again in this country. Human kindness is in scarce supply."

"There's not enough money for you to take the children. I'm sorry, but I don't want to touch our investments."

Mummy waves a blue airmail envelope in his face. "My parents offered to help with their fares. They want to see their granddaughters—it's four years since our last visit when Anne was still a baby."

Daddy gives her one of his looks—the one when he's tired of arguing with Mummy. "Very well, Tita. However, I repeat, we don't have much money and this kind of trip always turns out more expensive than you expected."

*

Maybe it's the altitude or the heat or the air in Mexico City, but both Anne and I are sick after we arrive. The doctor says we're adapting to another climate and the high altitude, 7,500 feet above sea level. Probably our stomachs aren't used to the food here; and it's the hot, dry season when more people get sick because it's so dirty outdoors. The breeze blows clouds of dust down the street. In the afternoons maids water the pavement and leave black puddles. Or perhaps it's the food that's cooked in oil instead of butter. What's nice is that Anne and I have a bottle of Coca-Cola to drink at lunch.

A polio epidemic breaks out. A little girl who we played with a week before comes down with it. Mummy and Granny are both scared. They won't let us go out because we might catch polio from germs in the street. Anne and I still have our rubber dolls that a friend of Mummy's gave us on our last trip here. My Laurence is nice and clean, but Anne's Peter is black with dirt and she loves him so much that she chewed him up. All that's left is half his head, his body, and part of an arm. Granny takes Peter away from Anne because she's says he's unhygienic. Anne cries so hard that she can't speak, only gulp, and she keeps crying until Granny promises she'll give Peter back as soon as the polio epidemic ends.

The little girl dies, and though it's sad, we're lucky we didn't catch polio from her. Anne asks Granny to give Peter back to her, and Granny says not until after the epidemic ends. Then she tells Anne that Peter has gone to doll hospital. She buys Anne a doll with real hair and a pretty dress, and says it's nicer for Anne to have a girl than a boy. Anne keeps asking for Peter. In the end, Granny tells her Peter died in doll hospital and won't be coming back.

For a moment, Anne stands there looking at Granny as if

she doesn't believe her. Then she screams, a scream that sounds like an ambulance siren that goes on and on, and she yells, "I hate you, I hate you, I hate you!" at Granny. Mummy comes rushing in and tries to calm Anne down, but when she's like that, no one can except for Daddy, and so Anne doesn't stop until she can't scream anymore.

Mummy has another operation on her leg. She says she hopes it's the last one because it was hard for the doctors to sew it up. She has to stay in bed for a week, and then she needs crutches. "I used crutches for two years," she says. "I'd hoped never to use them again." Everyone says she's very brave and makes a fuss over her, and brings her flowers and little gifts. "What a difference from England," she says. "There, people were hardened in the war and they have little sympathy for those in pain."

A lot of people in Mexico like to complain about their aches and pains while in England you keep quiet about them. Sometimes, it's like a competition about who is worse off or who has more problems. Now I understand why Mummy is always complaining because that's what everyone else does here. It's the custom, as they say.

*

We're going to be flower girls at Mummy's cousin Aggie's wedding. Aggie looks more like Mummy's younger sister than Aunty Laura as she's also short and doesn't have a bosom, but her eyes are brown instead of Mummy's hazel. Aggie's always laughing and telling jokes.

Mummy's sister, Aunty Laura, takes us to Sears Roebuck to buy white organdy dresses with little puffed sleeves and a bow in the back, and long skirts so we can wear them to the wedding and when we make our First Holy Communion.

Granny gives Aggie a bridal shower. Anne and I are there as well, though Mummy tells us to go help to have things ready.

I think she wants us out of the way so I dawdle outside the half-open door.

Everybody is giggling except for Granny who makes a sound like a snort. "Tita, you shouldn't say things like that!"

"Mother, stop being so old-fashioned. In the eyes of God it's not a sin for married people to see each other naked."

I let out such a loud gasp that if they weren't laughing so much, they would have heard me. I just found out that when a man and a woman marry, they have permission to see each other without any clothes on, and it's not a sin. I get the shivers thinking this.

I eat too much potato salad at the shower, four helpings and three the day after. I have tummy trouble. Granny says God is punishing me for being so greedy and I won't be able to be a flower girl after all. But Mummy says Anne can't be the only one, and I have to wear my new dress. She gives me chicken consommé to help settle my stomach. I'm wobbly, and I'll have to come straight back home after the wedding, which will take place at Granny's brother, Uncle Nacho's house, instead of in a church because the groom, Bruce, isn't Catholic. Granny's cousin, the "Pater," Monsignor Freyria, Canon of the Cathedral of Puebla, is coming to marry them.

The wedding invitations say half-past-six in the evening, though everybody knows the wedding will start around eight o'clock. Being on time in Mexico is different from being on time in England. If someone asks you over, they tell you to be there an hour or even two before they mean it. You don't arrive on time because people aren't ready.

Uncle Nacho phones to say some Americans who don't know how things are done in Mexico arrived at half-past-six. He needs Mummy to help him out because he has to dress and the waiters are setting up tables and chairs.

Mummy still has to put on her face. So Granny takes us

and we help Uncle Nacho entertain the Americans until people arrive around eight. He opens two bottles of champagne while everyone waits for the Pater Freyria to get there.

Aggie arrives at half-past eight and she's rushed into a bedroom where she can stay out of sight. Bruce, who is chubby and Aggie says looks like a flea, is already drinking champagne because he's so nervous. His face is very red, and he has the hiccups. People clap him on the back and tell him to drink water upside down. He can't have hiccups at his own wedding.

It's almost nine when the Pater phones to say his car broke down on the highway, and someone's giving him a lift. He's going to be very late.

Mummy, who just arrived, says, "Aggie shouldn't be shut up in a bedroom. Forget about formalities. She'd better enjoy her own wedding reception. Anyway, they're already married." In Mexico people have to be married first by the law before a priest can marry them.

"Suppose the Pater never arrives?" I ask.

Granny says, "Then they can't be married today."

"What about their honeymoon in Acapulco?"

"Since they are legally married," Mummy says, "I don't see why they can't go on their honeymoon and have a small religious ceremony on their return."

Granny looks like she'd spit at Mummy. "Tita, they're not married in the eyes of God."

"For Pete's sakes, Mother, this is the twentieth century."

At half-past-nine the musicians have to leave because they have another engagement. It doesn't seem to matter much since everybody is drinking champagne and enjoying themselves. Even Aggie, who says she doesn't care if Bruce sees her in her wedding dress before the wedding.

By the time the Pater arrives at ten o'clock the party's in full swing. There's barely enough time for people to sit down for the ceremony while he changes into his priest's robes. Uncle Nacho puts on a record, and Anne and I start walking down the red carpet. It happens so fast that Anne doesn't have a chance to go to the cloaks—or the bathroom as they call it here—first.

It seems like the Pater tries to make up for arriving late with a long sermon. He goes on and on until everybody is fidgeting and whispering and making little noises. Later, I hear Mummy say he didn't have all his wits about him as he'd had one too many on the way here.

Bruce's hiccups come back. He goes "Uck, uck," trying to swallow them. He sounds like he's choking. Aggie gets the giggles, and I do as well. Then Bruce holds his breath until he turns purple, and it must help because his hiccups stop.

Anne is hopping around, but she can't wait any longer—she has to go to the cloaks before she has an accident. She asks Aggie and Bruce for permission. They don't hear her, and she pulls Bruce's sleeve and says a bit louder, "Uncle Bruce, may I be excused?" And he still doesn't answer her.

Anne can't hold it in any longer. She dashes up the red carpet, leaving little spots on it along the way. I don't think anybody else notices them except for me.

My tummy is making funny sounds and the worst thing in the world is about to happen—I'm about to stink up a smell. I scrunch up my bottom to keep it in. *Dear God, I promise I won't be a glutton again.* He must hear me because it comes out quietly and whooshes its way out under my dress. Even if people get a whiff, they won't know whose it is.

At the altar Bruce's hiccups come back as he says, "I do," and Aggie is laughing when she says "I do," and she goes right on laughing. It doesn't matter. Now they have God's permission to go away on their honeymoon and see each other without any clothes on.

*

36

I'm standing outside Granny's room where she and Mummy are talking. I like to do this, listen to what grown-ups say when they don't know I can hear them. It's one way to find out what's happening. Grown-ups don't always tell children the truth.

"How I dread that cold climate in England," Mummy says.

"You chose your own path." Granny doesn't sound very understanding.

"If I'd known what I was getting into, I would never have been married in the Catholic Church. Frankly, Mother, we should have gone to a justice-of-the-peace as Jimmy wanted."

Granny makes a sucking in sound. "You were married in the Church, and there's nothing you can do about that. For better and for worse."

"You're too narrow-minded, Mother. I'm not the only one who made a mistake during the war and lived to regret it. 'O, that my tongue were in the thunder's mouth! Then with a passion would I shake the world.'"

"Please, Tita, don't quote Shakespeare at me. I don't appreciate it."

But Daddy does. How can the things that make me happy, like Daddy and living in England, make Mummy unhappy?

Mummy changes the subject. "Jimmy can't pay for our return passages."

"Didn't he warn you he couldn't afford to pay for this trip?"

"Even so, I'd think if *his* mother wants to see her granddaughters back in England, she should be prepared to pay for the privilege."

"Perhaps he hasn't asked her, and she has no idea," Granny says.

"She's an old miser counting the coins in her money bags."

A few days later Mummy announces to Granny and Grandpa that Daddy is sending the money for our passages back to England on the biggest liner in the world, the *Queen Elizabeth.*

"That must be the most expensive liner," Grandpa says. "I thought he didn't have the money for your return trip."

"I suppose he sold one of his inventions," Mummy answers, but it doesn't sound like Daddy at all. I think Mummy is saying that to keep Granny and Grandpa happy.

*

We go by train all the way from Mexico to New York. It takes four days, but we have a compartment to ourselves. Just before we reach the border at Laredo, the train stops in the middle of nowhere, and Mummy's friend Uncle Harry gets on. Mummy asks if he stopped the train and he says, yes, he has to talk to her before we cross the border. He brings two girl dolls and comic books for us, and a box of chocolates, a big bunch of flowers, and a pair of earrings with red stones in them for Mummy.

"Oh, Harry," she says, when she opens the box and sees the earrings, "I can't accept these," but she tries them on and likes them so much she decides to keep them. "I'll have to say that my sister gave them to me. Children, remember, they were a present from Aunty Laura."

Uncle Harry says he will accompany us as far as San Antonio. "I don't think that would be a good idea," Mummy tells him, and they talk in the passage outside the compartment. I open the door a little way to hear what they're saying. Uncle Harry is crazy. He wants Mummy to come back to Mexico City and marry him. For a moment, before she answers, I'm terrified she will say yes. Aren't we going home to Daddy?

Mummy gasps as if Uncle Harry had hit her. "I wouldn't dream of doing such a thing. I belong with my husband in England."

Uncle Harry insists. "You belong in Mexico. I can give you

38

and your children a beautiful home and all the things you ever dreamed of. You'll live like a queen."

Mummy says, "I'm deeply honoured by your proposal, Harry. I wish I could accept it, but I can't leave the father of my two children." There's a silence, and they both make funny noises like clearing their throats.

Mummy asks, "Are we sailing on the *Queen Elizabeth*?"

"Don't worry about that," he says. "It's paid for, and if you insist on returning to England, at least you can enjoy the rest of your trip."

It looks like Uncle Harry won't be traveling to San Antonio with us after all.

"What a pity," Mummy says when he leaves. "He'd give us a good life, but I know where my duty lies. Anyway, he's too old for me."

In New York we visit Mummy's godfather, Mr. Waswick. He lives at the Plaza Hotel, when he isn't in the Bahamas or Canada where he owns houses. Mummy tells us to be on our best behaviour. Mr. Waswick is eighty and doesn't have any children of his own—though he's been married three times. And watch out for his wife Di, who isn't a nice lady. She's forty years younger than he is, and she married him to get her hands on his money.

The first time Mummy met Mr. Waswick, she had just graduated from the American High School in Mexico City. She was wondering what to do with her life when he turned up out of the blue. He took one look at her and told her to pack one suitcase because he was taking her to New York and buying her a whole new wardrobe. Mrs. Waswick, his second wife, took her shopping at Bonwit Teller and Saks Fifth Avenue.

"That Mrs. Waswick was a lovely lady," Mummy says. "A great loss."

Then Mr. Waswick sent her to Sarah Lawrence College

where she met Mr. William Shakespeare when she studied dramatic arts.

Mr. Waswick is a kindly old gentleman who can hardly rise from his chair. I know Di isn't pleased to see us because she moves her lips a little the way some grown-ups do when they pretend to smile. She's wearing a black dress with a sparkling pin like a bow underneath a great big shoulder pad. With her bright red lipstick and long red nails and black hair she looks like the wicked witch in *Snow White*, and her voice is all syrupy like the witch's too. "How old are you, little girls?"

"I'm eight and Anne's six," I say.

"What do you fancy for tea?"

Anne says, "Baked beans on toast."

Mr. Waswick chuckles, but Di says, "You don't have baked beans for tea at the Plaza. How about sandwiches and cakes?"

My, what they bring us on the trays is disappointing. Not worth eating. Biscuits with fishy black and brown and red rubbish on top, and tiny sandwiches with salty pink stuff inside. And small cakes like for a doll's tea party, filled with red strawberry bits that make me feel icky, with gluey icing, or stuffed with whipped cream or custard.

I can see Di doesn't like it one bit when Mummy is affectionate with Mr. Waswick. She sits on the arm of his chair, and Di looks like she wants to throw her out of the window. I've seen other ladies give Mummy that look, and I know what it means. Mummy is prettier than Di. And that makes Di mad.

I have to go to the cloaks. Di says walk down the passage and choose any bathroom I like. My, this is a big apartment. Three bathrooms, one silver and another pink and the last is black. I choose the silver one and sit like a queen on the most comfortable toilet seat I ever sat on.

Mr. Waswick has his chauffeur drive us all the way to Long Island to Anne's godmother's house. It's the biggest car

40

I've been in, with a glass behind the front seat so the driver can't hear what we're saying. "It was a very satisfying afternoon," Mummy says. "My godfather slipped me five hundred dollars when Di wasn't looking. I'm sad to say, if he doesn't watch out, that gold-digger will take him for everything he's worth."

*

We have a wonderful view of New York Harbor from where we stand at the railing of the *Queen Elizabeth*.

Lots of people are having goodbye parties, and drinking champagne. We go into the ballroom, with its great chandeliers, and then to take a look at the swimming pool and the playroom that is too small for children like us to play in it, and the cinema where we can see a movie every day.

The ship sails at midnight, and Mummy goes up to the deck to say goodbye to her country. I stay awake for a glimpse of the Statue of Liberty through a porthole as we sail past.

On the second day we run into a storm. It must be a big one because the *Queen Elizabeth* rolls a bit. Mummy's glad it hasn't bothered her because she has an invitation to dine at the captain's table. From then on she's out every night with a man from Egypt. He's very rich, Mummy says, and he's never dressed himself in his life because he has a body servant to do it.

One afternoon Anne and I have a fight, and she runs off by herself. I'm fed up looking after Anne. I find Mummy in the Verandah Bar with the man from Egypt. He's annoyed because I interrupted them, but I want Mummy to know that Anne doesn't behave herself with me. "Anne ran off," I say, "and I can't find her anywhere." Mummy gets all worked up. "Suppose she's fallen overboard?" she asks, and she calls a man to help look for Anne, and he calls someone else. They search high and low, the whole ship, even other decks, but Anne's nowhere to be found. By then Mummy's a nervous wreck, certain Anne's fallen overboard, and the captain should stop the ship and go back

41

and look for her. The man from Egypt says the captain can't do that, there's a schedule to be kept and passengers depend on it, including him because he has a very important appointment in London. They decide Anne will turn up, and maybe they missed seeing her.

All along I've been telling Mummy to check our stateroom and at last she agrees, but only because she wants to lie down.

That's where we find Anne, lying on her bunk reading a comic book.

"We turned the ship upside-down looking for you," Mummy shouts at Anne. She's so relieved that she's angry. "I thought you'd fallen overboard. How could you do this to me?" Anne sits there with a satisfied smile because she got everyone's attention.

Every day we go to the movies and see *Gone With the Wind* and *The Bells of Saint Mary's* and *Showboat* and *King Solomon's Mines* and *Treasure Island*.

We steam into Southampton in September, after five days at sea and six months away from England. There's a long line of people on a kind of balcony waiting for passengers. We can see Daddy amongst them. Anne is annoyed because instead of waving to us, he's talking to a lady.

We get down from the ship, and I run into Daddy's arms. Anne hangs back but when she sees him hugging me, she runs up to him. There's our Rover, which after the new cars in Mexico, looks old. When Daddy spends ages cranking it, Mummy tells him, "No one in Mexico cranks their cars. Everyone has brand new American ones."

"I'm thinking about selling it," Daddy says. "Too expensive to keep up."

"What will we do without a car?"

"Make the best of it," Daddy says. "How was your voyage on the *Queen Elizabeth*?"

Mummy tells him she sat at the captain's table one evening, and met Lord and Lady Blah, and Mr. and Mrs. So and So. The trip from Mexico City was most enjoyable, including the train ride. Then she says, "Oh Jimmy, how I missed you. I'm so glad to be home at last."

6

MUCH ADO ABOUT A BOX

Three days before Christmas, two men carry a big box to our doorstep where it sits, like a rich friend come to call. Its sparkling silver wrapping and large golden bow promise a treasure inside. No card, only a silver label with Mummy's name on it.

"My word, that's a flashy present," Daddy says.

"'It beggars description,'" Mummy says. "'I am queen of this day's happiness.'"

"Looks like it cost a pretty penny. From your godfather?"

"Probably." The glint in her eyes gives her away. She knows who sent it.

The box is so heavy that Daddy has to push it into the living room. "What on earth is inside?" He shoves it next to the tree.

She shrugs. "We'll have to wait until Christmas to find out."

Daddy has warned us that Santa Claus is rationing presents this year and not to expect much. So when Anne and I go downstairs early Christmas Day to see what he brought us, we scream in delight at the pile of presents under the tree.

"He must have got extra rationing stamps for good little girls," Daddy says, though Anne, who misbehaves all the time, has as many presents as I do. But my doll, Rosamund, is prettier than hers. Rosamund looks like a film star in a bright red taffeta gown and a gold cape. I saw her in a store window and pressed my face to the glass, wishing I could hold her. Mummy told me, "I'm sorry, Penny, we can't afford an expensive doll like that one." Now, thanks to Santa, she's mine. He also brought me two books, *Black Beauty* and *Robin Hood*. I now own thirty books.

Daddy gives Mummy a pressure cooker. The last one blew up, shooting bits of beef stew all over the kitchen and onto the ceiling.

"How thoughtful of you," she says, kissing him on the cheek.

Mummy gives Daddy a silk tie with navy blue stripes from Harrods, an elegant store in London.

"It's very nice, Tita," he says and sets it beside him on the sofa.

"Why don't you wear it today?"

"I'd rather wait for a special occasion."

"Today is a special occasion," she says.

With a sigh he puts it on. I can tell he doesn't want her to get annoyed. She's always on at him about how he's let himself go.

The only Christmas present left under the tree is the silver-wrapped box with the golden bow.

I gulp with excitement. "What can it be?"

"It's a present from me to me," Mummy says. "Since it's Christmas, I thought why not give myself a present as well?"

It's kind of funny that she's giving herself such a big present, but Daddy says, "Excellent idea, Tita, you deserve it," but his eyes scrunch together, making a deep crease between them.

Mummy's face is flushed and happy and naughty at the same time. She takes off the paper and folds it up to use later on. She opens the top, and I peek inside and see objects

45

wrapped in tissue. She takes one out, pulls off the paper, and gazes at it. "Royal Worcester," she says in a reverent voice. Anne and I help her unwrap some large plates, all white with blue and gold rims.

"We already have a perfectly good set of china," Daddy says.

Mummy makes a face at him, wrinkling her nose like Anne does when she's misbehaved. "Jimmy, stop being such a spoilsport."

"They're not as pretty as our Talavera plates," Anne says.

"Royal Worcester is real china," Mummy tells her.

She takes the tissue off a large round bowl and places it on the sideboard. I can see she likes it best of all. "A soup tureen," she says.

Daddy's eyes are so close together they almost sit on top of his nose. "Tita, we can't afford lavish china like this. You will have to return it."

"I can't do that." Mummy's head is turned downward so I can't see her face.

"Why not?" Daddy asks.

"As the Bard would say, 'I am not bound to please thee with all my answers.'"

"I'll turn on the kettle," Daddy says and walks out of the room.

"Why's he annoyed, Mummy?" I ask. We don't often see him that way.

"Because he can't afford to give me what I want." She looks as if she's about to burst into tears. "What a pity your father has to be so awkward about this on Christmas Day."

We go to Christmas services and say thank you, dear God, for all the presents. And please, make things better for Daddy next year. It isn't his fault he can't find a job when so many other men are out of work, and he's doing his best with his inventions.

Outdoors, it's cold and sleety, but indoors, the fire in the living room warms the house, and the smell of turkey roasting in the oven tugs at my tummy. Mummy went to midnight Mass, and she stays at home putting the final touches, as she says, on our Christmas meal.

Mummy has set the table using the new china, though Daddy says it's too formal and doesn't go with the red and gold tablecloth. The blue-rimmed white plates seem unfriendly, out of place; it's like I'm sitting at someone else's table.

I can hardly wait for Daddy to carve the turkey and for Mummy's stuffing to spill out in a stream of flavour. He's always careful, but this time, he digs the knife in so deep, you'd think he wanted to carve the new platter. He serves everyone else and then gives himself a big helping. "This looks delicious, Tita. I'm pleased we have turkey this year." Daddy sounds a lot like me when I'm trying to be polite and have to force out words.

"Last year I was in King's Ward." Mummy gives him a Look.

"Last Christmas, we had chicken," Anne says.

"You'd be eating chicken again if my godfather hadn't sent us this turkey," Mummy adds.

"Nice of the old codger." Daddy doesn't look up. "Please convey my thanks. I always enjoy my meal, whatever it is. How about you, girls?"

"I like turkey more than chicken at Christmas," Anne says.

"This is the most delicious meal ever," I say.

Mummy isn't eating much, moving food around on her plate. All of a sudden, she puts down her knife and fork and says, "'Now is the winter of our discontent.'"

Daddy stops eating and stares at her. "Don't you think you're overdoing it?"

"If there's one thing I know, it's my Shakespeare."

"Then what's the next line?"

47

"You know what I mean," Mummy says, sticking out her chin.

"It's 'Made glorious summer by this son of York.' Now, what on earth has that got to do with us? At least I don't quote Shakespeare out of context to suit my purposes."

"I lost my appetite." Mummy sits there watching us eat. The air's so thick with what they aren't saying to each other that I'm a bit queasy, as if the turkey and the stuffing and the gravy have gone off. I still eat everything and have a second helping.

In the afternoon Daddy, Anne, and I walk over to Granny's for tea. Mummy stays at home resting. She says that since Daddy sold the car, he can't expect her to go out in this awful weather. "Why should I have to sacrifice myself to see your mother? I deserve to relax after staying up half the night trussing the turkey and then spending all morning long in the kitchen."

Once a year on Christmas Day, Granny has a coal fire in the living room. The rest of the year, no matter how cold it is in her house, she doesn't light one because of the cost and the mess. Aunty has made sandwiches with tinned ham and a Christmas cake with white icing and lots of raisins. "Rena used up our egg and sugar rations in it," Granny tells us. She gives us the littlest of smiles and our presents, navy blue woolly vests that she knitted herself. I hope I won't have to wear mine because wool makes my skin itch. She hands Anne and me each a pound note. "This is not to spend," she says. "I want you to start saving your money for when you need it."

We walk back from Granny's, full of Christmas cake and wellbeing, sliding on the ice, and laughing about all the cake we ate. When we get home, we take off our coats and go into the dining room. Daddy puts on his new jumper that Granny gave him.

The new china is laid out on the sideboard with the soup tureen in the middle. Mummy is dozing in her armchair in the dining room, and she looks at us through bleary eyes and says, "What did Granny give her granddaughters?"

We show her the vests and the pound notes. All she does is raise an eyebrow and look at Daddy.

"It's the spirit of Christmas that counts," Daddy says.

"The spirit of Christmas, phooey! Tell that to your mother. If ever anyone lacked the milk of human kindness, it is she. If it hadn't been for my godfather, we wouldn't have had a Christmas at all."

"What does your godfather have to do with our Christmas?"

"Can't you guess, Jimmy?"

Daddy's voice is as stinging as the sleet outside. "Dammit, Tita, can't you stop for one day?"

I sit bolt upright. I never heard Daddy say anything like that before.

Mummy's face screws up as if she's about to burst into tears. "I just wanted to make everyone happy."

Daddy glances at us, and then he pats Mummy's arm and says, "I'm sorry, Tita, I want us to be happy too so let's enjoy the evening." He puts on the wireless to listen to the King's Christmas message.

When it ends, Daddy says, "The King seems optimistic that the economy will improve next year."

"That's what the King said last year," Mummy answers.

The Christmas Day Special Music Hall begins. Daddy and Anne and I love listening to it and singing along, with Daddy singing the loudest. Mummy doesn't join in. It's in full swing when she starts again. "Jimmy, why can't you stand up to your mother? There she is, sitting on a gold mine, and all she gave the children for Christmas were those awful woollies."

Daddy sings louder.

"If she won't help us out, why don't we emigrate to Canada

as my godfather suggested? We'd be better off."

Daddy stops singing. "Please, Tita, not now."

"'Sometimes I must be cruel to be kind,'" she says.

Please, Mummy, it's Christmas Day. Leave Daddy alone.

She stands up and walks over to Granny's presents where we left them in their red and green paper, takes out our vests, puts them to her nose and sniffs.

"They smell of mothballs. I bet your mother unravelled old sweaters to make them. How can she expect her granddaughters to wear these things? They'll come out in hives." She shakes the vests as if shaking off dust. "Here's what I think of your mother's presents." She grabs them, wrapping paper and all, marches to the front door, opens it, and throws them out into the slush.

Anne and I rush after her. "Mummy, why did you do that?" She just shakes her head.

We bring them back in and hang them on the heater. The wet wool stinks as bad as our old woolly knickers, blotting out the homey smell of the fire.

"The children deserve better than this." Mummy's lips tremble. "Jimmy, I tried so hard to give you all a happy Christmas."

"What *did* you do, Tita?" I hear something in Daddy's voice I've never heard before. Anger. "Where did the plates come from?"

She gives him a clenched-teeth look. "You don't have to know."

"I think I do," Daddy says.

"*There'll be bluebirds over, the white cliffs of Dover,*" Vera Lynn is singing on the radio. Usually, Daddy sings along with her—but he isn't singing now.

He stands up and walks to the sideboard, lifts the precious soup tureen and drops it onto the floor where it breaks into bits.

Mummy's scream catches in her throat like a gurgle. "Jimmy, don't. Not my china!"

As if he hasn't heard her, he lifts a hand and drops a plate on the floor, then another, and another.

Anne and I jump on him, pulling at him, howling, "Stop it, stop it, Daddy!"

He does, but there's no expression on his face as he glances at the pieces strewn across the floor. Without a word, he walks out of the room and we hear the door slam.

Mummy runs to the door and shouts after him, "Damn you, Jimmy!" and some bad words she'd told us never to use. All she gets back is a mouthful of wind. She sits in her chair, bent over like someone who's been hit in the stomach, sobbing into a hanky. "Your father's the most ungrateful man. I wanted you children to have the best Christmas of your lives, and he ruined it for us."

We pick up the pieces. They fell on the carpet and some aren't broken. "Look, Mummy." I try to cheer her up. "This plate is a bit chipped, that's all."

She leans over and takes it from me. For a long time, she stares at it. Then, wiping her eyes, she gives us a small smile. "Children, I'm sorry … you had … to witness this." Her words come out choppy like little waves. "I shouldn't have thrown out Granny's vests, but your daddy shouldn't have got so annoyed. Don't worry; he'll get over it and fix the plates."

I learn this about good china. Once it's mended, if not for the faint lines crisscrossing the plates, you'd hardly know it was broken in the first place.

Except for the soup tureen.

"Some things are too broken to mend," Daddy says.

7

A CASE OF NERVOUS FUNCTIONAL DISORDER

There's a netball game at school today, and I don't want to be in it. I'm not any good at netball, even less so when it's raining. So I tell Mummy I have a bad tummy ache. "It sounds like you ate something that disagreed with you," she says.

Here goes. Another lie. "The nuns gave me custard yesterday."

"Drat those nuns. Can't they get it through their heads you're allergic to milk?"

Mummy read all about allergies in her *Ladies' Home Journal*. She decided I must be allergic to milk because I never liked it and spat it out when I was a baby. That's when I made up the story that custard made me sick. The truth is, I hate pudding or stewed fruit swimming in custard, the way they give it to us at school, and an allergy seemed a good way out.

Mummy phoned Sister Augustine, the head sister at the convent. She had never heard of food allergies, or that some foods can make you sick. So she was doubtful.

Mummy insisted. "Penny's had a delicate stomach ever since our last trip to Mexico. Do you want a child to get sick over a bowl of custard?"

"I suppose it's one of those new American illnesses," Sister said, and she would look after it. The nuns stopped giving me custard and instead, gave me an extra helping of pudding or stewed fruit. All the other girls say how lucky I am to be half-American and have an allergy.

The nuns are funny about things like that. Mummy says they're living in the Dark Ages. A few weeks before, I had a bit of a cold. I couldn't find a clean hanky and Mummy gave me some paper ones to take to school instead. A lot better than blowing your nose on the same old dirty hanky until it's wet and sopping and all the germs stay on it. But very few people in England know about paper hankies. They have just come over from America.

I did as Mummy told me to and threw them into the wastepaper basket after using them. The very next day Sister told the class that paper hankies are dirty things and spread germs, and we're forbidden to take them to school.

So who is right?

Mummy or the nuns?

*

Anne is having tantrums again. She throws all the things on top of Mummy's dressing table out of the window—her Elizabeth Arden's and perfumes and her grandmother's silver hair set. They fall on the grass and, though nothing breaks, the face powder comes out of its box, and the top comes off her Chanel No. 5, and perfume leaks onto the grass. Anne hides Mummy's crucifix from her plane crash and says she flushed it down the toilet, and it isn't until Daddy talks to her nicely that she gives it back.

Then Mummy screams at Anne and Anne screams at Mummy. I'm certain almost everybody up and down Sea Avenue can hear them.

Mummy tells Daddy, "Anne's a troubled child."

"Nonsense, Tita. Anne's as normal as any other seven-year old. You have to know how to handle her."

"She's always been overactive. Remember how you had to

53

put bars across the windows to stop her walking on the roof or jumping out of the upstairs bedroom."

I remembered Anne doing that to scare Mummy. She'd jump out of the window and land like a ball on the grass and everyone would come running. Then she'd cuddle up to Daddy as if she was hurt when all she had was grass grazes.

"It's her way when she wants attention," Daddy says.

Mummy tells him. "I can't cope with that child. I'll end up back in hospital."

One morning, Anne can't get up. She can't move her legs, like the little girl in *Heidi*.

Daddy doesn't believe her. "She's making it up."

But Mummy does. She asks Daddy, "Why do you always have to be such a doubting Thomas? It might be polio. A little girl we knew died of it when we were in Mexico."

Daddy asks Anne to try and move her legs. "Anne, you know you can walk. Don't you want to play? Do you want to lie here all day long?"

Anne sits on the edge of her bed and puts her feet on the floor, but every time she tries to stand up, she falls over.

"Try moving your legs," Daddy asks, and she scrunches up her face like she's pushing very hard, and her legs move a little bit, but that's all. Then he says, "If you can walk, we'll go to the films to celebrate. But you can't go to the films if you can't walk." Even that doesn't work.

Mummy begs Anne to walk, and when she doesn't, Mummy is angry at God for letting all these calamities befall her family. Then she takes me with her to church to pray for Anne to walk.

Anne has all the attention she could ever want. Doctor Waller comes and bangs a spoon on the soft spot under her knees and her legs don't budge. He makes her try to stand up and her legs buckle. The doctor says he's baffled, though he has good news—it isn't polio or infantile paralysis. If Anne still can't move her legs in two days, he will call a specialist to diagnose this. In the meantime, he'll have to quarantine us in case it's some kind of tropical disease.

"It's over a year since we returned from Mexico," Mummy tells him.

"But you have had visitors from Mexico," the Doctor says.

"People like the Mexican Ambassador don't carry tropical diseases around with them," Mummy says in a hoity-toity tone.

Doctor Waller isn't certain. "Who knows whom they've been in contact with? The Amazon jungle in Brazil is noted for its tropical diseases, and Mexico must have its fair share."

"Mexico," Mummy says, sticking her chin up, "is farther away from Brazil than it is from England. And we didn't go to the tropical part. We stayed in the city." The good doctor isn't convinced.

The specialist comes and examines Anne. She doesn't have a fever or any other symptoms, so he rules out a tropical disease or infection. And she seems to be in perfectly good health. It might be a nervous disorder of some sort, and he wants to put her under observation. Which means Anne will have to go to hospital in Shoreham, next to Brighton, and the doctor will send an ambulance for her. Although he has lifted our quarantine, the hospital will keep Anne separate from the other children until they find out what she has.

Anne doesn't hide her smile as they carry her out of the house on a stretcher and put her in the ambulance. She's loving all the attention.

Mummy gives her a bag of toffees, but as soon as Anne arrives at the hospital, the matron takes them away. She tells Anne that all the children share their sweets, and they are only allowed a few each day. Daddy and Mummy visit Anne as often as they can, and once I go along as well. Anne is all by herself in a glass room, and we talk to her through the window. A nurse helps her stand up, and she takes a few steps leaning on her to show us she is better.

"She's starting to walk," Mummy says.

"She never stopped," Daddy adds.

The specialist does lots of exams. He says she isn't truly paralysed, even though she can't walk. He thinks she might have something called Nervous Functional Disorder. It means her motor system has been affected by extreme emotional anxiety. "Your daughter is very worried," he tells Mummy and Daddy.

Worried? About what?

Anne is away in hospital two months. By June Daddy is impatient, and he knows how to make her walk. He leaves a box of chocolates on a shelf where Anne can see them though they're out of her reach. The next day, the top layer is gone. Only one explanation—Anne got out of bed and ate them.

Why did Anne keep it a secret that she could walk?

"I was afraid you'd be angry," she tells Mummy and Daddy.

How long has she known?

"A week," she tells them, "but I'm not sure."

"Rubbish," Daddy says. "Anne was making it up all along. Tita, if you hadn't made such a fuss, this would never have gone so far."

The specialist has a talk with Mummy and Daddy. He thinks that whatever caused the Disorder is there in our home.

"It's your fault, Jimmy, for spoiling her while I was away in hospital."

"More likely, Tita, she got it in her head that hospitals are wonderful places where she would have lots of attention."

On her first night at home, after we're tucked in bed, Anne says, "Penny, will you tell me a story?"

I don't answer. Then she asks again and I keep quiet.

So she asks, "Why are you being mean to me?"

"Because you make things up and everyone believes you," I say in a nasty voice that makes her cry.

I sing, "Cry, baby, cry, stick your finger in your eye," until she begs me to not to tease her.

"Only if you tell me why you pretended you couldn't walk."

She sniffles and snuffles and then it comes out in a rush. "I wanted to stop Daddy and Mummy from fighting. I don't want them to get a divorce."

"What do you mean—a divorce?"

"I heard them talking, and Mummy wants to go back to Mexico, and she will marry *el Doctorcito,* who's still waiting for her."

I sit up in bed. "*El Doctorcito?* Where did you get that idea?" Mummy was engaged once to the Little Doctor, as she calls him.

"I heard her say *el Doctorcito* is waiting for her." She's crying too hard and her words come out in gulps. "So I pretended I couldn't walk."

Next day, I ask Mummy about *el Doctorcito.* "He's a nice man," she says, "but rather dull. I received a letter from him a few months ago that he was getting married. At last."

Don't grown-ups realize their children worry about them? As much as they worry about us? They have all those grown-up problems, but at least they're grown up and can do something about it. If you're a child, you can't do anything.

8

NO MORE FAIRY GODFATHER

I used to think Mr. Waswick was Mummy's fairy godfather. Every time he visited London, she'd see him at Claridge's Hotel, and she always came home with nice things for us. Now it looks like his wife Di has stopped him from seeing Mummy.

"Mark my words," Mummy says, "that gold-digger will take every cent he's got."

She hasn't heard from Mr. Waswick in a while. She phones Claridge's, and he hasn't stayed there since last year. He didn't send his usual gift of a hundred quid at Christmas, and he hasn't answered Mummy's letters. "I fear he may not be well," she says. "Or Di has a grip on him. Nothing good can come from that marriage."

It's half-term on a sunny May afternoon. We get out of school early on a Wednesday and we don't have classes again until Tuesday. I've made friends with a new girl at the convent who just came back from India. She goes on the same number 31 bus. I do something I've never done before—take someone home for lunch without asking permission first.

Nobody's in the kitchen. Mummy can't have forgotten Anne and I are coming home early. Then we hear her shrieking upstairs.

I bound up the stairs and find Mummy, in her dressing

gown, standing in the middle of her bedroom shouting, "That bitch! That bitch! I'll kill her!" while Daddy tries to calm her down.

He sees me come in and says, "Hush, Tita, the children are home."

Mummy's face is a mess, red and blotched and her eyes are swollen, and black mascara marks on her cheeks. "My darling Penny. This is the worst day of my life." She waves a postcard at me. "That daughter of darkness, Di, has done me out of my inheritance. I swear I'll have her head for this."

Daddy says to me, "Di Waswick sent a postcard saying Mr. Waswick died six months ago."

"My godfather's not cold in his grave and she's in the South of France with her new fiancé. She must have poisoned Mr. Waswick to get him out of the way."

"He was an old man, and he wasn't in good health," Daddy says.

I think of all the things Mummy counted on doing with her inheritance: paying bills and our schools, another trip to Mexico, and new clothes, and a new car. What will we do now?

"Jimmy, any idiot could see she was in a hurry to lay her hands on his money."

"He wasn't the first rich old man to leave a young widow."

"A young widow so greedy that she has to keep everything for herself. And look at whom she's going to marry—Antonio Davi, the Argentine polo player. He used to be married to Blanche Madson, the supermarket heiress, and before that to Lottie Bowden, the bleached blonde with the big tits. Just think what he'll cost Di. My godfather must be turning over in his grave. And what about me? He promised to leave me enough to be comfortable the rest of my life."

"You can't know for sure," Daddy says.

"He always said he'd remember me in his will."

"He must have changed it."

"My godfather would never have gone back on his word. It was that jaded showgirl, Di, who wanted all his money for herself. Where are my cigarettes? I left them there. I must be going out of my mind with grief."

"Here they are, Tita."

"There's something fishy about Di waiting six months to tell me. She didn't say when the funeral took place or how he died. I'd better look into it."

"Don't even consider that. You won't get anywhere."

I'm thinking of my friend waiting downstairs. I gulp and say, "I asked someone to lunch."

Mummy makes a face. "I'm in no condition to entertain guests."

Daddy says, "Don't worry, Tita, I'll go down and make sandwiches. And Penny should attend to her friend." On his way out he gives me a wink.

"A few more minutes, Penny." She lights another cigarette and puffs away. "Mr. Waswick may have decided not to leave me anything because your daddy asked him to finance his inventions. I'm sure that annoyed my godfather. He was funny that way. He cut me off once before, when I got engaged to a man he didn't approve of." She wipes the tears on her cheeks. "He opened my eyes to another kind of life and then dropped me like a hot cake. We made it up, but Di came along and ruined everything."

Ten minutes later Daddy calls out that lunch is ready.

Mummy wipes her face and stands up. "I'd like to meet your friend. I hope she will forgive me for being in my dressing gown at this hour. I need a drink, though a whole bottle of brandy wouldn't be enough for me to recover from the shock of my godfather's death."

*

60

Even though Mr. Waswick died, this has been the best year in my life. In February, sweets rationing ended, and for the first time ever, I bought a Mars bar and finished the whole thing off by myself.

In June it's the Coronation. You'd think England was having a great big party. Everyone is celebrating. They take down the billboards about the million men out of work, and people stop complaining about how awful life is since the war—though some do complain the government is spending too much on the Coronation. Butlin's Fairground gives free passes to every school child in the country. Better still, Coca-Cola has arrived in England though I like Mexican Coca-Cola more because it's sweeter. Anne and I share one on Coronation Day while we watch the ceremony on a neighbour's new television set that she bought for this occasion. Mummy says watching the Coronation in black and white on a small screen doesn't do it justice. She'd rather see it later in all its pomp and ceremony on a big screen.

I'm really excited because we're going to Mexico this autumn. For months, Mummy's been trying to buy passages on a ship sailing all the way there, such as a freighter of the Swedish-America Line. They don't stop in New York. We're on a waiting list because they only take a few passengers at a time. After we'd waited for months, I wrote to them on my own, without telling anyone, and said we urgently needed to go to Mexico to visit my grandparents who are old and sick. I told them Grandpa has Parkinson's and Granny is blind and my mother has to have an operation on her leg that she can only get there. They replied we were at the top of their list. So I expect we'll be sailing before Christmas.

*

I dream the tide is coming in much too fast, and the waves are getting bigger and bigger. I scramble up the beach, trying to get away from them, but a much bigger wave comes along and almost catches up with me. Just before it sweeps me away, Daddy holds out his hand and pulls me to safety.

I wake and call out to him. He comes as always. I ask, "What would happen if a wave came up the shingle and Sea Avenue? Would it knock over our house?"

He smooths my forehead. "That big wave again? Don't worry. Big waves don't come this far. They don't ever get as far as Granny's house and that's a lot closer to the beach."

Daddy is always right. So I go back to sleep feeling safe and snug in my bed because the big wave will never get me here.

9

LITTLE PITCHERS HAVE BIG EARS

I've just been expelled from the Brownies.

Tawny Owl, the old lady who leads the Brownies, asks me into her den to have a word with me. She says, "Penny James, you've been making up stories."

My face goes red. I don't know what she's talking about. Her stony eyes behind her glasses make me shiver. "What stories?"

"Stories. Fibs. Let me see." She reads from a paper. "You told Heather your mother had been in a plane crash in Mexico. With the American president's—Mr. Roosevelt's—nephew, no less."

"That's true." Did I break some Brownie law, talking about Mummy's plane crash?

She holds the paper close to her face. "You also told Heather your mother was rescued from the flames by an Indian. He thought she was an angel." Tawny Owl's face is so hard you'd think I'd tried to kill Heather. "What an imagination. Did you think you could get away with tall tales like that?"

"It did happen. I swear it did." My voice comes out squeaky and my face is burning.

"You've been telling stories to everyone. Here it says you told Judy your grandfather rode with bandits during a

63

revolution in South America. In Mexico, I believe. It seems to me that you've been reading too many adventure stories. Well, Penny, Brownies don't tell lies. What do you have to say for yourself?"

"It's true. All of it."

"Now, Penny, the Brownies don't like girls who make up stories to feel important. I'm afraid we must ask you to leave the Brownies, and we'd like to have a word with your parents."

I can't hide my indignation. "My parents will tell you it's all true." I'm almost shouting. "And I don't want to be a Brownie anymore. They're silly and," I borrow one of Mummy's favourite words, "narrow-minded. And Mexico is in North America. Not South America."

As I run out of her den, there's surprise on everybody's faces. I run past them and out onto the road and as far as I can before slowing down.

I hate the Brownies. And their horrid uniform that looks like a wrinkled brown bag. The other Brownies don't want to be friends with me because I don't go to the same school. Heather is the only one who is nice. She has such a sweet face. But she's friends with Judy, who isn't nice. I thought if I told them those things about Mummy, it would make them like me. Maybe I was showing off.

Why didn't they believe me when I told them about Mummy's plane crash? They had seemed to at first, but then their mums said I was making up stories. People don't always believe what you tell them. Nobody else's mum has been in a plane crash; though some dads crashed in the war.

Joining the Brownies was a big mistake. I've had to sing their silly songs and play their silly games and wash the dirty dishes the fairies leave in Tawny Owl's sink. Now that is a made-up story. You tell me, Tawny Owl, do fairies leave dirty dishes for other people to wash up?

I reach our house. I'll be very quiet, and maybe Daddy and Mummy won't see me come in, and I won't have to tell them why I'm not a Brownie anymore.

The baker's boy comes out from the back of the house. "The stuff's on the table," he says. He gets on his bike and rides away.

The back door's unlocked. I'm going past the kitchen when the smell of fresh baked bread reaches out to me like a cloud. It's coming from the brown paper bag the boy left on the kitchen table. There are two loaves inside, one white and one brown. I can see the crunchy golden crust around the white loaf. Makes me think of a haystack just begging to be slid down. I put out my hand. The loaf's still warm from the oven.

Nobody will miss a piece of crust.

It tastes like salty honey, crackly and chewy.

Oh dear, the loaf's lopsided. I'd better pull a piece off the other side to even it out. No, that makes it worse. You can see where chunks are gone on both sides.

If I eat the rest of the crust Mummy and Daddy may think the loaf came that way. Without a crust? It does look neater. Anyway, Mummy cuts it off when she makes sandwiches—dainty ones like at a garden party—but Daddy might notice.

Mummy and Daddy are walking up the drive. I can hear her loud voice, the same as when they go to the movies in Littlehampton and come back late, we can hear her all the way from the bus stop. Daddy has a pleased voice, like a purr. He seldom makes it louder, not even when Mummy shouts at him.

They mustn't find me in the kitchen. Not with all the crust gone and the loaf looking bald. I put the paper back around it, and stick it into the bag. They'll think it came that way.

I hide behind the kitchen door. They never close it so they won't see me here.

"The children aren't home, yet," Daddy says as they come in.

"Penny's with the Brownies and Anne's with a friend. Back to what I was saying, I'm taking both girls with me. They belong with their mother."

"They're my daughters as well," he says, "and I want to keep them here."

"You'll be lucky to keep anything."

"Can't you lower your voice? Don't want the neighbours to hear you."

Instead, she says, "I don't give a damn if they hear me . Everyone knows we're in trouble. Face it, Jimmy, your inventions aren't working out. If you want to save our marriage and this house, you have to start working. Even if it means emigrating to another country. The girls are young enough to adapt, but time goes by very fast. I can't believe Penny's already ten."

"I'll consider it, Tita. Now why don't you lie down? You're upset because of what Mr. Adams told us."

"Damn it, Jimmy, of course I'm upset. The bank manager just told us that we're deep in debt. For Pete's sake, where's your head? Did you lose it in the war? I don't know what we'll do about schools when we come back. We may have to send them to the village school."

Oh no, not the village school. With horrid little boys who want me to do rude things with them. One of them asked me to play *bugger* with him on the beach. I said no, thank you, because it didn't sound very nice. I asked Mummy what *bugger* meant. She didn't know, so she asked Grace who said we should never, ever say that word. It's a bad word like *puta* in Spanish. Now, when Anne's mad at Mummy she shouts *bugger* and *puta*.

"What do you expect me to tell the nuns?" Mummy asks. "I've already humbled myself, and because we're Catholic, they're charging us less for their tuitions."

"They can give them scholarships."

"Yes, but scholarships won't solve our financial problems.

It's best for us to go to Mexico while you get on your feet."

"If I can find the money for a patent for my new invention, I can have it out by next year, and we'll be sitting pretty after that."

"Jimmy, for once in your life, be practical. 'Or have you eaten on the insane root that takes reason prisoner?'" She stamps out of the kitchen and I hear her climb the stairs, placing one foot heavily and pulling up the other like a little girl.

While Daddy goes into the larder for bread and butter, I slip out without him seeing me.

At supper, Daddy says, "A funny thing happened today. The white loaf came without a crust. I wonder if one of the elves that live in the trees around the house had been nibbling on it."

*

I wake up and hear Mummy shouting at Daddy. This happens quite often at night. I get out of bed and stand in the doorway, listening. "I can't put up with this anymore, Jimmy. No money and this climate's ruined my health. I can't do housework with my bad back, but we can't afford Grace. At least in Mexico, I can employ a maid for next to nothing."

"Then you will be better off there for the time being," Daddy says. "But we have to think of the children and where they want to live."

"If you want us to come back to England, you will have to pay our return passages. Will you do that, Jimmy? You do want us back, don't you?"

"Of course I do, Tita." He sounds like he's saying that because she asked him and not because he's certain.

Why do grown-ups have to decide what's best for us? They're not always right and we're at their mercy. If they do something wrong, it goes wrong for us as well.

It's very hard being a child.

10

LORD OF THE OCEAN

Bonfires of golden leaves fill the air with a smoky smell. Tousled haystacks stand like cottages of dead grass in bare fields. There are so many apples on the trees that people give them away. Grace makes baked apples, apple tart, and apple pie. The nuns give us stewed apples for sweet at the convent.

We go down to the beach. It's late October and the beach is deserted except for two people walking their dogs. The tide is halfway out, and the wet sand is dark brown, and the waves are small and yappy.

By the time we come home from school, it's dark. Daddy makes our tea—our favourite cheddar cheese and Marmite sandwiches and apple tart. Mummy and Daddy are being very nice to each other. They have stopped fighting since the day we had our typhoid vaccination.

Who would have thought an injection would hurt so much? My arm blew up to almost twice its size, and it felt like someone hit it with an iron rod. Mummy said it was probably the old-fashioned needle that Doctor Waller used because an injection shouldn't make us so sick. She telephoned him, and he said it was a normal reaction to typhoid vaccinations. She put down the receiver and shook her head. "Sometimes I wonder if Doctor Waller knows what he's doing."

"For Pete's sake, Tita, he's been practicing fifty years."

"That's exactly what I mean," she said.

Anne's arm was swelling, too, and our temperatures had gone up. Daddy asked Mummy what could he do to help, and she got mad at him.

"Jimmy, if you really want to help, ask your mother for money for the journey. Or do you expect us to cross the globe without a penny to spare? I don't have my engagement ring to hock." She waved her hand with its bare fingers at him. Since her godfather didn't come to London ever again, she had lost her ring after she pawned it to pay the grocery bill.

"My mother has her own way of doing things," he said.

"Will you ask her or do I have to?" Mummy asked. "Otherwise, what do you expect me to do for cash, Jimmy? Sell myself to sailors on the docks?"

"Damn it, Tita, don't you ever let up?"

I stared at him in surprise. He grabbed the silver cigarette box on the coffee table, which had been a wedding present from his men. "This should fetch a few quid."

"You're not selling that," Mummy said, and they had a kind of tug-of-war over the box. Mummy won. She sat back and hugged it to her as if it was the most precious thing in the world. Daddy looked at us sitting there—we were quiet because we were feeling ill—and he told Mummy, "Why don't you put the girls to bed while I see what I can do?"

Daddy went to Granny's and came back with ten quid that she sent us for the journey.

"We're going halfway around the world and stopping on the way. Do you expect us to manage on ten quid?" Mummy asked.

"It's all she could give me today," Daddy said. "I'll try to get hold of more tomorrow."

The next day he went off, but not to Granny's, and came

back with thirty pounds. "You're going to be on the ship most of the time, so this should do it," he told Mummy. "But don't ever ask where I got it."

*

On our last evening at home, Mummy is calling Daddy "Jimmy dear," and saying how much she's going to miss him and England as well, despite the climate. But this time, she warns, Daddy will have to pay our passages back. He can't expect other people to pay for them.

He tells her that he has great confidence in his inventions, and some man who has heard about the catamarans is coming to talk to him about them, and he'll send for us as soon as things work out.

"Promise me you won't sell Carlyon" Mummy says. "The children will need a home to come back to."

"The children will always have their home here," he tells her.

*

We take the train to London. At Victoria Station Daddy asks if we'd like some sweets. Of course I want a Crunchie Bar and Anne a Mars bar, and so he buys us two of each. One for now and one for the journey. We're lucky that sweets rationing ended because before we never ate a bar by ourselves; Daddy would cut one Mars bar into four slices, one for each of us.

At the travel office we have to wait for the other passenger, a Mr. Pickford, who's late arriving. He's a small man in his thirties with slicked-back hair who, when he arrives at last, greets Mummy with, "Hello, Duckie," as if he knew her very well. She stiffens and says, "Hello," in her formal voice. I don't think they're going to be friends.

By the time we pull up at the side of the ship, it's dark. The *Vretaholm* is a freighter belonging to the Swedish-American line and it's carrying cargo all the way to Veracruz, Mexico. A

70

crane is hoisting tractors on board. The journey will take four weeks, from October 29th to the third week of November to get there, stopping off in Miami, Florida, and Havana, Cuba.

Two men in leather jackets help us up rickety stairs to the deck. A steward carries our luggage to our stateroom. It's as big as the one on the *Queen Elizabeth* with two small beds and a sofa that turns into a bed.

"This is quite nice," Daddy says, trying to be jolly. "Your home for the next month."

We go up on deck to say goodbye. Anne holds onto Daddy and says she doesn't want to leave him. She's been changing her mind all week.

"If you stay," Daddy tells her, "you'll be sorry you missed out on this trip. But Penny will tell you all about it." He knows that Anne can't bear to lose out on anything I do. She gives a vigorous nod and says, "I'm sorry, Daddy, but I'm going to Mexico after all."

I swallow as hard as I can to stop myself from crying, and when I can't quite keep in my tears, I look down at the ground so nobody will see them and say a gruff, "Goodbye Daddy." Next I know, he almost swings me off my feet in a bear hug.

"Remember, Penny, now that you're ten, you're a big girl. It's your turn to look after Mummy and Anne."

He kisses Mummy goodbye. I bite my lip and look down again. When I lift my eyes, Daddy has reached the stairs. I want to run after him, but he waves and disappears into the darkness.

*

What a pity to start our journey with a storm in the Bay of Biscay. It has raged for two days. We're lying on our bunks, and Mummy's on the sofa bed. The ship rolls onto its side and all we see through the porthole is water. Pans clash, one after the other—dang, dang, dang—in the galley. The tray falls off Mummy's bed making a mess on the floor; it's the fourth time that happens. Mummy calls the steward to clean up—again. He keeps bringing us trays of food even though we leave most of it. "You will feel better if you eat," he insists, but we're too seasick. Anne keeps asking if the ship is going down. Mummy tells her no, it's a sturdy ship, and not to worry, but then she starts praying. When Anne asks again, Mummy tells her, "I didn't survive a plane crash to drown at sea," and Anne shuts up.

We're nine passengers: the three of us, a dashing young man named Sverri, another lady who's travelling with her two little boys, Pieder and Hans, Mr. Svenson, who's going to Miami, and Mr. Pickford. We all have dinner with the captain, the first mate, and the engineer. The first evening on board Mummy is gay, and laughing, smoking lots of cigarettes and drinking something called *snaps*, which is Swedish firewater. That is, until she finds out, though everyone speaks English, at mealtimes they speak Swedish. The only person she can talk to is Mr. Pickford. Then the storm hits, and it doesn't matter who speaks what or where. We all stay in our staterooms.

On the third day, the storm dies down, and we're not rolling as much as before. By afternoon, I'm bored lying there and making up stories in my head. My tummy's so empty it hurts. I'm woozy, but hungry. Mummy and Anne are sleeping. So I get up, put on my clothes and take my hat and coat, and go out. I don't see anyone in the passage or in the galley.

Tea is laid in the lounge. Sliced pound cake and nobody except me to eat it. I have a slice and then another, and I wait. After five minutes, I have another, and since it looks like nobody is coming to tea, who will know the difference if I eat the lot? Maybe I should leave one slice. Don't want people calling me greedy.

I'm not seasick anymore.

I'd like to go outside and see how tall the waves are. There's no grown-up around to ask permission so I can do as I like.

The door leading out to the deck is heavy, and I have to pull the handle really hard and then push with all my might to open it. As soon as I step outside, the wind hits me and I almost fall over. I'll have to watch out. I can't see a single person on the deck. I walk towards the bow and look at the oncoming waves. What a disappointment. They're quite high, but not half as big as I expected. I watch for several minutes. They seem to be smaller until here comes one that's so big I can't see over it to the next. The ship lurches up and down it, while I hang onto a railing until we're in a sort of valley between waves. I take a few steps and the ship leans over, and I grab a rope to keep my balance. These waves are bigger than they seemed at first sight.

There's a great big one in front. Up we go on it, and over and down the other side. Like being on a ride at Butlin's. I'm covered with spray, but it doesn't matter, it's so exciting. I'm lord of the ocean: Old Jack, or Captain Horatio Hornblower, or Sir Francis Drake. I'm master of this ship.

The wind is so strong it pushes me from one end of the deck to the other. Then, I grab onto a mast, turn around, and struggle against the wind to the other end where it isn't as strong. I race back with the wind pushing me from behind and grab onto a mast in the nick of time. I keep on doing this, like a sailor in a storm. I'm braver than anyone else, the only person who dares to be out on the deck.

A sailor comes up the stairs. He sees me and makes wild gestures for me to get off the deck. I pretend not to understand. He walks over to me and says, "This not gut for little girl. Too danger." He takes my arm and pulls me all the way to the heavy door, opens it and says something like, "*Fars vin*," and pushes me inside.

I go down the stairs to the bottom of the ship, just above the boiler room, where the sailors live. They're playing cards, and smoking cigarettes, and drinking *snaps*. I meet the two cooks, one very fat and one very thin, and Johannes the mess boy, who's seventeen and has freckles and curly golden hair and a snub nose. He's playing the accordion.

The fat cook has arms like tree trunks. He holds one out and tells me to hit it as hard as I can. He laughs when I do; it's like hitting a pole. He gives me a small glass of *snaps*. It burns my throat. How can they like this stuff so much and drink it all the time? I suppose I'm too young to appreciate it. Someone grabs my glass and says, "Not gut for little girl." I'm glad not to have to drink the rest of it because it made me dizzy.

When I go back to our cabin, Mummy and Anne are awake. "Where were you?" Mummy asks. "I was worried."

"Don't worry," I say. "I'm doing very well on my own."

At dinner, there's only the captain, the engineer, Mr. Pickford and me, so everybody speaks English. What a pity Mummy's too sick to be here. She would have had a good time. We eat pickled herring with sour cream, and roast pork with mashed potatoes and apple sauce, and chocolate pudding for sweet.

*

Up close the sea is lemony green, but grey from a distance, and why are all those white bubbles on top? Up we go and over, though never as hard or high as in the storm. We're sliding rather than bouncing. Just when I have that thought, we tilt over on one side, bump upright, and tilt again. I hear the usual crash in the galley. Pans are always banging in there.

Dear Daddy, how are you today? I'm trying to send you my thoughts with the wind. If you're out on the beach you can pick them up. But will you know how?

I've been thinking about my name. I like Penelope but I don't want to be plain old Penny with a "y" anymore. Penny is such a silly name. When I'm grown up, I'll use Penelope, but until then, I'll be Pennie with an "ie" at the end

*

Anne and I play with Pieder and Hans. Pieder is a bit shy, but Hans wants everything his way. They don't speak English, but we understand each other. We play shooting with a bow and arrows, and hide-and-seek, and chase each other around on the deck. After a while, I'd rather be alone with my thoughts. I sit at the front of the deck and look out to sea. It goes on forever like an eternal blue field. There's no wind and no noise except for the ship's engines. Whole schools of flying fish follow the ship, leaping around in our wake.

After two weeks at sea, land is in sight. One afternoon, while we're going through the Bahamas, Mummy and the ship's engineer stand together at the railing and drink gin. Why does Mummy want to be friends with the engineer? He has a rusty-red face and wispy hair, and his tummy bulges out of his trousers. She's crying on his shoulder and telling him about Mr. Waswick, who used to have a home here, and about Di, who diddled her out of her inheritance.

Late that evening, because it's so hot, we're in our underwear and Mummy's got on her Merry Widow corset when there's a knock on the door. Anne opens, and the engineer barges into our cabin. He's also in his underwear, vest and shorts, and his face is redder than ever. He has a bottle of *snaps* with him.

Mummy grabs a shawl to cover herself, and tells him, "Go away, this is no time for a visit." He gives her a silly grin, and sits right down on her bed and offers her some of his *snaps*.

Mummy says no, thank you, and will he please leave us alone? Instead, the engineer tries to pull the shawl off her, and she lets out a cry and clutches it to her and tells him, "Keep your hands to yourself." He tries again, and she holds the shawl with one hand and pushes him away with the other. It looks like they're having a little game, and so we join in trying to pull the shawl off Mummy.

She stops smiling. Her face is grim. She says to the engineer, "Leave me alone," in a serious voice. It isn't a game after all. Perhaps she'd rather not have the engineer see her in her Merry Widow with its hooks and bones and stuffing where her breasts should be. She tells the engineer, "If you don't leave at once, I'll report you to the captain."

"Why are you upset?" he asks. "Don't you want a little fun?"

"Not the kind of fun you want," Mummy tells him. "And certainly not in front of my two children."

The engineer's red face fills with surprise. "I'm sorry," he says to us, "I do not have evil intentions." He stands up, wobbling a bit. His eyes have a crooked look, and he stumbles out of the room. He forgets to take his bottle of *snaps*.

"Why were you so annoyed at him, Mummy?" Anne asks.

"The engineer wanted to do nasty things to me in front of you two," she says. "He's like those dirty old men I'm always warning you about." She goes on to say that sailors are starved for women, and we'd better not be too friendly with them because some of them might like little girls—and not in a nice way—and to report anyone who tries to hug or kiss us.

After that the engineer stops having dinner with the passengers.

We reach Miami, and the Americans won't let Anne and me off the ship because we don't have visas. Mummy didn't live long enough in the U.S. to give us the right to be Americans, which makes her mad as anything at the American immigration officers. She tells them we're more American than most Americans because her ancestors came over just after the Pilgrims. And, "This McCarthyism is going too far. Do these little girls look like Russian spies?"

When Mummy wants something she usually gets it, so she convinces the immigration officers to let us into the country

LORD OF THE OCEAN

for one day. We go to the beach, a long stretch of golden sand, and there are only two other people there. One is wearing a two-piece bathing suit. "That girl can wear it because she has a nice figure," Mummy says. "It's a pity Americans have such bad skins." One of the girl's cheeks is covered with pimples. "That's because they eat a lot of greasy foods."

It's November, but the water is warmer than on the hottest day in Rustington. Mummy says, "Soon this beach will be crowded when they build hotels here." It's nothing like our beach, but it reminds me of Daddy. I miss him. Going to the beach is not the same without him.

*

Havana must be the most fun place in the world, with lights and glitter and happy people singing in the streets night and day. The harbor is filled with brightly lit gambling ships from Miami that bring Americans here to the casinos. We meet a couple on their honeymoon who have come over for three days to try their luck, as they say. We take a look inside one. People are playing cards or watching a little ball whirl around until it settles on a number. It doesn't make any sense to me, especially since Mummy says some people lose everything, even their shirts, in there because they can't stop gambling.

The best part of Havana is the Morro Castle with its dungeons and torture chambers. The guide tells us about the prisoners who couldn't escape because the sea is full of sharks. There's a life-size, wax statue of a man in a *garrote* being choked to death. We love it, but Mummy's shocked to find out that Anne and I are so bloodthirsty. Havana is also dirty and we get fleas walking on the docks. Mummy buys some awful smelling liquid to wash our hair, and she pulls the fleas out with her long nails and squashes them.

Then Mummy meets Antonio, who's a manager at the docks, and she's happy to have somebody to talk to in Spanish.

77

She goes out with Antonio to a big casino, and they win some money. They use it to take us to an early show at the Tropicana that Mummy tells us we will never forget. It's mostly showgirls in bathing suits balancing fruit baskets on their heads while they sing and dance. *The Greatest Show on Earth* was more fun. They take us to the pictures. Mummy didn't know that first they're showing a grown-up film, *A Streetcar Named Desire*. She asks, how can Cubans let children in to see that film, but since we're there, we might as well stay. We won't understand it.

My, grown-up pictures are boring. Anne falls asleep. Most of it's about a man in what Americans call a t-shirt who's very rude to a lady who behaves like she's going to burst into tears. In the end men take the lady away because the man in the t-shirt drives her crazy. The next film is about a beast that keeps destroying everything in its path. When the beast is wounded in New York, it bleeds all over the streets, infecting people, and they die. Mummy says it gives her the willies, and she'll be outside in the bar with Antonio because she needs a drink to steady her nerves. She goes out with Antonio for the week we're in Havana until we leave for Mexico.

"We were just two ships passing in the night," she says.

*

There's a storm in Veracruz, and the captain says we can't land until it blows over. We will have to sit out at sea for a day. "Surely, there's something you can do," Mummy asks. "We're already five days behind schedule," but he says he isn't Jesus to calm the waves, and that's that.

In our stateroom Mummy says, "Damn that stubborn Swede. If he only knew how things work in Mexico, he'd give them some money to send a tug to bring us in."

By nighttime the storm has died down. I can't bear the stillness now the engines have been turned off. Mummy wouldn't like it if she knew I was up, but she took a sleeping pill. Johannes has promised to play his accordion on deck as soon as we can see the lights in Veracruz. I go down to the sailors' quarters and say goodbye to the cooks, and then I go up to the deck with Johannes to hear him play.

The lights of Veracruz aren't friendly anymore. I don't want to land in Mexico. I'd rather keep on sailing for the rest of my life.

11

A DIFFERENT WAY OF LIFE

The *Vretaholm* docks at nine in the morning. Mummy makes us put on our little girls' party dresses with polka dots and lace frills at the hems and cuffs. I've spent almost a month wearing my blue jeans only to have to get into a silly dress the same as the one Anne is wearing.

Mummy's sister Aunty Laura and her brother Uncle Artie are waiting for us right there on the dock. Aunty Laura looks glamorous in a bright red dress, with her golden hair in a coil on her head and some loose down her back. Everyone calls her *La Guera*—Blondie.

Uncle Artie is wearing a funny, checked blue-and-yellow jacket that makes him look very American. Mummy warned us to be careful with him because he's been touchy ever since he came back from the War, after parachuting into Normandy on D-Day, and tramping through France and Germany.

We're spending the day in Veracruz because our plane to Mexico City doesn't leave until the evening. We go to a noisy terrace café in the main square, Los Portales, where a band that sounds like our band at school is banging away. We have to speak at the top of our lungs to be heard. The sun shines so brightly that colours jump out at us: purple, crimson, orange, and green. The air is thick with a mix of foul cigarettes and

Cuban cigars and cooking oil and fried fish. If I weren't drinking a bubbly Coca-Cola, I'd be really sick.

Who should we see wandering around but Mr. Pickford? Mummy shouts, "Mr. Pickford," across at him, and when he comes to our table, she greets him like a long-lost friend and invites him to join us.

Everyone is drinking tequila—a Mexican *snaps*—with a red thing called *Sangria* on the side, so Mr. Pickford tries one. He makes a face and says he'd rather drink a rum and Coke.

The waiter brings a tray with glasses of Coca-Cola, and I grab one. It doesn't taste like it should, too sweet and gives me a funny feeling inside. My sight is blurred, and I'm a little dizzy. The sun's hotter than ever and the fans are going full blast. My dress is as heavy as a winter coat.

Aunty Laura is eating little toasted green chilies one after the other. Mr. Pickford asks her what they are, and she says with a wicked smile, "Why don't you try one?" So he pops it into his mouth, and oh dear, he goes so red you'd think he's about to explode. He finishes his Coca-Cola in one gulp, and Aunty Laura passes him hers to drink as well. Everyone laughs, and Uncle Artie says, "Aw, that was mean of you, Laura," but we all knew, and nobody warned him.

Mr. Pickford is a good sport and he says he should have realized; he lived in India where food is very hot. From the way Aunty Laura was eating them, he expected Mexican chilies to be milder, and he needs to drink another rum and Coca-Cola.

So that's why mine is so sweet. I'm having a grown-up's drink with rum in it. Yucks. Give me a real Coca-Cola, fast, I tell the waiter. I hope I don't get drunk or sick.

Mr. Pickford has one drink right after the other, and he behaves as silly as the rest of them.

A beggar in rags comes up to our table. His hands are black, and he's missing two fingers, and his bare feet have long nails that curl underneath. Uncle Artie gives him a peso to stop him whining for the love of the Virgin Mary, and go away. Next you know, we're surrounded by beggars. Aunty Laura runs out of change, and Uncle Artie shoos them away.

Another band of musicians called *jarochos* keep strumming tunes and singing verses in rhyme about everybody. The music is so noisy that people shout when they talk. The musicians shout back at us, making up verses about us. Aunty Laura translates:

Two little princesses,
A beautiful sight,
Come down from Heaven,
To give us their light.

Little princesses. Hot sun. Shouts mingled with music. My ears are ringing. My eyes are closing. We're in Mexico at last.

*

The day after we arrive in Mexico City Mummy decides we're going back to England. Straight away. All because of a squabble with Granny-in-Mexico.

Grandpa tries to cheer Mummy up, but she keeps saying she knows when she's not welcome. "Children, don't bother unpacking. We're sailing home on the *Vretaholm.*" She phones the people in Veracruz to keep our trunks, and not to send them by train, and she wires Daddy that we're on our way home. She says she'll borrow the money for our fares to England. Then she talks it over with Grandpa and calms down. She tells us, "My father has convinced me to stay a few more days, but that's all."

For a week it's back and forth while Mummy decides. Daddy sends a wire saying to stay put. What can Mummy be thinking if we just got here?

One of Mummy's old school friends calls to ask her out. Since all her nice dresses and her fur coat are in one of the trunks, she has to send for them. As soon as she's unpacked her evening dresses, she goes out.

Every night.

Granny and Grandpa live in the Colonia Condesa, where they have lived since Mummy and Aunty Laura were little girls. It used to be an elegant neighbourhood, but now it's rundown and shabby. Uncle Artie pays the rent for this house, and he has a bedroom downstairs that he doesn't use much. Most of the time he's away working for Pemex, the national oil company. Rich people, like Aunty Laura and her husband, Uncle Bob, and Americans, live in big houses in Lomas de Chapultepec, where it's cleaner and there aren't any beggars.

Granny's older sister, Aunt Carlota, who looks like a fierce little blackbird, has an apartment near us in the Edificio Condesa, a long block of apartments where Mummy lived when she was growing up. Aunt Carlota's apartment is on the first floor. One night she awoke to find a man holding a knife to her throat. He didn't do anything to her, but he did steal her good jewels, including a tiara her grandmother had worn when she was presented at court in London. Everyone tells her to move, that an old lady shouldn't live there on her own, but Aunt Carlota won't budge. After the burglary she put iron bars on her windows and a triple lock on the door. She's lived there for thirty years, and she intends to stay until she's carried out in her coffin.

Everyone speaks English, though they mix in words in Spanish all the time. Uncle Artie says that's what comes from living in a country where you speak Spanish everywhere except inside your home. You have both languages in your head. I don't expect that to happen to me. Why bother to learn Spanish if we're going home to England in a few months?

This house smells of the rooftop where the linens are washed and dried, and of sick old man and cigarettes. Grandpa smokes a pack of Raleigh a day, and he has a dreadful cough and spits out yellow gobs. He takes a cold bath every morning. Even when he's not going anywhere, he insists on getting properly dressed in his grey suit and a shirt with collar studs. Granny has to do them up, but she's too blind to put the studs on without catching the loose skin on his neck, and he yells, "Goddammit, Amada, you're pinching me." Once he's downstairs in his armchair, he smokes and drinks black coffee. When he lights his cigarettes, he's always burning his fingers because his hand trembles from Parkinson's Disease. Two of them are black because he's burnt them so often.

Granny's room smells like a church from the candles she lights in front of the big crucifix in a glass case on her altar. When they're not lit, it smells damp like Queenie, her Boston terrier, and Granny freshens it with lavender Colonia Sanborns—eau de cologne.

On Sunday, we go with Granny to half-past-one Mass at *La Coronación*. The church is always packed. We have to push and shove to reach a bench where Granny can sit down, but often there's no room for Anne and me to sit, so we stand with the group of latecomers at the back. It's hard to concentrate on the Mass when I'm crushed and poked in the ribs and barely able to breathe, and all the incense the altar boys swing around goes up my nose.

In this city they're always building something or fixing the streets, and they never seem to finish. In front of the church there's a building, the Cine Plaza, that was started when Mummy was growing up. Nothing's been done to the rusty construction in twenty years, and probably nothing will be done to it until it falls down in an earthquake. Some men are working at the corner of our street, and the rat-tat-tat of the drill keeps up all day long. It gets on Mummy's nerves, and she sends the maid with five pesos to give to the man to switch off his drill. The man takes off for the day and leaves a big hole in the pavement with a red rag around it so people won't fall in. Seems that here, if you give people money, they will stop doing whatever they should be doing. The next day he's back drilling again and Mummy lets him finish his job.

The park playgrounds have orange dust, and it's blown around by the wind and stings my face. The games are broken, and the metal seats on the swings and the slides are so hot they burn the back of my legs. The patchy yellow grass has dog's business on it and mangy old mongrels share the shade under the trees with beggars who come up to us, holding out their hands and saying, "*Por el amor de Diós.*" Everything is "for the love of God" or the Virgin, but God doesn't seem to care much for Mexicans since most are poor. I learn to shake my head and look the other way.

Granny is a professor at Mexico City College where she lectures on Mexican history and culture. It doesn't matter that she's blind—she's been giving her lectures for years and knows them by heart. She has someone come over to read her students' papers to her. Mummy says her mother is crazy to take the bus to work, but Granny can't afford taxis. Since she has a white cane, someone always helps her or offers her their seat. At least she takes a first-class bus because the Mexican *camiones* are a real menace, and they rattle as if they're falling to bits. It costs thirty centavos to ride on a first-class bus, which has proper seats though the covers are torn and the springs poke out, and only eight people are allowed to stand. A ride on a second-class bus, with benches on both sides, costs twenty centavos, and it's packed with as many passengers as it can hold, mostly standing, with people hanging on, even outside on the steps.

The food in this house is not very good. Always soup, usually chicken consommé, to start and then chicken. Grandpa says, "We eat so much chicken in this house that we'll all end up looking like chickens." Anne and I fill up on Coca-Cola.

People don't eat proper desserts. Only fruit after the main course. I never thought I'd miss Aunty's rhubarb and gooseberry pies, but I do. Apples are so expensive—one peso each—that we rarely buy them. I love *Cajeta*, like liquid toffee that you eat with a spoon right out of the jar. Also I can buy twenty *chiclosos*—Mexican toffees—for one peso, and I eat most of them myself, though I have to share a few with Granny and Anne.

They don't sell real tea in Mexico, not the black kind we like to drink, so we have to ask people to bring us Lipton's tea when they come in from the States. Here they drink *te de manzanilla*, that's camomile tea, but it's yellow and tastes like sweet boiled water.

In the evenings we go out with the maid to the bakery to buy *pan dulce* for supper—cakey *conchas* and crisp *orejones*. A woman outside the store makes *quesadillas*. She takes a little dough, pats her tortilla into shape and fills it with potato or cheese, throws it into the steaming oil in her pan, and the *quesadilla* comes out crispy gold.

Sanborns, an old restaurant in downtown Mexico City, is Grandpa's favourite place. Americans like it because it has a soda fountain, purified water, good coffee, and American food. Mexicans like it because it has good drinks and Mexican food. Grandpa likes it because he can sit there for hours drinking coffee and seeing people he knows. When Grandpa was a foreign correspondent, he went to Sanborns every day. The waitresses, dressed like Mexican peasant girls, don't pay attention to customers until they've been sitting there fifteen minutes, but they always bring Grandpa his coffee straight away.

Usually, Aunty Laura sends her car to take him, but once when she can't send it, he decides to go with Anne and me. Granny and Mummy are out, and there's no one to stop

Grandpa. He puts on his hat and off we go. Since he refuses to use a walking stick, he has to lean on me. We hurry to catch a bus at the corner. I try pulling him on the bus and Anne pushes him from behind, but he's too heavy. Luckily a man gives him a hand up, and the bus driver waits and doesn't take off leaving Grandpa in mid-air. Then Grandpa won't let anyone help him sit down. Instead, he grabs onto the handhold while he takes a tottering step until the bus moves and he falls into a seat. His legs are too stiff to bend, and he stretches them across the aisle and people trip over them. Every time the bus turns a corner, Grandpa slides in his seat and hangs on for dear life, all the way downtown to the Centro. Luckily, a man helps him off the bus.

We sit at a table near the entrance and two older waitresses come over at once to say hello and bring him a small cup of thick, very black coffee. Anne and I both order apple pie, but after we finish there's nothing to do but sit there while Grandpa watches people come in and out. This continues for over an hour until he spies some men he knows, and sends us over to their table to tell them we're his granddaughters and to say hello from him. We hesitate—the men look like gangsters in films, but we give them the message and at once, they come over to pay their respects to "Connie" their *amigo*. Everyone calls Grandpa "Connie," short for his surname, "Constantine."

Two hours go by and we're still there when Mummy rushes in. "Papa, what were you thinking? You're a stubborn old man asking for trouble."

"Pennie and Anne helped me," he says without looking up.

"Two little girls. Lord, grant me patience." She pulls out a chair, sits, takes out her cigarettes and lights one with a shaky hand.

"We came on the bus," Anne tells her.

Mummy looks at him in despair. "It's a miracle you ever got here."

"Nonsense," Grandpa says. "There was nothing miraculous about us getting here. If you expect me to sit and rot in my chair at home, then you have no idea what I'm made of."

"That's the problem, Papa. I do know. That's why you shouldn't expect two little girls to bring you to downtown Mexico City on a bus."

"Next time," Grandpa says, "we'll come in a taxi."

*

A week later, Grandpa is gravely ill. Granny asks her cousin, the Pater, to come from Puebla where he's canon of the cathedral, and see Grandpa before he dies.

Grandpa's not a Catholic—he's a Unitarian, and he wasn't baptised and never goes to church. But Granny begs him, since he's on his deathbed, to let the Pater baptise him a Catholic. She says it will make her very happy to know Grandpa's soul is taken care of, and he will go straight to Heaven. Grandpa can hardly speak, but he moves his head, and they think he's agreed. So the Pater baptises him and gives him the Last Sacraments.

Grandpa gets better almost at once. Granny says it happened because he was baptised. Grandpa says, "Stuff and nonsense. What's this about me being a Catholic? I never wanted to become one, and if I'd had all my wits about me, I wouldn't have agreed. I'm definitely not a Catholic."

"Yes, you are, whether you like it or not," Granny tells him, "and there's no going back. A conversion is a conversion, whatever the circumstances, and you should be grateful you're alive."

"Alive for what?" Grandpa yells. "To sit in my chair for the rest of my life?"

12

A TROUBLED CHILD

We've been in Mexico six months.

I have a plan. I won't learn to speak Spanish, and if I can't speak Spanish, sooner or later, Mummy will have to send me back to England.

Anne is homesick too. I tell her, "We'll sit in our chairs and close our eyes and pray very hard to God to take us home. Maybe when we open our eyes, we'll be in Rustington."

God isn't listening. From what I can see He doesn't listen much to prayers in Mexico. Things keep going wrong even though people are always lighting candles and praying for their lives to get better. People complain all the time—about the servants, their health, and how the country has gone downhill since President Miguel Alemán left office.

One afternoon I'm standing outside Granny's bedroom door eavesdropping. She's talking to Aunty Laura about me. "I don't know what's happened to Pennie," she says. "She used to be a good child, but she's becoming more like her mother every day. She's rebellious, and I can't control her."

I don't want to be like Mummy. I'd rather be nice like Daddy. But in Mexico I'm not nice or good. I don't like doing the things Granny asks me to do.

What's the point of putting on my First Communion

dress, which Granny can't see I've grown out of, and going to the church to offer flowers to the Virgin? Why offer her flowers when the church is already full of flowers? Only because it's a custom in May for little girls in their First Communion dresses to offer flowers. Anne doesn't want to do it either, but she says yes to please Granny. I end up doing it so as not to hurt Granny's feelings. What about my feelings? I don't see the point of all this fuss about the Virgin. In Mexico the Virgin is very important since the Virgin of Guadalupe appeared to Juan Diego, a poor peasant, hundreds of years ago. She's so important that people go on pilgrimages to the Basílica de Guadalupe and walk on their knees for the last mile or so. So why complain about having to go to a church ten blocks away?

"Pennie's always been a good child," Mummy says, "Mother, try to understand how hard it is for her to adapt to this country."

The truth is, Mummy and Grandpa are nasty to Granny, and Granny and Anne are nasty to Mummy, and Granny doesn't like me much, so why can't I be nasty as well?

*

I'm reading *Quo Vadis*, and I'm at the part where the early Christians are being fed to the lions. I wonder what it's like to be torn to pieces by wild animals. Anne wants to play, and I say no, leave me alone, and she goes and tells Granny I'm being mean to her.

Granny comes in and says, "Pennie, why won't you play with your sister?"

"Because I'd rather read this book."

She makes a hissing sound. "*Tsss ...visiones*," meaning that's nonsense.

Thanks to Granny, I'm stuck in this house. She won't let us go out alone because someone might kidnap us, though we do behind her back. If she forces me to play with Anne, I'll think up an interesting game.

How about setting fires? Little ones. Find out if it's true that wool can't catch fire. Mummy told us she didn't have bad burns on her body from her plane crash because she was wearing a wool suit, and wool doesn't burn. So I'm out to prove a point.

We start with a little stack of matches and make a tiny bonfire, and light it on the shaggy wool carpet in our bedroom. Mummy's right. The carpet doesn't catch fire. We try a few more times, making each stack a bit larger than the last, and nothing happens except for a few black spots where the carpet was singed.

We can't keep on lighting fires on the carpet because someone might notice the spots. And little fires aren't much fun. How about setting a bigger one? In the garage? The floor is cement so that's not a problem, and there are lots of Grandpa's old newspapers that will make a much better fire.

At first, we set a little one, but it burns out almost at once. So we set a bigger one and watch the flames rise almost to the ceiling. We have to be careful because the maid's room is upstairs and we don't want it to catch fire. I'm excited watching the fire grow, and the flames leaping upwards, and having to control them. After a while we're quite expert at setting fires. And at putting them out when they're too big.

One afternoon Granny calls us, and we have to put out a fire in a hurry. Or we think it's out until the maid comes in shouting the garage is on fire.

Aunty Laura, who's visiting, runs outside, grabs the hose and douses the flames. It was almost out, just some smoke, but she insists it could have gone upstairs to the maid's room or sideways to the house. Did we want to burn down our grandparents' home?

I try telling her we didn't mean to set the garage on fire,

and we were very careful, and it wouldn't have caught on because it was mostly smoke.

"How do you know that?" Aunty Laura is used to her four sons doing this kind of thing, but we're nice little girls who shouldn't be playing with fire. "Have you started other fires?"

Anne's face turns bright red.

"Where?" Aunty Laura asks in a serious voice.

Anne gulps and says, "The carpet in our bedroom."

"Those don't count as fires," I say, but the damage is done.

Aunty Laura goes upstairs and inspects the carpet and finds the little black patches. "Whose idea was this?"

"Mummy's," I say.

Aunty Laura slits her eyes and shakes her head. "Come on, Pennie. Your mother did not tell you to set a fire."

"She told us that wool doesn't catch fire."

"Where did she get that idea?"

I tell her about Mummy's wool suit in her plane crash. Still, Aunty Laura has a forbidding expression on her face. When Mummy comes home, Aunty Laura tells her, "Your daughters almost burned down the garage. It's your fault for putting ideas in their heads."

Mummy is shocked that her comment would have such results. Aunty Laura accuses her of neglecting us and letting us put our grandparents' lives in danger.

In the end they decide it was my fault because I'm the older one, and it was my idea. Anne's my little sister following my instructions. Aunty Laura calls me a *pyromaniac,* and she says I have dangerous tendencies that need to be watched. If I ever light a fire again, I will be sent to reform school. Understood?

How unfair. I wasn't trying to burn down the house but she's acting as if that was my intention.

From then on, I stop smiling. On purpose.

Mummy asks, "Why do you have that rebellious look?"

I say, "Because I'm unhappy here. I want to go home to England."

"We can't return until your father sends for us."

I narrow my eyes the way she does when she's annoyed and say, "Ask an uncle to help us like you did last time." That makes her mad, of course, but I don't care. If everyone thinks I'm rebellious, then I'll behave that way.

I do look up *pyromaniac* in Webster's dictionary; the word comes from the Greek *pyro*, meaning fire, and a compulsion to set fires. I look up *compulsion*. "An irresistible urge to behave in a certain way, especially against one's conscious wishes."

That isn't me. I don't have an irresistible urge to set fires. How unfair to be called something I'm not. I've learned that once grown-ups believe something's wrong with you, they keep on thinking that way even when you try hard to be good. They don't forgive and forget. They remember and blame you for things you didn't do.

*

When we start school in Mexico, I find out three important facts. The most important is who you are related to or who you know. The second is that in a Mexican bilingual school, students don't really speak English, they just study it there. Third, going to school with boys is very different from going to school with only girls.

The school year begins in February and not September like in England. The long vacations are in the winter and not in the summer. Our school is called Kensington, which sounds very English, though there's nothing English about it. Once the other children find out I'm not related to the queen and don't know her, they lose interest in me. Especially since I don't speak Spanish and the children don't speak much English. I'm in Fifth Grade and Anne is in Third Grade in the same class as our cousin Felipe, and she's learned to speak Spanish.

The most important children in the school are Luis and

Leon. Their father is a famous architect and a friend of the president, so everybody wants to be friends with them. Luis, who is in my class and is very stuck up because his father is so famous, calls me a *perra inglesa* meaning English dog. I'm annoyed and call him a *cochino Mexicano* meaning Mexican pig. It's only fair. Luis tells his father who calls the headmistress who sends a message that she wants to speak to me. "Why did you call Luis *cochino*? In this country, that is considered very offensive. *Cochino Mexicano* means 'dirty Mexican.' It's an insult, especially coming from a foreigner."

I tell her I didn't know it was an insult; I hardly speak any Spanish. She says, "Even so, you insulted Luis and you should apologize to him."

"What about him calling me 'English dog'?"

"That isn't an insult," she says.

I go up to Luis and say in English, "I've been told to apologize for calling you a *cochino Mexicano*, but I'm not sorry." After that, he leaves me alone.

For Anne it's different. Felipe helps her make friends. A boy asks her if she wants to be his *novia*, and she says yes, and another boy asks her and she says yes to him, and to a third boy before she finds out they all asked her to be their girlfriend.

One afternoon Anne and I hear shouts outside our bedroom window. Two of her boyfriends are fighting each other on the grassy part of the sidewalk. They're making a racket, and kids and maids are coming over to see what's going on. I have a bright idea. "We'll invite them in. They can fight in our patio, and we'll charge fifty centavos to anyone who wants to watch."

I tell the boys that if they want to keep on fighting they have to do it inside. They don't want to stop until the next-door chauffeur pulls them off each other and shoves them into our patio. Six maids and four kids pay Anne fifty centavos each

94

to watch the show. It's supposed to last half-an-hour with us cheering the boys on, but they're wrestling each other rather than fighting, and after a while, we lose interest. And Grandpa is shouting, "Who's making all that noise?" So I tell everyone to leave. The boys are last, both with dirty, sad faces that they haven't won Anne as their girlfriend.

*

After a month, I advance to Sixth Grade English, but I'm sent back to Fourth Grade in Spanish. I don't care. We're sure to return to England this year, so it doesn't matter what grades I get in Spanish. I sit at the back of the class and daydream. When Miss Elsa, the teacher, asks me something, I answer, "*No entiendo.*"

The school sends a report card every month, and Granny asks, "Why aren't you doing better? Anne has nines and tens in Spanish, but you have fives."

It doesn't make sense to learn to multiply and divide the Mexican way when I already know how to do it the English way. And why should I change my straight English handwriting into a lot of slanting loops? I've had to learn to spell words the American way so they won't be marked as wrong. The only interesting subject is Mexican history. What a surprise when I turn a page and see a picture of Granny's grandfather, Ignacio Mariscal, in my history book. From then on, I get a good grade in this one subject, which makes the teacher think I know more Spanish than I let on.

I have an argument with Luis. Half in English and half in Spanish. "Mexico," he says, "is a free country because it's a democracy and the people vote for the president. England is not a free country because it's ruled by a queen, and she's not elected by the people."

"England is a monarchy." I know because I studied this at the convent. "But the Queen doesn't rule, Parliament does,

95

and the people vote in a Prime Minister or out if they want him to resign."

Luis doesn't seem to understand so I say, "Have you heard of Winston Churchill?"

"Oh, yes, he's a famous man. A hero, my father says."

"After the war he and his party were voted out, and he was no longer prime minister. Then two years ago, the people voted for him to come back. That's democracy."

Luis asks his father which country is more democratic. His father tells him that Mexico is a democracy, even though the PRI party has always been the party in power, and each president stays for six years. In England, despite the queen, the people can vote in a prime minister and a party and get rid of them whenever they want a change. England is another kind of democracy that works. He tells Luis that he should become friends with me and that way he can practice speaking English. So Luis and I shake hands and make it up.

*

We're three quarters through the school year, and we're still here in Mexico. My teacher tells me I may not pass Fourth-Grade Spanish unless I make a big effort. If we're in this country next year, I might end up in the same class as Anne.

I go outside in front of the school where I can be alone, when Luis comes up and asks, "What's the matter?" I tell him and he says, "I know how you can pass Fourth Grade. The same way I did. Just beg Miss Elsa to pass you. She has a kind heart."

"I don't have a famous father like you."

"Isn't someone in your family famous? Doesn't your mother know the president or someone important?"

"No, I don't think so."

"Someone who used to be important?"

Granny's grandfather, Ignacio Mariscal. He's in my history book; he must have been important. I take a photo of him out of Granny's album and show it to Miss Elsa. Surely she won't flunk someone whose ancestor is in the history book. She doesn't believe me—how can an English girl have an ancestor who signed the Mexican Constitution? She calls Mummy to ask if it's true. It must help because in the end, I pass Fourth Grade Spanish. Thanks to my great-great-grandfather. Goes to show that in Mexico, it's very important to be related to someone famous.

13

UNCLE IAN

In Mexico, we have some uncles who are not real uncles. They give Mummy flowers and perfume and presents, and sometimes they give us presents as well.

She goes out so much that Granny tells her off. Mummy says Granny is old-fashioned and narrow-minded. "What can I expect from a mother who didn't learn the facts of life until three months after she was married?"

Gosh, I'm ten and I know the facts of life. So does Anne because I told her. I thought when people were married, like Aggie and Bruce, they had to know what to do next.

"Why didn't Granny know what to do?"

"Before she met Grandpa, she was going to be a nun," Mummy says. "I imagine that's why no one told her, and she wasn't curious to know. Then Grandpa proposed, and they had to get married in two days before he was sent to Veracruz. I have no idea why her mother or one of my aunts didn't have a little chat with her before the wedding."

"So how did she find out?"

"After she'd been married three months, she confided in an American woman that she was worried she wasn't doing something right." Mummy clears her throat as if looking for the right words. "The American woman told her what to do, and I was born seven months later in the St. Louis Hotel in New York City."

The way I understand it, the American woman must have told Granny she had to take off all her clothes when she got into bed with Grandpa.

Yucks. Granny and Grandpa?

"I don't know how my parents made three children," Mummy says. "My father's a Puritan and my mother's so innocent."

Every Saturday afternoon, Anne and I go to the movies. We like going with the maid on the bus to a cheap movie house where they show two films for two pesos. Mummy takes us when she can, and we go to a first rate movie house like the Cine Roble, but we never arrive on time and miss the first part of the film. So we have to stay and watch almost an hour of shorts before the film starts again. By the time we come out, it's late. On Saturday evenings most taxis are full, and we can spend up to an hour finding one that's empty, and they charge extra at night. The outing comes out to around thirty pesos, including popcorn and snacks, which is a lot more than Mummy can afford as she has to borrow the money because she doesn't have any of her own. She prefers taking us out with the uncles, when they want to.

One Sunday, we go with her and Uncle Pepe to the Jockey Club. He gives Anne and me five pesos each to bet on the horse races. At first I win ten pesos but I lose it all on the next races. Anne's luckier and ends up winning twenty pesos.

Then there's Uncle Agustin, an old boyfriend of Mummy's, whose wife, Lucia, is Mummy's best friend. Uncle Agustin is short, tubby, and very dark with a few black hairs on his head that look like pieces of thread glued to it. He speaks English with an American drawl, and likes to call us "his nieces from Arkansas" to tease us.

Grandpa doesn't understand their friendship, and he put the "spanner in the works when Agustín was courting me," Mummy says. "Agustín has a fine mind and we communicate on an intellectual level. He's a writer, an artist, and a patron of the arts."

Uncle Agustín also has a publishing house, and he's promised to publish Mummy's book of poetry once she finishes it. She tells everyone who will listen that she should never have let herself be distracted from her goal to be a writer. "All those years of being a drudge in England took it out of me. And Jimmy made fun of my efforts."

We go to lunch on Sunday at Uncle Agustin's house in San Angel Inn. From the outside, all you can see is a wall off a cobbled street with a front door and a garage. Inside, the house is enormous and built around a courtyard with grass patches and a fountain in the middle. There are two living rooms choc-a-bloc with antiques. Mummy says you're likely to find a Ming vase there next to a Diego Rivera painting next to an Olmec figurine.

Uncle Agustin has four children, two boys and two girls who become our friends. We all fill up on Coca-Cola while we wait for the group of about ten grown-ups to finish their drinks and appetizers. By the time we have lunch, it's almost five o'clock.

The dining table is long enough to fit twenty people and is laid for a banquet with silver cutlery and cut crystal glasses and silver plates under each food plate. But the food is the same *sopa de fideos*—noodle soup—and the same red rice you find in almost every Mexican home, and slices of boiled meat in a watery tomato sauce, and *frijoles refritos* on a silver platter that a servant holds out to each of us to serve ourselves.

Uncle Agustin opens two bottles of wine and makes a great to-do about how it's an exclusive French vintage wine that cost him the earth. Only Mummy seems to appreciate it, so between them, they drink a lot of the wine themselves, and Mummy gets a bit tiddly. The other grown-ups taste the wine, but wash down their meal with Coca-Cola or Carta Blanca beer.

*

Daddy is taking his time sending for us. Mummy says it looks like he's abandoned us, and Grandpa and Granny can't support us forever. Mummy has applied for new resident papers because she lost her Mexican residence when she stayed out of the country for too long. It may be a while before her new residence comes through and meanwhile she is not allowed to work.

"I don't know what to do," she says. "I can't go out on the streets and sell myself to support my two children, but if I have to, I will."

The only way she can work is part-time for friends. She finds a job in an antique store three afternoons a week where she makes enough to pay for our personal expenses and her beauty parlor and her cigarettes. Uncle Agustín gives Mummy some translations and they keep her busy, but not enough to cover all of our expenses.

Uncle Artie pays the rent and a lot of the bills. He's thirty-two, and one of these days he'll want to get married and have a home of his own. Mummy says that he may have come back from the war a hero, but he's a changed man. He drinks too much, and he's going out with a burlesque entertainer called Tongolele who dances half-naked in a nightclub.

Because of her book, Mummy starts attending sessions in English at *El Centro Mexicano de Escritores*—the Mexican Writers Center. It's not long before she's saying she's an "intellectual" and does not want to waste time with people who don't stimulate her mind. All she talks about is her book, and the writers at the Centro, and how some are liberal and controversial, which means they write things that shock people. There are other, more serious writers like a Scotsman, Ian, who wrote a book called *Mexican Parade*, and he gives Mummy a lift home after each session. One day at lunch, she keeps talking about how much she's learning from him.

Grandpa says, "I know that man, and he's full of hot air. I wouldn't give his book the time of day."

Mummy stares at him as if she can't believe what he said. "But, Papa, Ian has a wealth of knowledge in his fingertips."

"Knowledge in his fingertips does not translate to knowledge in his head," Grandpa tells her.

"It's an intellectual friendship."

"Rubbish," Grandpa says. "That man is not befriending you for intellectual reasons."

Mummy puts down her knife and fork with a clatter. "Papa, can't you understand a platonic relationship between a man and a woman? Ian is interested in my mind. And he's been happily married for thirty-four years."

"May he remain happily married another thirty-four years," Grandpa says.

Mummy's book is called *Flight and Other Poems*. "Flight" is about how she endured pain after her plane crash. Another poem is called "Flight From Loneliness."

What is Loneliness?
The Loneliness of neglect.
The wife whose evenings are spent
Cleaving to the scraps of her life
As a beggar counts his bread.
While her spouse
Companionship his own,
Dozes in a chair, like a drone.

"Did you hate living with Daddy?" I ask her after reading it.

"Of course not, Pennie," she says. I don't always believe her, and this is one of those times. "I love your daddy, but when you write poetry, it's more about your feelings at that moment, and not always the truth. It's called poetic license."

What will Daddy think when he reads it?

One of her poems is about me before I was born. "To My Unborn Child."

My child, What Future do you face?
Safe in your mother's womb
You curl yourself in peace and warmth
Still blind to this world's painful sights
You sleep unmoved to cries of Hate,
Or to an earth, which burns in flames!

Her book is published in July 1954. She buys herself a toreador blouse with a sparkly tie, and has her picture taken. It comes out in the newspapers, and there's a big photo of her in the window of the Librería Misrachi downtown. She appears on television, though she doesn't say much because a well-known commentator spends most of the time talking about flying saucers.

I don't like Mummy's photo. She looks stuck up in it. I don't like her *toreador* blouse, and I don't like her being an intellectual. There's something else I don't like about her nowadays—she's not the Mummy we knew in England. There she was more like a mother—cooking meals, and when we came home from school, and to talk to in the evening, and chatting with us even when she complained. Here, she's out a lot, and she doesn't cook at all, and she doesn't have much time to spend with us.

One Sunday Uncle Ian, as Mummy tells us to call him, comes for us in his big black Cadillac. He looks like a walrus, with a big stomach, and a toothbrush moustache and not much of a chin, which makes his head seem too small especially since he's wearing a bow tie. He tries to be nice, but he talks to Mummy as if we weren't there. I think he's the kind of grown-up who believes children should be seen and not heard.

He takes us to his home in the Lomas, an English style house with a pretty garden, where we meet his fox terriers and his wife, Aunt Ethel, who has gray-red hair and lots of freckles. She cooks a proper Sunday lunch, roast beef with roast potatoes and carrots and peas, and lemon cream pie as the sweet. The best meal I've had since coming to Mexico.

Uncle Ian's two sons are also there. The older one, who's engaged, is with his fiancée, and the younger one, who's fifteen, goes to the American School. They have two daughters but one is a nun in Monterrey and the other is married in Ciudad Juárez on the Texas border.

The next Sunday they invite us again, this time to Lake Tequesquitengo where they have a house. We swim in the lake and their sons take us out in the motor boat and even let me run it for a few minutes. Uncle Ian and Aunt Ethel say we're welcome to come back whenever we want. I like them both very much.

They take Mummy to the state banquet at Palacio Nacional for the Emperor of Ethiopia, Haile Selassie. Uncle Ian is invited because he's honorary consul for Norway.

Grandpa says Haile Selassie has no business here in Mexico except to waste a lot of people's time and money. What is a country like Ethiopia hoping to get out of a country like Mexico? Oil trade agreements? Or perhaps the Emperor is feathering his nest in case he is ousted from power.

A photograph of Mummy, Uncle Ian, and Aunt Ethel comes out on the front page of *Sociales*. Mummy is standing next to Uncle Ian, as if they were together, while Aunt Ethel pokes her head out from behind them.

On Saturday, a week later, Mummy tells me that Uncle Ian

has to go to Tequesquitengo to pay some bills. Aunt Ethel can't accompany him, so he has invited Mummy to go along, and would I like to accompany them? Just me, not Anne, because Uncle Ian wants to know me better.

It's not much fun with them on my own. Uncle Ian buys a roast chicken and potato chips and an apple pie for lunch, but I'm a bit bored, after we finish eating and he and Mummy decide to take a nap.

Uncle Ian says, "There are plenty of books here for you to read. Have you read any by Agatha Christie?"

"Well, no, she writes for grown-ups."

He says, "Try this one, *Sparkling Cyanide*."

There's nothing else to do but read. I can't go in swimming by myself, so I spend all afternoon reading while they take a very long nap. By the time they're up I'm well into the book, and I've become an Agatha Christie fan.

*

I must say Uncle Ian is very helpful. He comes and collects Mummy and takes her where she wants to go. He's also helpful to me. Once, when Grandpa and Granny are out, Mummy asks him to wait in the living room, and he takes a look at Grandpa's books.

"Which books have you read, Pennie?" he asks.

"*Jane Eyre* and *Wuthering Heights* and *David Copperfield*," I say.

"You should read some of the short stories in the anthologies," he says. "*The Necklace* by Guy de Maupassant and *The Black Cat* by Edgar Allan Poe."

Thanks to Uncle Ian, I discover a whole lot more to read in this house. It's important because in Mexico it's not easy to find books in English, and if you do, they're very expensive.

Anne doesn't like Uncle Ian at all. She says that when he smiles or laughs, he's pretending, and the only good thing about him is his house in Tequesquitengo.

I'm trying to sort out how I feel about him. He's one of those people who you can never be sure of. Sometimes, when he says he's pleased to see us, I don't think he is. His mouth smiles but that's all. He can be rather abrupt or put-off easily. I can tell from the way he turns his head, like forcing it. And he smells like a damp towel that's been used over and over and never dried.

14

ONCE I HAD A SECRET LOVE

It's the middle of the night, but light comes in to our room from the street lamp outside. Not like our bedroom in England where the blackout curtain kept it dark. Here we have Venetian blinds and dusty, gauzy curtains, which haven't been washed in ages.

I'm trembling. Any minute now, a big, hairy, black Monster will come crashing through the window.

The Monster is loose in Mexico City. He's coming our way.

Monsters are like uncles. They pursue beautiful women like Mummy. They know where to find them because they can smell them. And her room is right next to ours.

I can't tell anybody. Since I scare Anne with horror stories, everyone will think this is another one. How I wish I could call out to Daddy as I used to, and he'd come and make everything all right.

Night after night I lie awake, waiting for the Monster and praying to God to save me from it. Though what good does it do to pray if I'm in a state of sin? Maybe that's why the Monster is coming for me.

It's Mummy's fault. She wants me to help her with her problems because she has nobody else to turn to. Not Anne or Grandpa or Granny or Aunty Laura. They wouldn't understand her reasons for doing what she is doing. I don't either, but she thinks I do.

One afternoon she's going to take me to see *Calamity Jane*. We're in a hurry to arrive at the cinema on time—or that's what I think—but as soon as we've walked a block, Mummy asks if I can go to the grocery store and make a phone call for her. To Uncle Ian.

"Why don't you call him yourself?"

She fidgets, and looks around, and at her feet before she says, "Aunt Ethel might answer, and I'd rather not speak to her."

"Why?"

Mummy's lips press together as if she doesn't want to tell me. Then she says, "I'll be honest with you, Pennie. Aunt Ethel doesn't like me anymore."

Oh dear. What did Mummy do?

Her expression is shy and sly at the same time. "Can you keep a secret? A grown-up secret? Don't tell Anne because she will tell your grandmother, and I don't want her to know."

I hate Mummy's secrets. She can never keep them for long; in the meantime, it's like I'm carrying a heavy suitcase of her belongings.

She tries to sound serious, but she can't hide how pleased she is about what she's telling me. "Uncle Ian is madly in love with me. I wanted him to keep quiet about it, but he's gone and asked Aunt Ethel for a divorce so he can marry me. That's why she's upset."

I stumble backwards as if she'd walloped me in my tummy. Aunt Ethel is such a kind lady, and we enjoy seeing her on Sundays. "What did Aunt Ethel say?"

"She said she's a good Catholic, and she won't give him a divorce. He's moving out anyway because he says the marriage is over and has been for a long time, and he will marry me, come hell or high water."

"But you're married to Daddy." My head whirls. How can Mummy leave Daddy and marry Uncle Ian?

She sighs as if it pains her. "Pennie, I have deep feelings for your father, but our love died a long time ago. As Shakespeare put it, 'Love is a smoke made with the fume of sighs.' Uncle Ian has offered to pay for my divorce. He wants to make things happen so we can be together. I asked him to hold his horses because I need to think what this will mean for you and your sister."

I have an awful taste in my mouth. Spit fills it. I'll be sick right there in the street. I swallow the spit, but it comes back, and I make a sound like I'm about to vomit.

Mummy says, "Get it out and then take a couple of deep breaths." I lean over and throw up yellow stuff. She pats my back and strokes my forehead as I breathe deeply. "Please, Pennie, don't take it that way. I haven't said yes. I told Ian I'd think it over. Try to understand my situation. Sometimes need impels us to take steps we would not consider otherwise."

I gulp back the panic welling up inside me and take more deep breaths. She puts her arm around me, but I shrug it off. "I'll phone Uncle Ian's house."

I don't know what to say if Aunt Ethel answers. Luckily, nobody is there.

By the time we reach the movie house, the film has started and Doris Day is singing "Once I had a secret love." She sounds happy, but Mummy and Uncle Ian's secret love will make a lot of people very unhappy when they find out about it.

I can't concentrate on the film. Does this mean Mummy isn't going back to Daddy? I think about Uncle Harry when he stopped the train, and how we always returned to England. Maybe it will be the same way with Uncle Ian.

We stay to see the beginning and I have to listen to Doris Day singing about her secret love all over again. I'll never forget that song.

After the movie we have supper at *La Flor de Lis*. Mummy tells me how she used to come here when she was my age. They have the best *tamales* in Mexico, though tonight everything tastes thick and pasty.

Mummy asks, "You do like Uncle Ian, don't you?"

I stick out my lips. "Yes, but I like Aunt Ethel more."

She raises one eyebrow as she often does when she doesn't agree. "You have only seen her good side. Believe me, she's put poor Ian through the mill."

I play with the *tamale*, squashing it with my fork and moving the pieces around my plate.

"Stop pouting, Pennie, it gives you a doughnut mouth. Try to understand my position. Now that your father's abandoned us, because that's what he's done, abandoned us, I will probably have to divorce him anyway. Granny and Grandpa and Uncle Artie can't keep on supporting us forever. We need someone to look after us, and Uncle Ian is well off." Until at last she says, "Beggars can't be choosers. If I marry Uncle Ian, it will be to put a roof over your heads."

"I don't want that roof."

Mummy is married to Daddy, and Uncle Ian is married to Aunt Ethel, and that is how it should be. Anne and I want Mummy to stay married to Daddy, and I'm certain that Uncle Ian's sons want their father to stay with their mother. If they get divorced, everybody is going to be mad at everybody else. What's more, Uncle Ian is an old man of sixty, and he has grandchildren. And he smells like a damp towel. How can Mummy want to kiss him? Or, if they're married, sleep in the same bed and let him do things to her?

Mummy puts on one of her anxious faces. "Don't toy with your food, Pennie. I thought you liked *tamales*."

"These don't taste of much."

110

She wrinkles her brow; she already has a line between her eyes.

"Uncle Ian gave me a little money to spend on myself, and I thought I'd give you a nice treat." Her voice is much louder. "Stop looking at me with mutiny on your face. Try to think like an adult for a change. You're almost eleven and grown up for your age. So get this through your head. Your father is not sending for us, and Uncle Ian is offering us a home."

She's asking me to betray Daddy and to tell her it's all right for her to commit a mortal sin. For that is what it will be, if she's divorced and remarried. If I agree with her, then I will be committing a mortal sin as well. That will make me a sinner, an outcast from the Church, and on a path to Hell.

*

As long as I'm the only one who knows about her secret love, Mummy keeps calling me into her room to confide in me. I don't want her to confide in me, or tell me her secrets, or what was wrong with her life with Daddy. I want her to leave me alone.

She always starts by saying, "Please close the door, Pennie. There's something I have to tell you." Anne is suspicious and feeling left out. Over and over, Mummy says the same things. "No one understands my position. Nor the sacrifices I've had to make. I lost my engagement ring when I hocked it to put food in your mouths. All those presents and trips, where do you think they came from? Heaven? Your father wasn't much help. And if he really loved you, he'd have sent for you by now."

And, "We're alone in the world. My parents can't keep us anymore. I don't have working papers, so I can't get a job. How will I support you? The only solution is for me to be married."

"It will be a mortal sin to divorce Daddy and marry someone else," I remind her.

Mummy grabs my arms and digs her long nails into

my skin. She can be nasty if I don't agree with her. "Damn the stupidities your grandmother's been putting into your head. She's trying to poison your mind against me. If I don't marry someone, we might as well starve to death. God understands that."

I don't think so. From what I gather, God isn't very understanding. To make sure, I ask the priest the next time I go to Confession. He's very firm about telling me that nobody who is married in the Catholic Church can ever be divorced, whatever the reasons, and they should never marry again because it wouldn't be a true marriage and they would be living in sin. If they do marry in a civil ceremony, they will be excommunicated, which is rather like growing horns on your forehead. It gets worse. A good Catholic shouldn't have anything to do with a person who's been excommunicated. So I know that if I say, "Yes, Mummy, marry Ian," I'm committing a mortal sin.

Another thing is that if she's divorced, we won't go back to England for a long time. I can't bear the thought of not seeing Daddy again, perhaps not for years.

I try hard to hold onto my memories of home. At night, when I can't sleep, I walk through Carlyon in my mind. I put the furniture in place, piece by piece, starting in the dining room where we spent most of our time. There are Daddy and Mummy's leather armchairs on either side of the table with the wireless on it, and the dining table with the flaps pulled out, and the rust-red carpet that's a bit frayed at the edges, and the red curtains which are faded from the sea light. I look out the window at our front garden.

I belong there, in England, not here in Mexico.

*

Anne has found out. She has a rebellious expression as she asks, "Is it true that Uncle Ian wants to marry Mummy?"

When I say yes, Anne shouts, "I won't let her." She runs

into Mummy's room and screams at her. "I won't let anybody take Daddy's place. Never, never!"

Mummy tries to calm her down, but it's no good. Anne keeps screaming her head off. When Mummy offers her five pesos to behave herself and be nice to Uncle Ian, she throws the money on the floor. It takes a while for her to simmer down.

Grandpa and Granny find out because of the way Uncle Ian is behaving. He telephones Mummy all the time and comes by for her every day. He draws his car up outside and bangs his horn twice so she will know he's there, and then he sits for hours waiting for her to finish getting ready and come down.

Granny calls him "That Man" because she refuses to say his name out loud. She says Mummy is risking her soul going out with him, and can't she think of what she is doing to her children? She stops talking to Mummy, unless she absolutely has to.

Grandpa says a man Uncle Ian's age has no business hanging around Mummy like a lovelorn calf or banging his horn to tell her he's arrived. "The man has no manners, and I'm sure he's not in his right mind. If my daughter marries that lunatic, it will be over my dead body—" but since Grandpa is very old, I know his dead body won't be enough to stop Mummy.

On my eleventh birthday Uncle Ian brings a cake for my party. It's chocolate, but the icing is a mud color. All the same, it tastes good and everyone likes it.

Uncle Ian wants to take us out, Anne and me, and make friends with us. Anne doesn't want to go, but when I tell her that I'm going anyway, curiosity gets the better of her. He takes us to an ice cream parlor where they serve Mexican ice creams made with water, *Nieves*, they call them. Uncle Ian asks us about school, and then he talks about his children the rest of the time. He's not interested in anything we have to say.

At the end of the afternoon when we come back and

Mummy greets us and ask how everything went, Anne says to Uncle Ian, "I won't let you take my daddy's place, and I'll never let you marry my mother."

Uncle Ian turns so red you'd think he was about to blow up. I can see how he'd love to give Anne a telling off. He can't because she says, "Thank you for the ice cream," and runs inside.

Mummy says, "Ian, don't let her bother you. Anne is very attached to her father, but she'll get over it." Doesn't she know that Anne will never get over Mummy divorcing Daddy? Nor will I.

Somebody has to be on Mummy's side, so I'm trying hard to do as she says and think like a grown-up. It's a pity Uncle Ian has to divorce Aunt Ethel, but if he will take care of us, and we'll have our own home, and Mummy will be happy, it might not be such a bad idea.

Who can I ask for help? God's not answering. I have to make up my own mind.

It takes six months but in the end, I tell Mummy, "Yes, I understand. It's for the best that you marry Uncle Ian."

Ever since, I've hated myself.

I can't go to Confession, so I can't take communion. I try one day and the host falls off my tongue onto the plate. God doesn't love me. I committed a mortal sin, but it is Mummy's fault. She made me do it.

That's why God isn't saving me from the Monster. I think the Monster is the devil, and one of these nights, he'll crash in and claim my soul.

15

CHANGES OF HEART

A lot of people besides Aunt Ethel and Granny and Grandpa are angry with Mummy and Uncle Ian. The way Mummy puts it, half of Mexico City is against them because Mexican Catholics are narrow-minded and self-righteous. Uncle Ian has been a pillar of society and attended services at the Episcopal Church, Christ Church, every Sunday, for many years, but even the British community is turning its back on him and Mummy.

Aunty Laura and Mummy aren't talking to each other because Aunty Laura called Uncle Ian a *"Viejo libidinoso."* I look it up in English. Libidinous, which Grandpa's Oxford dictionary defines as "full of lust" and "lascivious passion." I suppose it means Uncle Ian is consumed with lust for Mummy.

The only person who is nice about everything is Daddy. He writes to say he will give Mummy a divorce, and he hopes she will be very happy with Uncle Ian. He also says how kind of Uncle Ian to agree to support us, though, of course, only for the time being until Daddy has enough cash to send for us.

Instead of being pleased, Mummy is furious. "Now, children, see how easily your father is relinquishing all responsibility for you to another man."

In a way I know she is right. Up to now I'd secretly hoped

GETTING RID OF IAN

that maybe Daddy would say, *No, think it over, Tita, don't hurry your decision.* Or he might say, *Go on, Tita, marry the man, but I want the girls to come home where they belong.* His giving in so easily is like a huge iron door has swung shut, locking us outside Carlyon and Rustington and England. Once more, he's let us down.

I try to understand. Daddy has other things on his mind. A gale came in, and the waves went all the way up the shingle and battered his catamaran to bits. Daddy has lost his wings. He's as marooned as we are.

It's been months since Uncle Ian moved out of the family home, and Aunt Ethel still won't give him a divorce. Maybe she'll be like Aunt Carlota, whose husband went off years ago to live in sin with a lady in Oaxaca. Mummy says that after all that time, it becomes a common-law marriage, as good as the real thing. Though she herself would never consent to be Uncle Ian's common-law wife or become "the back streets of his life."

One evening Uncle Ian telephones Mummy to say he must see her at once. She is worried.

"I think Ethel is up to something. She's being very sneaky. She told Uncle Ian she might consider a divorce, but he'd have to talk to Father Fenton at St. Patrick's first."

Mummy sits with Uncle Ian in his car outside the house for about an hour. When she comes in, her mascara has run and left marks where she rubbed it. "I'm in shock," she says. "What do you think that viper Ethel went and did? She got Father Fenton to make Ian take an oath never to see me again. He came to say goodbye. I've burnt all my bridges because of him. I should have realized he was going through a middle-age crisis, and he'd go back to Ethel. Damn that priest! I hope he rots in hell."

The doctor gives Mummy some pills for her nerves. She takes two and closes her thick curtains and puts on her sleeping mask. "I need darkness to nurse my broken heart. 'I am a wretched soul, bruised with adversity.'" She stays in bed the rest of that day and for the next two days. She refuses to eat anything except some chicken broth, and only because she says she needs to keep herself alive for "my children's sakes."

Granny is happy her prayers have been answered but annoyed that Mummy is carrying on so. "Tita always has to make a drama over everything."

On the third day Mummy sits up and asks, "What will I do now? I suppose I'll have to ask your daddy if he will take me back. Or maybe I will find someone else." She has lunch with Uncle Pepe. "I need a shoulder to cry on," she says. Another evening they go out dancing. Then she has the suspicion that Uncle Ian is following her. "I'm sure it was his Cadillac parked around the corner today, and I think I saw it yesterday, as well."

"Why can't that man leave you alone?" Grandpa asks. "Hasn't he caused enough trouble?"

"I haven't the faintest idea why he's following me," Mummy says, but she can't hide her smug expression.

As Mummy tells us, the next time Uncle Pepe brings her home, Uncle Ian is lying in wait outside the house. As soon as the car stops, he charges over, pulls open the door, and yanks Mummy out.

Mummy cries, "Ian, Ian, behave yourself!" so loudly that we run to the bedroom window to see what's the matter. Uncle Ian has grasped Mummy's arm with one hand and is shaking his other fist at Uncle Pepe. "Please, Ian, don't hit him!" Mummy screams. They're making enough noise to wake up the whole block.

Uncle Ian shouts at Uncle Pepe. "I'm warning you to keep your distance. If you ever try to see Tita again, I will maim you for life."

I wish they would fight over Mummy the way Anne's

boyfriends fought over her. No such luck. Uncle Pepe is not the fighting type, and Mummy begs him to leave. "I would hate any harm to befall you on my account." So he gets into his car and drives away.

The next day she tells us Uncle Ian wants her to take him back. It turns out that since he's a Protestant, a Catholic oath doesn't count, and he's decided to break the one Father Fenton made him take.

In the end he wears down Aunt Ethel, and she gives him the divorce. On condition that she keep the houses in Mexico City and in Tequesquitengo, the motor boat, and most of their belongings. He keeps his Cadillac, his favorite armchair, a few pictures and other items, and the family silver. And his war medals. Even their fox terriers are dog-divorced. Uncle Ian takes Mac, the male, and Aunt Ethel keeps Ida, the female.

Mummy says, "What an old bitch Ethel turned out to be. She took Ian to the cleaners."

I suppose that losing your husband after all those years would make even the nicest person a bit nasty, especially since she can never marry again because she's a good Catholic.

*

Mummy and Uncle Ian have to wait a year for their divorces to be final before they can be married. During that time, Mummy loves him and is going to marry him one week, and the next she's thought it over and has decided not to. Sometimes she says that if Daddy is willing, they will make a new start. Every time she changes her mind she expects us to believe her. We're all mixed up. It's hard not knowing what will happen in the future.

"Just make up your mind, Mummy. Please?" I ask her.

She gives me one of her serious looks and says, "Maybe I should send you to boarding school in the United States." As if that would solve anything.

But there's no getting rid of Uncle Ian. He has made up his mind for both of them.

Mummy says she's divided between her devotion to the Lord and her heart. Except she isn't sure of her heart any longer. "But I don't want to hurt poor Ian," she says. "Not after he's given up everything for me." And, "He's so much older. If I marry him, I'll be losing out on what little youth is left to me."

And, "I have to admit that Ethel was a good wife to Ian. The trouble was she didn't fulfill his intellectual needs."

And last, "If I call it off, I will have to return my engagement ring."

Uncle Ian has given Mummy an engagement ring with a big, square, perfect emerald from Colombia. Or, it was perfect until I tried it on. I was admiring the way it looked on my finger when Mummy, who was on the phone downstairs, called me. I leaned over the balustrade to answer her, and it fell off my finger onto the marble floor below. Now it's a cracked perfect emerald.

One day, Mummy has a long talk with the Pater and decides it isn't worth risking her immortal soul for Uncle Ian. This time she seems serious about breaking up with him. I'm sad, not because of Uncle Ian but because we won't have a home after all, and we won't have the nice meals I'd been looking forward to, like the ones Mummy made in England. I'm longing to move out of Granny's house. Anne is happy there, and she doesn't like Uncle Ian because deep down, she still hopes Mummy and Daddy will make it up though I tell her that's impossible.

Uncle Ian waits a week, and then he drives up and parks his car outside the house and sits there waiting for Mummy to come out. She sends the maid to tell him to leave, and he sends back a message that he will wait there until doomsday if he has to.

After several hours, Grandpa asks, "Doesn't the man have

anything better to do? I have a mind to tell him to get lost."

"Ian will tire and give up," Mummy says. Uncle Ian doesn't. He goes off for a while but comes back around six o'clock and rings the doorbell. He pushes aside the maid who opens the door and barges straight into the living room where Grandpa is sitting in his armchair. I'm there reading to him from *Wuthering Heights*.

Uncle Ian is all red and blustery and he seems a bit nervous. "I've come to ask for your daughter's hand in marriage," he says.

Grandpa gives him a sour look. "I thought you'd already decided to take it, with or without my consent."

At that, Uncle Ian's expression is uncertain. "It would make a big difference to Tita if she knew you were on our side."

"Well, I'm not," Grandpa says huffily. "You're much too old for my daughter. Unfortunately, she will do what she wants regardless of what I say."

At that moment Mummy slams into the living room and pummels Uncle Ian on the chest and shouts, "Didn't I tell you that you're not welcome in my parents' house?"

Right then and there Uncle Ian drops to his knees and begs Mummy to marry him, please, because he can't live without her. She is his life—his love. "Baby dearest, all I want is to give you the happiness you so richly deserve."

Mummy wilts and her eyes are all soppy and her mouth opens in a silly grin. "Oh Ian, my darling Ian," she says in a sighing voice. "I'm overcome with emotion." She holds out her hand to him. "I will marry you."

He gets to his feet and gives Mummy a jerky embrace. Then he turns to Grandpa. "I apologize for intruding, but I needed to ask you for your daughter's hand. I'm very glad this matter has been cleared up."

Off they go happily together.

"My word, what a disgusting exhibition," Grandpa says,

and he snorts. "For the life of me, I can't understand what Tita sees in that man."

16

WHERE'S MY PLACE IN LIFE?

Uncle Nacho has offered to pay our tuition. We're attending an all-girls school in the elegant part of the city, the Lomas, run by American Ursuline nuns. Mummy says the nuns only accept girls from the best families, and thank God Uncle Nacho is paying for everything as our schoolbooks have to be imported from the States. "Those American nuns must think we're all rolling in money," she says.

This year I'm doing Seventh Grade English and Fifth Grade Spanish. On my first day I make friends with Anna, who's English-Argentinian. She comes to school half-day as her mother teaches her in the morning the subjects she'd be learning in England. I spend the night with her, and her mother lets me miss morning school in Spanish and take a lesson with Anna. From then on, I go to her house quite often. But Anna's parents are very Catholic and they disapprove of Mummy. Once, when they come by for me and Mummy greets them in the car, Anna's father turns his head away and doesn't say hello.

Mummy is upset. "I don't want other people influencing you against me," she says.

Mummy's jealous. The truth is I've found a home away from home with Anna and her parents, and her English mother is willing to teach me, as well as Anna. Anything helps as when I go home to England, I don't want to be that far behind my class.

From the start, my grades in Spanish improve in my new school. My Fifth Grade Spanish teacher, Miss Martha, is quite pretty with long curly hair. She wears bright red lipstick, and her sweaters are so tight that her breasts stick out in points. She's always ready to help with my schoolwork. As a result, I'm trying harder and I'm no longer bottom of my class in Spanish. It helps that some of the girls come from very rich families and can't be bothered to study, and they get lower grades than me.

Anna and I share first place English as we easily beat the Mexican and American girls in our class. We're both more advanced in reading than what they teach us at school. Our Seventh Grade reading book in English has stories about the saints and the wondrous things they did, and it's written for much younger children and not twelve-year-olds who read real books at home. Anna and I are disgusted. "It's insulting," she says, "that we have to pay top fees at this school and not receive value for our money." She's repeating what her parents say. Her mother is thinking about changing Anna to the French Licée, where she will get a much better education.

These American nuns are very different from the nuns in England and not because they're American. Nuns in Mexico are not allowed to wear their habits in public, and these nuns look more like country ladies in white tops and gray or navy blue cardigans and skirts. The school principal, Mother Thomas, is so pretty I wonder why she became a nun. One day she tells us she heard the Call. "When the Lord asks you to follow him, it's as clear as a bell. You can't ignore it, not even if you would rather be married and have children."

I'm worried about the Call. It would be God's way of telling me how to save Mummy's soul. Unless someone does something drastic, she will end up in hell. Mummy doesn't think so. She says God in His mercy knows why we do what we do. But if He sends people to hell for sins like not going to church on Sunday, or for seeing French films, will He have much sympathy for people who break the Seventh Commandment?

Mother Thomas tells us to pray for sinners' souls and not despair over whether they will be saved. "Remember that God gives every sinner a chance to repent before the moment of death." She tells us a story about a man who jumped off the Golden Gate Bridge in San Francisco and killed himself. His daughter prayed and prayed for his soul, and one night she had a dream where her father told her that between jumping and hitting the water, he had asked God's forgiveness. "Although the last breath is the last sign of life, it may not be the last conscious thought," she says.

So there is hope for Mummy.

*

The day after my twelfth birthday I start writing a book called *The Glass Stag*. I've begun books before, but never finished more than five chapters. Daddy writes and says I shouldn't get my hopes up because it will probably end up like all the others I started. Mummy gives me a desk and promises that if I finish it, she will give me her Olivetti typewriter, so I can type it out and send it to a publisher.

When I'm writing, I forget all about Mummy and Uncle Ian and not knowing what's going to happen to us. I don't care about not belonging in Mexico and wishing I was in England with Daddy, or about girls who aren't allowed to come to my birthday party because of the Mummy and Uncle Ian scandal.

It takes me four-and-a-half months to finish my book. As I write "The End," it's such a triumph that I yell at the top of my lungs, "It's finished! It's finished!"

Anne comes running to find out what I'm screaming about.

"I've finished my book," I tell her and she asks, "Why are

you being stupid about it?"

I try to explain. "It's like when a woman has a baby."

She sits on the bed, dangling her legs and staring at the pile of notebooks that are the book. "How does it end?"

I read the last part of the last chapter to her.

"That's not very exciting," she says.

Anne wants me to write another book, this time with adventure in it. She keeps me busy, asking every day for a new chapter because she wants to find out what happens next.

Mummy insists on correcting my writing. She changes words like "a dull sky" into "a muted sky" and adds adjectives because she says it lacks description. Because of Mummy, the feeling of wonder at writing a book has disappeared. I don't think I did a good job anymore.

Funny about Mummy's own writing. She stopped after her book was published. I never will. It's the only good thing in my life.

17

THE HONEYMOONERS

Mummy and Uncle Ian invite thirty people to their wedding at the Hotel Prince. Uncle Artie is the only member of our family who will be there. Mummy threatened to never speak to him again unless he agreed to attend.

The day before the wedding she keeps saying she can't go through with it. "What should I do?" she asks. An hour later she asks us the same question again. What she really wants us to tell her is, "Mummy, you can't back out at this point, so please do marry Uncle Ian." What we want to tell her, after a year and a half of tears and shouts and arguments, is, "Mummy, please, make up your mind."

Now that I'm twelve, I know a lot more than I did when she started seeing Uncle Ian. Deep down inside, I do wonder how she can marry a man who made her divorce our father, or whether I can love Uncle Ian after he stopped us from going home to England. Anne hasn't accepted him, and she doesn't like him. "He will never take Daddy's place," she says.

Mummy goes to Confession, though Anne tells her it doesn't count, not if she plans to commit a mortal sin and be married again outside the Church.

"You would think I was about to commit murder." Mummy is all heated up. "Thank God, I'll be removing you from my mother's influence."

Granny comes into Mummy's room and asks, "Why risk losing your soul over that man?"

"Mother, I'm doing this for their sakes, to give them a home."

The softness in Granny's face disappears. "Why make your children bear the burden of your sins? They didn't ask you to divorce their father and marry that ..."

Mummy explodes. "Mother, I'm fed up with your religious mania. I'm so glad to be leaving your house forever."

Afterwards, Granny refuses to see or talk to her. Grandpa says if Mummy wants to wreck her life, it's fine by him, but he doesn't like her dragging us into it.

Once they are married, things will be better. Anne doesn't think so. Mummy tries to reason with her. "Do I have to drum it into your head that your father abandoned us?"

"If you marry Uncle Ian, I won't love you anymore," she says.

Mummy raises her eyes to the ceiling. "'How sharper than a serpent's tooth is a thankless child.' That's what old King Lear told his bad daughters Goneril and Regan. They took everything from him and left him to die on his own."

Anne runs to Granny, but an hour later I hear the two of them listening to Granny's *radio novela*, so maybe they aren't all that unhappy, after all. No one cares how unhappy I am. Because I'm twelve, they think I'm old enough to fend for myself. What about Daddy, who's all alone in our house in England? He must be unhappy as well. It will be a very long time before we see him. Instead, we'll be living with Uncle Ian and Mummy and trying to be a proper family.

On Mummy's wedding day, all morning long, she keeps saying, "I can't go through with it," and then, "I must." In the afternoon she goes to the beauty parlor. She comes home all done up and says, "Since Ian is the only person in this world willing to support us, I have to marry him."

She puts on her new powder-pink dress with its bolero top and a matching pink hat that hugs her head, and kisses us and Grandpa goodbye. "Wish me luck," she says and departs with the expression of a martyr going to the lions.

I'm glad. No more ups and downs. We'll have a home.

"Mark my words, she's making a mistake," Grandpa says to Granny.

"I dearly hope so," Granny answers, and kneels at her altar to pray for Mummy's soul.

*

Ten days after the wedding, Mummy telephones to ask Anne and me to join her and Uncle Ian on the last two days of their honeymoon in Taxco. Will someone put us on the bus to Cuernavaca? They will pick us up at one o'clock. We should wait for them on the grassy strip in front of the bus station, so they won't have to get out of the car.

Cuernavaca is a lovely place, if you go to someone's house or to a hotel. Not if you're standing in the middle of a busy street in a not-so-nice area. The sun beats down and dust swirls in the air. The place stinks of rotting fruit and smells of pee, and there's litter everywhere where people coming out of the bus station toss their rubbish. We're thirsty, but all I have is one peso and I don't want to waste it on a Coca-Cola. We'll ask Uncle Ian and Mummy to buy us one when they arrive.

Neither of us has a watch so we have to guess at the time. I ask a man and he says it's half past two.

"Why do you think they're late?" Anne asks.

"It's quite a way from Taxco."

"What if they had an accident?"

"Dear God, I hope not." What would we do? "Maybe their car broke down."

Around three o'clock, we're quite worried that Uncle Artie,

who put us on the bus, sent us to the wrong bus station. There's another for second-class buses, but Mummy wouldn't want us to ride in one of those. She and Uncle Ian must be on their way They must be on their way, that is, if nothing's happened to them. We're thirsty, and Anne wants to visit the toilet, and we're sunburnt, especially our noses. Anne's is all red. With her round face, she looks like a droopy clown. "Your nose and your peddle-pushers are the same color," I say and she tells me, "You look like a shrimp."

I spend my peso on a phone call home. The maid answers. Granny and Grandpa went to Aunty Laura's. So now we're penniless and the station clock says half past three. I tell Anne, "We'll wait half an hour more. If they're not here by four, we'll have to think the worst—they're not coming for us. We may have to beg for our fares home."

She scrunches up her face. "I'm not begging."

"I'm not talking about begging like beggars. We'll look for American tourists and ask them to help us. We can find them in the plaza; it's a few blocks away."

I promise the Virgin to pray three rosaries if Mummy and Uncle Ian come for us, and almost at once, his black Cadillac pulls up. He rolls down a window and says, "Get in." He tells Mummy, "You see, Baby dear, I told you they would be safe and sound."

"Why are you so late?" I ask. "We've been waiting for hours."

"I'm so sorry," Mummy says. "We lost track of time." She has a silly expression, as if she's embarrassed, yet pleased. "Are you all right?"

"We thought you'd forgotten about us," Anne says.

I can't hide my annoyance. "It's very hot in the sun and we're dying of thirst. Please, can we have a Coca-Cola?"

Uncle Ian turns and wags a finger at me. "You should know that I have a rule—no one is allowed to drink or eat anything in my car."

"Oh, but Ian, my poor daughters have been standing in the hot sun for over an hour."

"Two and a half hours," I correct her.

"It couldn't have been that long," Mummy says.

"Pennie said we'd have to beg for money to get home," Anne adds.

Uncle Ian jumps in. "Baby dear, children are tougher than you'd think. A little sun never hurt anybody."

Didn't he notice our sunburnt faces? "We were standing for hours in the midday sun."

"That sounds like the Noel Coward song," he says in a jolly tone. "The one that goes, 'Mad dogs and Englishmen go out in the midday sun.'"

Anne says, "I need the cloaks."

"I can't stop now. Why didn't you use the toilet in the station?"

"Mummy doesn't like us using dirty public toilets because we might catch something, and you told us to be ready outside when you arrived."

"Can't we make a short stop?" Mummy asks.

Uncle Ian looks impatient. "If we're not at the hotel by five, we won't be on time for the meal, and it's all paid for. I would hate to waste my money."

"Please try and hold it in until we get there," Mummy tells Anne. "It's only a half-hour drive."

"I've been holding it in for hours," Anne says.

"Then hold it in a while more," Uncle Ian tells her. "Just as well you didn't drink a Coca-Cola."

The trip to Taxco takes a bit more than a half hour because of the curvy road that winds around a mountain and then around it again and up to Taxco at the top. "It's a breathtaking view," Mummy says, "and the town is very pretty. It's famous for its silver. I bought a silver mustard pot and salt and pepper cellars. If there's time, we can take you to see the shops."

Uncle Ian shakes his head. "We already went. Why spend more money?"

The car makes another turn and Uncle Ian says, "Isn't this fun, all of us together like a proper family?" and, "Isn't it nice of your mother to want to share part of her honeymoon with you?" and, "Isn't it nice of me to share her with you while we're still on our honeymoon, ha-ha?" and "When I took my own daughters on long car trips, we used to sing as we went along. How about a song?" He starts to sing, puffing as he sings. "Oh give me a home, where the buffalo roam, where the deer and the antelope play..." My throat is dry from the sun, but I sing along to please him. Anne's in agony trying to hold it in, so she can't sing a note. Mummy's being lovey-dovey and cooing, "Ian dear this" and "Ian dear that." His "Baby dear" sounds silly coming from an old man like him.

My head is spinning from the curves. Uncle Ian stops singing and says, "Before we get to the hotel, there's something I want to tell you. From now on, I'd prefer that you call me Ian. It's how American kids address their stepfathers—by their first names. No more 'Uncle Ian,' please. Plain old Ian will do. I'm a simple man, and I like simple things."

We reach the hotel, way up at the top of a mountain, overlooking the town of Taxco, with a view of red rooftops and cobbled streets. It's very pretty, but we hurry to the bathroom and then to the dining room.

Mummy says, "We have a nice surprise for you, Pennie. They made a lemon meringue pie especially for us."

Uncle Ian says, "Isn't it well worth your wait?" We sit down to eat. I'm so thirsty that I gulp down my Coca-Cola. He frowns at me. "Don't drink it all at once because you're not getting another."

The spaghetti and baked chicken and fried potatoes are

so good, and I'm so hungry that I eat too fast, finish everything on my plate, and then my slice of pie. I ask for another slice.

"Don't you think you've had enough, Pennie?" Uncle Ian asks.

Mummy gives him a little girl's smile and strokes his arm. "Please, Ian dear, today's a special day."

He says, "Baby, if it will make you happy, she can have another slice, but only because this is a special occasion. However, in the future, Pennie, I want you to know that I do not welcome gluttons at my table."

That second slice of pie tastes like metal, as if it came out of a tin.

*

The next morning, Uncle Ian says, "Come and cuddle with us in bed."

Anne makes a face, but Mummy says, "Oh, yes, that would be lovely. Come on, girls. Like we used to in England."

But Ian is not Daddy, and in the morning he smells more than ever like a damp towel. I get in on one side of Mummy and Ian pulls Anne between them and puts an arm around her. He's trying to make her like him. "Now that we're a proper family." Anne looks very uncomfortable because he's stroking her and telling us how he used to cuddle his own daughters on Sundays, and he talks and talks about his daughters, and about when they were little girls like us, and Anne's squirming because she doesn't like him stroking her chest. Mummy doesn't notice. Afterwards, Anne tells her she doesn't like Ian touching her that way, and Mummy tells him this, and he's annoyed. He says he was trying to be close to her, but if that's the way she feels, he will never cuddle or show any affection to us again. Anne says she didn't want any affection from him in the first place.

*

Ian and Mummy find an apartment in Colonia

Cuauhtémoc in a building called the Edificio Nervión. At first we think that means the Nervous Building until we learn the Nervión is a river in northern Spain. The building is square and sturdy, ten stories high with four apartments on every floor and balconies with plants and flowers at each end. There are three doormen, Fausto, Chabelo, and his father old Don Matias. Don Enrique, the manager, looks like a bull. We're on the fifth floor. Mummy and Ian's bedroom, at one end of the passage, has its own bathroom with a shower, and there's another bathroom in the middle of the passage, which Ian likes more because it has a bathtub. Then Anne's bedroom, and mine at the end with a balcony. The living and dining rooms are one big room, which Mummy divides with a screen and a long turquoise sofa. Tall bookcases stand at either side of the fireplace.

Mummy isn't happy that our kitchen looks onto an inside patio and we can see into everybody else's kitchens and they into ours. She says the whole world will know what's going on in our apartment, and she puts up a curtain straightaway. The maid's room and bath are next to the kitchen and front door.

There are two elevators: a modern one for the tenants that has automatic doors; and one with a grating that has to be closed by hand, for servants and delivery boys. There's an incinerator chute to throw down the rubbish. There's a roof garden with a patio and swings for children to play on. If you look over the wall, you can see the Angel Monument on one side and almost to Polanco on the other.

Our building is nice, but not like the elegant Van Dorn at the other end of the block, which Mummy says is full of rich bohemians. Once she went to a party there where she met writers and artists and film stars, and French champagne flowed like water.

"A lovely party, my arse," Ian says "That place attracts the worst kind of people. Several politicians keep their mistresses in that building. There have been shootings, and not long ago someone jumped or was pushed off the tenth-floor penthouse. Remember the Francesca de Scaffa scandal, when her boyfriend turned out to be a jewel thief? It's certainly not the kind of place where nice people would want to live."

Who cares what he says? I'd dearly love to be a bohemian someday. Mummy says bohemians live on the fringes of society, which means I wouldn't have to worry about what society says about me. That sounds exciting.

I like having my own room. The walls are a pale yellow, the color I chose. Anne chose pink, a color I can't stand, but I don't have to share a room with her anymore. It wasn't easy because she's messy and I'm neat, and I like to read in bed while she wants the light off.

Mac, Ian's fox terrier, comes to live with us. Ian says Mac is half-human. "He doesn't know he's a dog," and we should treat him like one of us. Mac sleeps on Ian's bed, and in the daytime, he sits on Ian's wine-colored armchair in the living room. Mac is fat and sweet-natured, but he's so sad at being taken away from his old home that he pees on all the new turquoise and blue upholstered furniture, leaving yellow stains on them and on the carpet.

Ian hangs a big portrait of himself in the dining-room. He also puts up photographs of himself in his army uniform on a living room side-table and on top of the Stromberg-Carlson record player. In the First World War, Ian had been a colonel in the Argyle Sutherland Highlanders. Mummy calls him "the Colonel," when she speaks about him to other people, the same way she used to call Daddy "the Commander."

The coffee table is especially made with an oval glass top to display all of Ian's twenty medals. But he isn't like Daddy, who fought in both World Wars. Ian was here in Mexico during the last war. So how did he win all those medals?

18

THE RULES OF THE HOUSE

At our first meal together in our new home, Ian informs us he's a master carver, an art his father taught him, and he will show us the correct way to carve a chicken. His method is simple: make a slit down the middle of the breast with the carving knife, then grab the chicken and tear it apart with his bare hands. I don't know if he's joking. Daddy was always so careful about carving perfect slices.

After lunch, Ian tells Mummy he wants to have a little talk with us, just Anne and me, without her being present. He tosses Mac out of his armchair and sits in it, and we sit on the sofa facing him.

He smiles, a crocodile smile that looks like he's about to open his jaws and snap us up. "I'm aware that I can't take your father's place, but I will do my best to fulfill my obligations as your stepfather. Therefore, I expect you to fulfill yours." He's as pompous as a first-day teacher. "If you want us to be a happy family, you will have to observe a few house rules. I have written them out for you." He holds up two pages. "These should make it clear how I expect you to behave from now on." My stomach does a little dance, sort of a be-bop, thinking we will have to watch out, and this new home won't be anything like our old home

He puts on his glasses and reads. "First and foremost, this is your mother's house, and you are living here because it makes her happy. Her happiness should be of the utmost importance to you." He stops reading and says, "She's had enough trouble in her life. You will make sure her every need is met and do whatever she asks you to. So rule number one," he stares at Anne, "you must not upset your mother. If you do, you will be punished. Do you understand?"

Mummy flies into a rage all the time. How can we stop her from losing her temper and being mad at us? But we say, "Yes, Ian."

"Rule number two. The bathroom in the passage is for your mother's and my exclusive use. You may use the other bathroom to bathe in and satisfy your needs."

"But we have to cross your bedroom to get to it," I say.

He looks puzzled as if that hadn't occurred to him. "Well, then, I'll permit you to bathe in our bathroom twice a week in the evening, as long as you don't take more than fifteen minutes. But you must always ask permission first, and make sure it is convenient."

"What about ... you know, when we have to use the toilet?" All of a sudden I'm afraid of him.

"You will use the other bathroom to satisfy your needs. If we are in our bedroom, use the maid's, and at night, a good old chamber pot should do." Neither of us ask, what if we have to poop?

"Rule number three. Your mother and I treasure our privacy. You can have friends over on special occasions only, with our permission." This isn't new. We don't ask friends over because they get on Mummy's nerves, so we only invite them to parties.

"Rule number four. I want you to observe this rule without exception. The telephone is for your mother's and my exclusive use. You are not, I repeat, you are not to give this number to anyone. I will hang up on people who call you."

I manage to keep my face straight, while knowing this will ruin my social life. If my friends can't call me, will they want to be friends?

Anne asks, "Suppose it's an emergency?"

"If it's an emergency, they should say so," he says.

"Rule number five. Do not mention your father in front of your mother or put up photographs of him." I glance at Anne—her face is tight and rebellious. What about Daddy's photo on top of her dresser?

"Rule number six. If you go out with your mother, always ask my permission first. I must know where you are going and what time you are coming home."

"Like the name of the movie we want to see?"

"Exactly. Then I won't be worried something has happened to you."

"Rule number seven. No conversations allowed with your mother behind closed doors. Whatever you have to say to her, you can say in front of me."

There are other rules, a list of them, and he hands me two typewritten pages. "I trust you will take these to heart," he says. "As long as you keep those rules, there shouldn't be any problem. Remember, good daughters make good wives, and someday you will say, 'Thank you, Ian, for everything you taught us.'"

Before long, we forget the rules, and we pay the price. We go to the movies with Mummy, only to come home to a furious Ian. Have we forgotten his rule about asking permission first?

"It's my fault," Mummy says. "We were late, and I rushed them out."

"Don't cover up for them, Baby," he says. "That has nothing to do with it. This is a clear transgression on their part, and they should accept their guilt. However," he gives us his crocodile smile, "on this occasion, I am willing to overlook this with the condition that you never, ever go out again with your mother without my consent. I trust I've made that clear."

"Sorry, Ian." But we're left with the puzzling question. Why do we have to apologize?

Mummy says in a cold voice, "Ian, I'd like to have a word with you in private." As they head toward their bedroom, she says, "I will not allow you to bully my daughters." Their door slams shut, but we can hear them shouting for a while after that.

*

I hate mealtimes. Anne does, as well. We'd rather go without eating than sit down at the table with Ian. He stares at us with bulging eyes, pinning us with his gaze. I feel he's trying to invade my mind and take it over. I'm too scared to move, to think, to say a word. I put food into my mouth, but nothing matters except for his eyes, controlling me, and somehow he does it to Anne, as well. We sit there, controlled and frightened, until we finish everything on our plates and say, "Excuse me, please," and flee. Anne and I can't work out how he does it to both of us at the same time.

In the safety of my room, I decide he's trying to hypnotize us, the way Rasputin hypnotized the Tsarina of Russia. We do whatever he tells us without question. We're under his thrall—a word I find when looking up hypnosis—which means "the state of being in someone's power" or "a state of servitude or submission." I bet that's what he's done to Mummy—hypnotized her because she's not herself at all. Half the time she acts like a little girl, until she snaps at him, and his eyes grow big and mad-like, I can see him struggle to control himself and stop from doing something nasty. But Mummy is still Mummy, and she complains to Ian about everything—the maids, the food, where we live, her family, and of course, us.

"He's trying to hypnotize us the same way he's hypnotized Mummy," I say to Anne. She agrees. "It's always at the lunch table," she says. "Does he want us to stop eating?"

I'm sure that I will never forget Ian's eyes, and trying to avoid them by looking at the picture on the wall of Emperor Maximilian facing the firing squad. Then there's Ian's enormous portrait hanging next to the table. That gives the impression he's always watching.

*

Ian takes pills. Sleeping pills and tranquilizers and pills that give him energy. Mummy says that's why he has trouble sleeping. He's up at two in the morning, pacing around the apartment. Sometimes I awake and hear him walking back and forth or banging away on his typewriter. I suppose he's tired of being alone because one night he thumps on Anne's door and then mine. "Get your fat fannies out of bed," he roars. "Both of you. In the living room. Right away."

Why is he waking us in the middle of the night? I put on my slippers and dressing gown, and trudge into the living room. Anne's just behind. We stand before him. Something isn't right. His eyes are like marble—hard, cold, no expression, nothing in them.

"You need to comprehend your position in this household. At least servants work for their keep—whereas you do next to nothing." He picks up his glass of Scotch and has a drink. "You can't sit on your arses in my house. Here everyone does something. My daughters always knew they had to help out."

He talks about his daughters, who both live far away so he doesn't see much of them, and how well-trained they were when they lived in his house. One was married at seventeen and the other became a nun. After a while, he mellows. How much he loves our mother, and how he will do anything to bring happiness back into her life, and please, help him make

Mummy happy.

"Nothing you can do, Ian," I tell him, "will ever make Mummy happy."

His forehead wrinkles. "Why not?"

"She enjoys being unhappy."

"If she's not happy," he says, "there's a good reason, and it's for you to find out. Remember that your mother has endured numerous operations, and has constant health problems as the result of hardship and privations. From now on she should stop worrying and relax. I'm sure you must care enough for her to want to make her happy."

He runs out of steam after an hour. "You can go back to bed," he says as if he's doing us a favor, and he serves himself another whiskey from the drinks tray.

Next day I tell Mummy about this wee hours' talk, and maybe I exaggerate and say I fell asleep at school, but I want to rile her up enough to make her mad at Ian. For once, she doesn't get angry; she has a serious look and says she will talk to him about waking us up. Later, she tells me Ian says he never did such a thing. Either he's lying or he's forgotten, but we haven't, and it's two against one. Mummy doesn't want to believe us. "It must have been a mistake," she says.

*

The very first time I use "our" bathroom after lunch, I'm stuck there when Ian and Mummy come right back to their bedroom, and start doing "it." I've never heard anyone doing it, but why else is he groaning and Mummy moaning, "Yes, Ian, yes," and their bed is making a crazy whacking sound, and the headboard is banging on the wall that separates their room from the bathroom where I'm sitting on the toilet. Then Mummy cries, "Stop, Ian, stop, you're hurting me!"

A shiver runs through me, then another, and I have goose-flesh on my arms. Should I run in to defend her? No, they'd know I was in here, listening. But he's doing something to her, hurting her, and he won't stop. I'm all mixed up because I didn't know that doing it could hurt, though maybe I'm wrong because they're at it again.

I think about creeping past and hoping they don't see me, but that's too risky. Even after they finish, I don't dare come out because then they'll know I heard everything, and get mad at me even though I was in our bathroom. I'm petrified he'll come in here so I stand behind the shower curtain, praying he won't look and I won't give myself away. Sure enough, he comes in and pees and washes off in the washbasin and leaves. Then Mummy comes in. By now, I'm fed up and since I haven't done anything wrong, she can't be mad at me, so I wait until she's peed to step out from behind the shower curtain. She lets out a scream.

I say "Shut up, Mummy, Ian will hear you." He calls out, "Something the matter, Baby?"

She pulls herself together and says, "No, Ian, just coming out," and to me, she whispers, "What are you doing in here?"

"I came in to pee, and then you came into the bedroom, and I was afraid to come out."

"Did you hear anything?"

Anyone with two ears would have heard them, but I say, "Ian really snores loudly."

Mummy chooses to believe what she likes to believe. "Let me see what I can do to help you," she says, "Ian's lying down, and he's falling asleep. Wait a few minutes."

"This won't work," I say, "with the bathrooms. You have to tell Ian that we must use your bathroom sometimes. I haven't bathed in a week."

"You haven't bathed in a week?" she repeats. "You're absolutely right. I'll talk to Ian about giving you permission to use it."

A funny thing, Ian doesn't mind us bathing Mac in his bathtub or the wet doggy smell he leaves behind, but he doesn't want us to bathe there—as if we will leave some dreadful disease in the tub. When I tell this to Mummy, she says, "I thoroughly object to your bathing Mac in our tub." From now on, she says we should bathe him on the roof in the sink where the clothing is washed.

I'm angry with God for letting Mummy pull us into this mess. Why are we supposed to love God even when horrid things happen to us? Memories swamp me, as they always do when I'm unhappy, of Daddy and how loving he was with us.

I'll find a way to get even with Ian. Put tranquilizers in his food at lunch so he will sleep all afternoon. It's not a bad idea. I'll buy some Equanils, the sedatives Mummy loves, from the *farmacia* and see if they dissolve in Campbell's cream-of-tomato soup.

I mention this to Anne. "That way, he'll sleep all afternoon and our friends can call us."

She likes the idea and adds her own contribution. Why not break up the pills, turn them into powder? That way it will be easier to put them in Ian's soup.

Next morning, Saturday, he wants to have a little talk with me while he's having his breakfast. The drippy egg yolk has left a couple of yellow spots on his moustache. He picks up a piece of toast, ladles on the marmalade, and takes a bite before saying, "I want you to know, Pennie, that I appreciate your female concerns. After all, I have two daughters of my own." He smiles, the hearty smile I've come to hate. "As they would tell you, I can be very understanding. Therefore, I have no problem with your taking a bath so long as I know beforehand. Better still, ask your mother. But please, don't take advantage of my good nature. Two baths a week should be enough."

He waits as if expecting me to say something. What?

Thank you, Ian, for being so nice, and letting me bathe in your tub.

I tell him, "Yes, Ian, I'll make sure to do that," but I'm thinking, how many ground-up Equanils would it take for him to overdose and die?

19

WHO IS EATING AT MY TABLE?

One afternoon, while Ian is having his after-lunch nap, Mummy creeps into my room. We have to be very careful because Ian has ordered us not "to hold meetings with your mother behind closed doors."

"I have to talk to you," she says in a loud whisper, as she shuts my door.

"Mummy, you know Ian doesn't like us talking behind his back."

She raises her voice. "Damn Ian. I refuse to be cowed by his petty rules. Anyway, he took a sedative and he's fast asleep."

She sits on my bed, lights a cigarette, and speaks as if it pains her to say the words. "Ian has not turned out to be the man he led me to believe he was. Ethel was a saint to put up with him all those years. I can't believe I married such a man after your kind, gentle daddy who understood me so well. To tell you the truth, I'm thinking of leaving Ian."

If she expects me to be shocked, she's in for a disappointment. I knew she'd have a change of heart before long; she always does.

"I suspect Ian may not be quite right in the head." She takes a long puff on her cigarette and lets out the smoke very slowly, waiting for me to react.

They've been married six months. But you never know with her. She'll probably change her mind. I'm cautious. "What makes you think that, Mummy?"

This time she pauses before answering, as if she fears to do so. "What I tell you is for your ears only. Of the highest confidentiality. So keep it to yourself. I suspect that what Ian did during the war unhinged him, and let me tell you, he did things no normal person would dream of doing. Don't you have an ashtray in here?" She opens my balcony door to flick her ashes outside. "Your plants need watering," she says. "Ian rants and raves in his sleep, and I've learned some horrible things from him."

"Perhaps he has nightmares about the First World War."

"No, this was during the Second."

"Ian wasn't in it."

"Oh yes, he was, but he took an oath of silence not to tell anyone what he did." She sounds quite gleeful. "At night it all comes out."

"What did he do that was so dreadful?"

She shakes her head. "My lips are sealed. He swore me to secrecy, and they are not things I would want my young daughter to know. All I can say is that you children will have to be very careful not to anger him—he's capable of murder when he's angry."

She's acting, I'm sure, the way she does to draw attention. She uses a special voice, earnest and somber. I can't tell if she's trying to scare me or if it's really the truth.

"I'm frightened, Pennie," she says. "He's killed before—without compunction—and he might do it again. He told me he knows how to strangle a man in just seconds. He learned that when they trained him to be a spy."

A spy? Ian a spy? "When?"

"At the beginning of the war. You don't think they gave

145

him all those medals because they liked him. He earned them, every one of them, and not for doing nice things. In wartime anything is justified, including murder. Oh well, I shouldn't have told you that, but I had to get it off my chest. I don't want you to worry."

So why tell me those things? Of course I worry. When Ian is angry, he doesn't just get angry. He gets mad, and his eyes open so wide you'd think they would pop out. Suppose that someday he's so mad at something Mummy says that he strangles her, and he doesn't realize what he's done until it's over.

*

When we sit down to lunch, Mummy complains that the maid, Gloria, bought the wrong things at the supermarket.

Ian asks in a nasty tone, "Why didn't you girls do the shopping instead? I can't see that you've earned the right to eat at this table."

Mummy springs to our defense. "Ian, you have no right to say such things."

"In my time," Ian says, "if children didn't do their share, they went without a meal." He glares at us. "If they were hungry, they'd do more to help around here, instead of expecting to be waited on."

"I'm not sitting here while you bully my daughters." Mummy snarls like a dragon at him. "Pennie, Anne, we're leaving the table." She half-stands.

Ian slams his hand down on the glass table top and glares at us as if we were insects he'd like to squash. "Stay seated, all of you. All I said was that a little help would be nice."

I see the same tight expression on Anne's face as on my own. We'd rather skip lunch than sit there with him in that mood. I have to speak up. "Ian, we'd help, but we arrived from school five minutes before we sat down at the table."

He turns hard eyes on me and I shrivel under his gaze.

I'm not saying another word.

Mummy rings her little silver bell, and Gloria brings in a tray with the soup served with fried croutons on top.

Ian makes a face. "We had cream-of-tomato yesterday."

"I wrote cream-of-mushroom, but she couldn't read my handwriting," Mummy says. "So she bought this instead."

"What can you expect from a monkey who jumped out of the trees?" Ian asks. Neither of them notices Gloria's face flush with anger or the way she stomps out of the room.

Ian slurps his soup. If we slurped ours, Mummy would be annoyed, but she says he never learned proper table manners because his mother died when he was a little boy, and he was brought up by a bunch of servants.

"I've lost my appetite," Mummy says and she puts down her spoon.

Ian says, "I'm sorry about that, Baby," then turns on us. "How can you two sit there enjoying your food when your mother has no appetite for hers?"

"Why take it out on my daughters?" Mummy asks.

"Because it's time they got off their fat fannies and did something to earn their keep."

"I should have known we'd be a burden on you," Mummy says in her martyr tone.

Ian clenches his jaw and his lips barely move when he speaks. "I gave up a marriage of thirty-four years to be with you."

Mummy's nose puckers as if she's about to snort out fire. "Let me remind you that I wasn't the one who asked you to divorce Ethel."

He says in a menacing voice, "May I remind you that you used me, among other things, as your chauffeur?"

"I used you? What do you think you were doing to me?" She glances at us. "This conversation is not for your ears, children, you had better leave the table."

We scuttle away to our rooms, thankful that ordeal is over.

After lunch, they take a nap. A very long nap. Then Ian goes out, and Mummy calls us in to say they have made it up. She's lying on her bed with her Merry Widow corset pulled loosely around her. The room is hot and full of Ian's damp towel smell. "Open the window, please," she says, "it's too close in here." She's not trying to hide her smug look. As if she wants us to know what they were up to. She asks us to run to the *farmacia* and buy her cigarettes and Bufferin because, "I have a headache. Ian really wears me out. He can be so rough. I can't believe I married two such completely different men. One never touched me and the other won't leave me alone."

Anne's face wrinkles in anger. Can't Mummy see we don't like her saying this? She's told me all about her life with Daddy, from the first time they did it "after a pillow fight," to the last time before we left England. She says she needs to share it with me because sex was part of the reason why her marriage to Daddy hadn't worked out.

*

One evening Ian comes back late. His face is sort of green and drawn, and he's not well. He sits on the sofa, brooding and drinking his Scotch. Maybe because he and Mummy fought at the lunch table, but this time he didn't take a nap, just walked out of the apartment.

Mummy tries to patch things up. "Ian dear, please tell me everything is all right. I didn't mean to hurt your feelings."

He says, "Don't worry, Baby, I must have eaten something that didn't agree with me."

It's sickening to see Mummy being all lovey-dovey and concerned about him.

That's when I pull Anne into my room and close the door. "Let's pray for him to die," I tell her.

She takes a bit of convincing, but in the end, we go to church and pray and light a candle.

Three days later, Ian has a coronary thrombosis.

20

IAN SCOURS HIS SOUL AND
FINDS IT SORELY LACKING

For several days it's touch and go if Ian will survive. Mummy stays at his side, except when his sons come to relieve her. The only day she doesn't go to the hospital is out of respect for his daughter, the nun, who comes to see her father.

The next morning, one of Ian's sons calls to tell Mummy not to come to the hospital. From now on, he says, Ian's children will take care of their father. Mummy slams down the receiver. "Like hell they will! Those vipers took advantage of my absence and conspired to take my husband away from me."

She rushes off to the hospital but comes back sooner than expected, shouting, "Children, children, I need to talk to you."

Ian is dead. I feel like being sick.

Mummy stands in the middle of the living room, shaking her clenched fists at an invisible enemy, and screams, "Ian has lost his mind. He told me he doesn't need me anymore, and his own family will look after him. That's all the gratitude I get for everything I did. It took those snakes one day to alienate him."

She drops onto the sofa and lights a cigarette. She wrinkles her forehead and her eyebrows come together, and she narrows her eyes and bites her lower lip. "I know who's behind this. Ethel. She's been scheming to get him back. Now she's using her own children. Yesterday, they all ganged up on him and brought along that meddlesome priest, Father Fenton, who did so much damage once before."

Goody, goody. Dear God, I'm sorry I didn't believe you would help us.

She sucks on her cigarette as if breathing in fire, and the smoke comes out in one spurt. "I need a drink, Pennie. Bring me something to calm me down. A whisky—it's good for my blood pressure—with water and one ice cube. How can Ian do this to me? Ian, who nearly died in my arms the other night. I wish to God he had died before they could get their slimy hands on him. They told him if he didn't mend his ways, he would be condemned to hell, and poor Ian is in no condition to defend himself." She shouts at me. "Pennie, don't stand there like a bump on a log. Can't you see I'm on the verge of a nervous breakdown? Bring me a Kleenex—the whole box. I don't see how I will ever recover."

She drinks the whisky and smokes another cigarette. What has she done to deserve such a trick of fate? God must be punishing her for her sins. She should have heeded her parents' advice. Then she takes two Equanils to calm down.

"Don't worry, Mummy," I say. "Ian will change his mind."

Just in case, I go to the church and light another candle and pray that he doesn't change his mind. Mummy likes to say, "God works in strange ways his wonders to perform." This does seem God's way of showing us Ian doesn't have to die in order to get rid of him.

The next day Mummy goes back to the hospital. His sons bar the way into his room. "He doesn't want to see you," they say.

She tells them they have no right to keep a wife from seeing her husband, and the law is on her side, and she knows they have brainwashed Ian, and if she has to, she will raise such a stink they will end up ruing the day they ever crossed her path. So they agree to let her see him for a few minutes, as long as she doesn't agitate him.

"'Hell hath no fury like a woman scorned,'" she says when she comes home. "Oh, I have a tale to tell you, but first I need a whisky." She serves herself, a strong one from what I can see, and puts it on a side table next to where she's sitting. "Neither one of Ian's sons had the decency to leave us on our own." Her voice sounds like she's reciting romantic poetry. "Poor Ian looked so frail, and white, and haggard—those vultures have been draining the life out of him. Do you know what he told me? He wants to become a monk. Ian, of all people. Imagine him in a monastery. Ha!"

Anne and I sit there and listen to Mummy go on, and all I can think is our prayers worked, but it's too crazy to be true.

She holds out her empty glass and asks me for another drink. "I'm giving myself permission to get high tonight."

The Scotch bottle is half empty. I serve Mummy about half of what's left. If she wants to get high, that should do it.

She continues, "Ian said he'd had a revelation, the kind you sometimes have on your deathbed." She pauses and her voice cracks a little. "He saw that his true vocation in life was—you will never believe this—to become a monk. He intends to convert and enter a Roman Catholic monastery. I said, 'Ian, you're not cut out to be a monk.'" She stops, takes a deep breath, and her voice comes out in a gust of hatred. "But that son-of-a-bitch priest told him to heed the call of God. I didn't dare tell Ian that he'd been coerced into this decision, not with his two sons poised like Dobermans ready to tear me to pieces." She sounds like she's giving a performance; her voice varies from fierce to tragic to almost sobbing and back. "Ian said to me, 'Try to understand, Baby dearest, I have scoured my soul and found it sorely lacking. It looks as if we're not destined to be together in this world after all.' I asked, who was I to question his decision, and I would always carry his last words graven on my heart. He told me, 'Baby dearest, I will love you forever.'" Tears roll down her cheeks.

Mummy is getting woozy from the Scotch or the Equanils or both. She says, "I pray that his sons' reproductive organs wither and fall off. And that meddlesome priest ends up writhing in eternal agony in the seventh circle of Hell!"

Ian's sons come for Mac, Ian's portrait and photographs, the silver, and his other personal belongings. Mummy won't let them take Mac's armchair, the screen with Ian's prints, or the coffee table. She says she will call a carpenter to remove the medals from the table at her own convenience. In the meantime we cover the glass top with newspaper. What will Ian do with them? He won't need them in a monastery.

While Ian recovers, he stays with his married daughter in Ciudad Juárez on the Mexican-American border where he obtains a quicky Mexican divorce. Mummy agrees to it as long as he continues to support her until she can stand on her feet again.

No question about it, Mummy will have to start working. Her Mexican resident papers aren't a problem anymore because Ian is a Mexican citizen, which gives her the right to work. Though, to her, this is not an advantage. "How will we live off what I make as a teacher?" she says. "I should look for work in the States. Your Uncle Nacho has offered to pay for your boarding school there, so that's not a problem. After all, I did work in the Office of Censorship, and I know how to type. I might find a position as a social secretary to a millionaire in Texas."

*

"I don't believe he's sincere," Granny says about Ian's decision to become a monk. "He'll change his mind."

"I always suspected he had a screw loose," Grandpa says.

"That thrombosis took him over the edge. The man's a nutcase. They are all better off without him."

Granny tells Mummy that before she makes any decisions about our future, it might help to stay with the Pater at the cathedral in Puebla.

The Pater's apartment, at the back of the cathedral, was built four hundred years ago and we have to climb forty steps up a narrow staircase to reach it. Inside, it has stone walls and uncarpeted floors and furniture that belongs in the last century. Luisita, the Pater's housekeeper, flutters around making us welcome. She gives us *tamales* and sweet, frothy hot chocolate for supper. We don't like having to kneel on the bare floor to say the rosary afterwards. Mummy can't because of her Bad Leg, and so she sits on a chair instead.

The beds are the kind you sink into, with cushy pillows and heavy, embroidered sheets. The rooms have shutters that make them really dark at night, and Mummy says she is sure to sleep like a top. At first it isn't easy to fall asleep. Maybe it's the sensation that the night is full of spirits. As if the movement and voices and prayers of all the people who have been inside the cathedral are still there, a congregation of laments and praises somehow caught forever inside that great jeweled cavern.

The next day the cathedral bells awaken us, and every bell in the city is also ringing. We find out that all three hundred and sixty five churches in Puebla, one for every day of the year, ring their bells at the same time in early morning and early evening.

Anne and I attend early Mass with Luisita because the Pater gives it. Mummy says the last few weeks have taken their toll, and she will go at twelve o'clock. Hearing Mass in the cathedral is different from hearing it in a church especially when the choir is singing. You feel exalted, as if you will rise above this earth and join the angels praising the Lord.

Last night at dinner, the Pater told us, "This cathedral is the finest example of baroque colonial art in the New World." I don't know what that means, but I suppose it's because it is filled with gold decoration and paintings of martyrs and life-size statues, and little chapels with altars of gold and precious stones.

Every day we walk around Los Portales, an arcade that surrounds the plaza in front of the cathedral. It's lined with stalls and eating places. The air is heavy with the scent of fresh baked *pan dulce* and harsh coffee from Veracruz. We can hear café bands all over the plaza, in some places drowning each other out. The stalls are loaded with all kinds of sweets, and we buy walnut and caramel and milky *cajetas*, light and crunchy toffees, and candied fruit.

Luisita outdoes herself in the kitchen, making dishes like real *mole*, which was invented in Puebla. We watch her grind up different kinds of chilies with spices and chocolate and turn them into a thick red-brown sauce. Mummy says it would take her all day to make it using a mixer, but Luisita takes two hours to put it together though she already had prepared some of the ingredients.

Mummy says it's obvious the Pater likes good food—he's chubby—and he'd better watch out because on that side of her family, men like her grandfather who enjoyed their food too much died early of heart trouble. The Pater laughs and says God will take him when he wants to, whatever he eats, and Puebla is well-known for having the best dishes in Mexico. He's very funny and makes us, even Mummy who's been down in the dumps since Ian left her, laugh all through the mealtimes. He isn't like other Catholic priests who condemn her for her sins. "That is up to God to judge and not me," he says.

We see *Love Is A Many-Splendored Thing*, a film only for adults, but in Puebla they're not strict about letting us in.

Mummy says it's all right because she's the one who should decide what we can or cannot see. It's a true story about a woman who's in love with a married man. Her family, who are Chinese, don't approve at all, like Granny and Grandpa with Mummy, and it shows me how people think the same way all over the world. The ending and the music make me cry; though I try not to let anybody see. I imagine love can be very beautiful—even if it makes you unhappy.

The three of us are having such a good time that we stay on a few days more than planned

*

Ian phones. He's on his way back from Veracruz. Can he drop by?

Mummy is very cool to him over the phone. She says she doesn't know if she can see him because what will her uncle, the Monsignor, say about him coming here. Ian says if he has to wait downstairs until she appears, he will do so, even if it takes days. And wait he does. We can see his black Cadillac in the street. Ian is persistent, and he won't take no for an answer. Mummy doesn't give in, not after all he's put her through, but as it gets later and he's still there, she's concerned because he's out in the sun. Maybe she should have a word with him after all.

Mummy asks the Pater what to do if Ian insists on talking to her. The Pater tells her this apartment is part of a church, and everybody is welcome under God's roof.

As Ian climbs up the stairs, holding a large bunch of red roses, I know our peace of mind is over. He'll win Mummy back, despite her protests that she won't ever take him back, not if he goes down on his bended knees and begs her—which is exactly what he does as soon as he enters the room. There he is on his knees saying, "Baby, I love you more than life itself. Can you ever forgive me?"

"After all the anguish you put me through?" Mummy tries

to sound indignant, but she doesn't fool anyone. "What do you take me for? Why don't you ask Ethel instead?"

Within half an hour, he convinces her to have dinner with him. We know what that means. She will forgive him and take him back. Sure enough, she comes in late, and says, "I accepted Ian's new proposal. We need him to support us. I can't do it on my own. So call it a practical decision. But I don't know what to tell the Pater. What will he think of me?"

The Pater doesn't tell her off. He's not like Father Fenton. He tells her he's very sad that her decision will distance her from the Church. She asks for his blessing, and he gives it to her and to us, as well.

We're going to need it.

Ian and Mummy are married all over again in Cuernavaca. Quicky divorce—quicky remarriage. Back goes everything. Ian's portrait and photographs. We uncover the medals. Mac pees on the sofa and takes over the armchair, and again, Ian is in control.

He says he should never have left the Church of England in the first place. As for the monastic life, he took one look and knew it wasn't his cup of tea.

21

WHO IS LIVING IN MY HOUSE?

Ian's caught us breaking his rule of talking with Mummy behind closed doors twice, and he blames me. He's taken off my lock and threatened to remove my door if he catches us again. But Mummy keeps coming into my room, while Ian takes his nap, to talk about her troubles. She says things like, "Ian is a disturbed man," and, "I've found out some terrible things about Ian," and, again, "Ian is capable of murder." His mad eyes are scary enough, but that makes it worse. Now, when I hear him at night, I'm afraid he'll burst into my room and strangle me.

One afternoon she comes in while I'm typing my book. "I have to talk to you," she says in a theatrical whisper. "Don't worry. Ian took a pill and he's fast asleep. I want to warn you, and your sister, not to anger him—he's on the verge of exploding."

She gets a coy look, one that I recognize from the days when she went out with the uncles or Ian was courting her. Last weekend, she and Ian went to a party at Aunty Laura's house. Aunty Laura has given in about their marriage, but only because Mummy called and asked, how could her own sister close her door to Mummy and her new husband, but welcome other divorced friends? So Aunty Laura invited them over to smooth out hard feelings.

"There must have been sixty people there," Mummy says. "I was at one end of the room and Ian at the other, and I was talking to my old friend, B. J., who was at the American School with me."

I imagine the scene. Ian at one end of Aunty Laura's living room that's as big as our whole apartment. And Mummy at the other end talking to another man. Ian can't stand her chatting to other men, unless he's right there next to her. It turns out her old friend is also a divorce lawyer.

"I could see Ian looking at us with daggers in his eyes, though we weren't doing anything wrong. Ian didn't say anything until we were on our way home. Then he asked how could I flirt with another man under his very nose? He was sure my sister put me up to it."

"Aunty Laura would never do that."

"He thinks it's because Laura doesn't like him. Ian told me he was not surprised that I was so eager to go to my sister's house, to meet my old flames there. I swore that he's an old school friend but Ian said, 'I know what you said to him.' That was impossible; he was at the other end of the room. He told me practically word for word what I'd said."

Mummy is trembling. "Ian was trained to lip read, and to hypnotize."

Hypnotize? I was right. "But, Mummy, how can he lip read from that far away?"

"He knew exactly what I'd said. And he asked why the hell was I talking to a divorce lawyer about personal matters? He threatened that if I ever spoke to my friend again, he'd kill him with his bare hands."

"He said that to frighten you."

"Then he succeeded, Pennie. Those weren't idle threats."

"He can't go around murdering men who talk with you."

"I'm not implying that, but during the war, he had to …"

159

She catches herself. "I can't say anymore. Many people did things during the war that went against their moral beliefs."

"There wasn't a war in Mexico."

Her face changes and she actually looks proud. "Ian was in British Intelligence. He trained alongside some of the best fighters in the French Resistance. One of his friends, a Frenchman, was caught and tortured by the Gestapo. But Ian prefers to keep quiet about his role during the war."

"Then why show off his medals? What did he really do?"

Mummy stands and paces back and forth in my little room, waving her cigarette as she speaks. "Ian played a vital role in saving the United States from Nazi invasion."

"Honestly?"

She stares at me as if I asked a silly question. "He had a handful of people to help keep Nazi agents from infiltrating the U.S. through Mexico. The Mexican government was on the Allied side, but there were many German sympathizers in this country." She stops and seems to think about what she said. Then she lifts her head and her voice trembles. "I'm afraid I've given you the wrong idea about Ian. He is really a very brave man, worthy of respect. An unsung hero."

All on her own she has convinced herself that he's not so bad.

*

Mummy gives herself a new look. She gets rid of the dresses she brought from England because Ian doesn't want her wearing things from her former life. She prefers sober colors and fitted skirts and believes them more elegant and suitable for a woman almost forty. Her favorite is a navy-blue dinner dress with a bolero top, which she buys at Henri de Chatillon. Her hair is short with a fringe and a curl over each cheek. She calls it a Joan Crawford hairdo. Even her expressions change. She starts to speak like a queen giving commands, and she raises one eyebrow as if questioning or doubting, or she has a sneery expression if she doesn't like what you're saying. Or when she wants to show people she's suffering or for them to feel sorry for her, she talks in what Anne calls her "dying duck" voice. If they ask, "How are you?" she tells them in a moaning voice that she's unwell and all that is wrong with her.

Mummy and Ian go out most Wednesday and Saturday nights, giving us a chance to take long baths, and phone our friends, and listen to records on the Stromberg Carlson. Once a month, Ian goes to Masonic Lodge. Mother Mary Louise told us the Masons hold satanic rituals and take vows of secrecy because they don't want people to know they're in league with the devil.

Anne and I don't care what the Masons do. Not as long as they get Ian out of the apartment.

Every Thursday, he sees his sons, and that's when Mummy takes us to the films. Sometimes we come back late and he's there, waiting for us, sitting on the sofa and drinking Scotch whisky. He may have drunk a lot of whisky, especially if he's been home long before we come back. He hates for us to go anywhere with Mummy, even when we have his permission.

Mummy insists on seeing Grandpa one afternoon a week. Ian resents even that. He drops her off and is back for her an hour later, hooting his horn for her to come out.

One afternoon he announces he's taking out his son-in-law from Ciudad Juárez, who's here visiting, to see the sights. He leaves the house around four thirty in the afternoon and Mummy says why don't we see *To Catch A Thief* with Cary Grant and Grace Kelly?

We come home to find Ian sitting by himself, furious. Have we forgotten his rules about asking his permission first?

"If you children take advantage of my generosity, I may not be so willing to allow you to go out with your mother. I was worried because it was late with no sign of you."

"We couldn't find a taxi," Mummy says.

"Are your daughters too lazy to look for one?"

Mummy bristles. "If you call my daughters lazy, then how about your son who's too lazy to finish high school?"

"What gives you the right—?" Ian's cheeks turn purple and he falls back on the sofa, gasping for breath.

Mummy wilts. One minute she's angry—the next she's kneeling beside the sofa. "Oh Ian, Ian! What's wrong?" in her Shakespeare tragedy voice.

He seems to force out the words, "Baby dearest, don't ever leave me."

"I won't leave you. Of course I won't, Ian darling."

They go on. Ian gasping his love, Mummy swearing she loves him, Mac barking his head off and running around in circles.

After a few minutes Ian sits up. He says, "This must not happen again, Baby. You must always tell me where you're going. I'm worried not knowing your whereabouts."

Mummy gazes at him as if he's some kind of a god. "I promise, Ian, not to be so thoughtless in the future. But, please, my daughters were not to blame."

"On this occasion," he turns to us, "I'm prepared to overlook this transgression. But you are not, and I repeat, you are not to go out with your mother without my consent. I trust I've made that clear."

Mummy says, "Yes, Ian, it's perfectly clear. Isn't it, girls? And we're sorry for upsetting you."

By now I'm convinced Ian hypnotized Mummy. Before, she would stand up for us and for herself. Sometimes she was so fierce, it was embarrassing. Now she behaves as if Ian's taken out her guts and left mush in their place.

Where is the Mummy we used to know?

*

One of Ian's rules is that we cannot receive or make any calls on the telephone. So, every time the phone rings, we stop whatever we're doing and wait. Usually, he answers except when he's taking his afternoon nap. Even then he may come rushing out in his dressing gown. If it's a family member of ours, he hangs up on them. If it's a friend of Mummy's, he may tell them she's too busy to talk. If it's someone for us, he tells them, "11-22-33 is a private telephone," and hangs up. This has happened to my teacher, and a friend's parent twice, to uncles, aunts, and many others. If it's a boy, Ian says, "This is not a whorehouse," and hangs up. If Granny or Aunty Laura or some of Mummy's friends call and he answers, they hang up.

No one understands why we aren't allowed phone calls. We explain that Mummy's husband needs it for his business. We tell close friends to pretend it's a wrong number. They have code names. Nancy D. asks for the *Nevería Dulce,* and Anna F. for *Farmacia Ana.*

When I hear Ian say, "Does this sound like the *Sastrería León?*" I know it's Susi L. and run downstairs to call her on the public telephone in the lobby.

The worst are phone calls at lunch time.

Just after the new maid brings in the soup, cream-of-celery—which I'd better finish before they start fighting and Anne and I have to leave the table—the phone rings.

Ian's head rears up. We freeze. Mummy twitches. "Answer it," she says to the maid. "Tell them we're eating."

"Who was it?" Ian asks as the maid hangs up.

"They didn't say."

"Who did they ask for?"

"La Señora."

"That's all?" The maid nods and slinks away. Mummy shakes her head. "I have a bad suspicion that something's wrong with my father."

Ian says, "Call your parents after lunch." He spreads a thick roll of Philadelphia cream cheese on a slice of brown German bread and shoves it into his mouth. He claims he buys the cheese for Mummy, but he always eats it all himself. He never offers us any because he doesn't believe in wasting special things on children.

They argue about the phone call. Mummy is working herself into a tizzy about her father having another stroke and there's no way of knowing because Ian won't allow her family to call here.

He gags. Something has stuck in his throat. He stands up, clutching his napkin to his face as if he's about to vomit, stumbles to the sofa, and falls down on it.

"Ian, what's the matter?" Mummy cries, knocking over her chair as she rushes to him.

He writhes around like Victor Mature in the throes of agony in *Demetrius and the Gladiators*. Not a very good performance, but enough to convince Mummy.

"Oh, Ian," she screams. "Please, speak to me!" He's panting like a tired old horse.

"Children, children, do something!" Mummy shouts at us. "Ian's having another heart attack!" Mac joins in, barking and running around in circles.

Ian's been having these attacks quite often and always when they're having a row. Anne and I are certain he's pretending, as he's perfectly all right afterwards. But each time Mummy is sure he's on the verge of another coronary.

"Ian, please, don't die!" Mummy's performance is disgusting. "My darling Ian, don't leave me. Children, bring me Ian's pills." The doctor has prescribed some truly marvelous pills; they always work and save Ian's life in no time at all.

Mummy is sobbing and swearing eternal love; Mac is

barking and jumping up and down; Ian is groaning and flailing his arms. The new maid comes out of the kitchen and watches, fright on her face. I bet she'll have a tale to tell the other maids.

Anne brings the pills and hands them to Mummy. Ian shakes his head and closes his mouth tight, but she tells him, "Please, Ian, I can't live without you." He opens his mouth, she pops one in, and holds a glass of water to his lips. He swallows it and miraculously, he can talk.

"Baby dearest," he says, "If you ever leave me, I swear I will kill myself."

Within minutes, Ian is sitting up, and they're happy again. Off they go to bed where they spend the rest of the afternoon.

22

A HOME IS NOT WHERE YOU LIVE

Same old house
Same old road
Same old county
Same old country
Same old world

November 12, 1956

My darlings,

I'm afraid I have some bad news for you. I sold Carlyon. No use hanging onto it if I'm the only one living here.

Grace had already written to Mummy saying it was a while since Daddy had lived in Carlyon, and she thought he might be trying to sell it. Oh well, I suppose he didn't want us to know. Now where will we live when we go back to England?

I kept it going for three years after you left in the hopes you'd be coming back one of these days. Now that you will be staying in Mexico, there's no point in keeping it any longer. I hadn't told you before as I expected my inventions would pan out and I could send for you.

Next follows a full page in his horrid handwriting, all about his inventions and why they haven't worked out so far. The same old thing he's been telling us for years.

Pennie, I don't think it's a good idea to set your new book in

England if you're not living here.

It's too late to change places. By now, I'm on the twelfth chapter of *Lady of the Mansion*. I can always check my facts when I'm in England, that is, if he ever sends for us. Anne likes this book so much she keeps asking me to write more so she can find out what happens next. It's an improvement on *The Glass Stag*, which I rewrote twice and ended up with two-hundred-and-forty typed, double-spaced pages. Daddy sent me five pages of criticism, saying it was all right for a first try, but I can do better.

Please thank Uncle Ian on my part for all he's doing for you. I hope you're getting on well with him. How is Mummy? Is her back any better?

I think of you both all the time and miss you very much.

Love,

Daddy

England is so far away from Mexico that Daddy's letter took three weeks to arrive. When we left, Winston Churchill was Prime Minister and now it's Anthony Eden. These days, I'm more likely to know what's happening in the United States than in England. Dwight D. Eisenhower is President, and he's a general. I even know who the vice president is, Richard Nixon, because Grandpa says he looks like a crook.

In my memory it seems we were always happy living at Carlyon. I remember Mummy and Daddy fighting because we didn't have any money, but at least we had a home and we were a family. I suppose Carlyon will always be my home because I never want to have another. It's too hard when you lose it.

"What does your father have to say for himself?" Mummy asks.

"He's sold Carlyon." I'm trying not to cry in front of her.

"You see, I told you he would. You didn't want to believe me." She sounds as if she's won a last fight with Daddy. "It makes me sad to hear he had to sell Carlyon. I loved that house and we'd still be there if not for his damned inventions." She's thoughtful, long enough for me to say, "I have some errands," and move towards the door.

"Did your father send you anything?" she asks. "That house is worth several thousand pounds. You can't tell me he owed every penny. Doesn't he mind that another man is supporting his two daughters?"

I don't want to have a fight with her about this so I shake my head and dart down the passage to my room. She's sure to come after me. I grab my bag and a book and run out of the apartment, out of the building, down the street, away from her and her cruel words.

We will never go home to Carlyon.

Will I ever have a home again?

*

A month after Daddy's letter, we find one hundred pounds in five pound notes hidden inside the magazines for girls that Daddy sends us every month. I don't want to tell Mummy because she will want to use it to pay our school. Anne says we should tell her so she knows Daddy did send us money.

We tell her and Mummy asks, "Is that all your father sent?"

"That's all the money he could send," Anne says.

"He probably spent it on patents."

"It's the most he's allowed to send each of us from England. When he can, he will send more." We keep our money. I buy new shoes and two books with it. Anne buys herself a radio as her old one is conking out. The rest, she puts into a savings account.

*

Granny and Grandpa have moved to a little ground-floor flat on Calle Mazatlán, the same street where they lived when Mummy was young. We always have lunch there after Sunday

Mass. Sometimes Granny gives me a glass of sherry to drink with her and Aunt Carlota. I quite enjoy it, though I hide it from Grandpa, who'd have a fit if he saw. Grandpa hates three things: guns, liquor, and anything red

"What's that red stuff on your mouth, Pennie?"

Uh-oh.

"Go to the bathroom and remove it at once."

To please him, I wipe off some but not all of my lipstick. His eyesight isn't that good. Mummy says he hates red because of his Quaker heritage. He sees red as the color of violence and vulgarity, and guns and liquor as being the worst inventions in the history of mankind. Who would imagine Grandpa rode on trains with revolutionaries like Pancho Villa, or interviewed the gringo-hating bandit—his words—Emiliano Zapata?

Uncle Artie brings his *novia* Claudia to Sunday lunch. She looks a bit like Sofia Loren with the same lovely green eyes and big-busted figure, and she's as tall as Uncle Artie. After lunch, they sit at one end of the sofa, and I'm at the other end reading while Grandpa takes his nap. They think nobody is looking and they kiss, the kind of long kiss when they stick their lips together. Claudia shuts her eyes and a magical moment lingers about them.

In the afternoon Grandpa asks me to take his dictation. He's always writing to Time magazine about how American foreign policy stinks. He wishes "the U.S. would get out of Germany, Lebanon, Korea, Japan, Formosa and stay at home where we belong; heed (George) Washington's advice to beware of entangling alliances."

*

Uncle Nacho, dear Uncle Nacho, is dead. Aunt Carlota says that at first they thought it was food poisoning because he'd eaten some bad strawberries. What really finished him off, though, was the purge his manservant gave him, as it turned out he had a ruptured appendix.

We're sad; he was always kind to us and paid our school fees. Who will pay our tuition?

Mummy has a talk with Mother Thomas. "I really like that nun," Mummy says when she comes back. "She said both of you are a credit to the school. She's agreed to give you part-scholarships and if Pennie helps out in the school office after classes, she won't pay tuition."

I like the idea of helping out in the office and it's good to know it will help with my school fees.

"Mother said she will make a concession and let you go straight from Sixth Grade into Eighth Grade next year," Mummy says.

"What?" I feel horror rip across my face. "But I just finished Eighth Grade English with an A average. I'm going into high school next year.

Mummy says, "Then it must be a mistake."

I go to see Mother Thomas and straighten things out so I can start high school. She smiles at me the way nuns do when they're being firm with you. Her eyes are metal blue as she says, "I wouldn't be doing you a favor if I let you skip Eighth Grade. We're changing the curriculum, and you'll be studying new subjects. Latin, Algebra."

Two subjects that I will never use in this life.

"But I wouldn't be skipping Eighth Grade," I insist. "And last year, two of my classmates went straight from Seventh Grade into high school,"

"They were older than you. If I promote you, there will be too much of an age difference. You need to stay with girls your own age." Her lips pull into a thin line.

Why should that be a reason for me to do Eighth Grade all over again? Here I am writing books, and reading the Brontës and Charles Dickens and Pearl Buck and Edison Marshall, and she wants to hold me back.

"I'm afraid I can't promote you," Mother Thomas tells me. "Your mistake, Pennie, is thinking that you were in Eighth Grade when in fact all you were doing was reading and writing at an Eighth Grade level, but not taking the full curriculum."

When I tell Mummy, she says, "I'm sure Mother Thomas has her reasons." Before, she would have gone to see Mother Thomas and talked her into promoting me to high school, but now Mummy is distracted. Ian demands all of her attention most of the time and makes the simplest outing seem like a trip to another country.

Now I know what it's like to flunk a year. After getting straight A's.

23

THE INCIDENT OF THE LOBSTER

On doctor's orders Ian takes a Seconal tablet at night to sleep, and he likes them so much that he takes one in the afternoon, as well. He sees another doctor and gets another prescription so he can take more Seconals when he can't sleep. Then a third doctor gives him something else.

One day, he takes several pills in the afternoon. Then at night, he drinks a lot of Scotch and has a fight with Mummy, so he takes a bunch of Seconals and something called Noctec and passes out. Mummy calls the doctor. Usually, when Ian takes too many pills, the doctor treats him at home, but this time, he rushes Ian to the hospital.

That scares Ian enough to stop taking pills, except for one tablet before he goes to bed. By four in the morning he's prowling around, up and down the passage, in and out of the kitchen, or tapping away on his typewriter, working on his second book, a novel. He doesn't sleep all afternoon like he used to, and when the telephone rings, he comes charging out to answer it.

The conversation at lunch between Ian and Mummy—Anne and I aren't included; children are seen and not heard—is about Ian's book, a murder mystery about an older man who falls in love with a much younger woman, but his wife refuses to give him a divorce. Ian and Mummy don't talk about the last part in front of us, but I hear them commenting in the living room. Is it a book I'd like to read? I don't think so. Not after living through all the problems when two married people are divorced in order to marry each other. In the end, no one is happy.

One Sunday Ian takes us on an outing to visit friends in Cuernavaca. We know he's only taking us to please Mummy, and he behaves as if we're painted on the back seat. The house we visit has an enormous garden with the kind of thick grass where crawly insects and scorpions lurk. The trees are so tall the sun doesn't reach the swimming pool, making the water too cold to enjoy. The only one having a good time is Mac; he's playing with another dog, and from what I can see, doing things that two male dogs don't do to each other.

On the way home, we share the back seat with a smelly Mac, sticky from the other dog's slobber.

Mummy says to Ian, "Did you see Mac playing with the other dog? I think he may be queer."

Ian snorts. "Nonsense, he fathered a litter of five pups. He was having a little doggy fun."

As soon as we're home, we have to give Mac a wash before he can sleep on Ian's bed, which means scrubbing him in the bathtub, drying him off as best we can, and cleaning up afterwards. But when I ask Ian if I can have a bath, he says no, it's not convenient.

Mummy overhears and flies out of the bedroom, her eyes filled with rage. She raises her hand, and I think she's going to slap Ian, but he grabs it before she can.

"What kind of a man makes my daughters bathe a dog and then denies them the right to bathe themselves?"

"I thought you wanted a bath," he says, and he draws back as if expecting her to try to slap him again.

"That is for me to decide," she shouts. "I swear I won't have another bath until you let my daughters have theirs."

"Your daughters can have their bloody baths and go to hell!" he shouts back and he stomps into their bedroom and slams the door.

Mummy smiles. "Well, I put him in his place, didn't I?"

"Wish you would do that more often," I say.

"I'll have a serious talk with him," she says, "about this bath situation. Establish some ground rules."

What's the use? I smile and nod and let her think everything's all right because she's won a small battle tonight. Does she want to fight the same battle every day? Knowing Ian, he won't give in or change. At least today was a small victory.

Baths are our biggest problem. Ian gives us permission, but then changes his mind. He says we can use their bathroom on either Tuesday or Friday, as long as we ask his permission first, but it depends on his mood. Often Mummy shoos us away with a "Don't ask him now" or "It's not a good time." We bathe when he and Mummy are out, usually Saturdays, and it may be our only bath in the week. Early morning is not possible because that's precisely when he may need to use the bathroom. Even late at night, if we dare enter the bathroom, we're taking a risk that he may hear and come bounding out, furious.

I sweat or, since Mummy says a lady doesn't sweat, I perspire a lot since I turned thirteen. When I go to parties, I stuff Kleenex under my arms so as not to have dark rings on my dress. I need to bathe before because otherwise I'm sweaty and stinky.

One Friday evening, during the hot season, I haven't had a bath in four days. I mean to ask permission, but Ian is in a bad mood, so I put it off until too late. Ian and Mummy have gone to bed, and Ian doesn't like to be disturbed. Well, didn't he say we could have our baths as long as it wasn't inconvenient?

I have soap lathered all over when there's a bang on the door, and he yells, "Get out of there at once!"

"Just a minute," I say, but he shouts back, "I'll count to ten and then I'm coming in. One…" In my hurry, I dither between rinsing or jumping out of the tub, and by the time I make a move he's up to five. I grab a towel and am draping it around me when he yells, "Ten," and bursts in. He drags me by the arm, soapy and dripping, out into the passage.

"Didn't I tell you to always ask my permission?" His eyes have the wide-eyed glare that makes me feel like a fly he'll swat away.

"Sorry, Ian, I thought you were asleep." I run to my room and stand there hugging the towel to my body. How I wish, wearing only this wet towel, I could barge into their room, the same as he barged in on me, and scream at Mummy, "Look at what your husband did to me!" But by now Mummy's sleeping pill must have knocked her out, or she'd be in the passage shouting at him. To tell her would only make things worse, though, because Ian can't stand her getting mad at him.

When something like this happens, I'm angry with God for stranding us in Mexico with no way home. In the kitchen, I rinse off my hair in the sink and when soap gets in my eyes, I start to cry, which makes things worse. I have to decide how to get even with Ian. Suppose I slip some pills into his soup at lunch? Buy some Equanils and mash them into powder. Knock him out all afternoon. Get him out of the way for a while.

At Sunday lunch at Granny's, I tell the story of Ian hauling me out of the tub with nothing on.

Her mouth twists in disgust. "You were naked? I hope your mother intervened."

"I didn't tell her," I say, feeling quite saintly at having to bear such a cross.

*

Ian and Mummy ask her first cousin Aunt Carmelita and her husband Padín over to lunch. They're not religious, and they don't care if Mummy is married outside the Church. They're practically the only family members who, when they met Ian, got along with him. Padín has an important position in the Ford Motor Company.

It doesn't matter who is coming over, Mummy is always a nervous wreck. This time she's worse because the maid just left. "This is a disaster," Mummy says. "I don't think I can manage a whole meal on my own. What if something doesn't turn out right?"

Ian offers to help. "I'll go downtown to the San Juan market and buy some shrimp. And your daughters can make themselves useful and help prepare the food."

Mummy pulls herself together. Didn't she do the cooking for years in England? If we give her a hand, she will prepare the meal.

Mummy decides the menu. "We'll have jellied consommé Madrilene to start." There isn't much to making that. Campbell's beef consommé mixed with tomato juice, sherry, and Worcester sauce, left to gel in the fridge and decorated with chopped parsley.

She isn't easy to help in the kitchen. "You are mutilating the new potatoes," she tells us. We're better at whisking egg yolks for a Hollandaise sauce for the shrimp and Mummy makes Aunt Carlota's French dressing for the fresh asparagus. We go to Elizondo Bakery and buy a baguette and a variety of little French dessert cakes.

Whenever Mummy has people coming for lunch, she always sets her table the night before. "A properly laid table is an art," she tells us. She uses the lace tablecloth Aunt Carlota embroidered, Ian's family silver, and the Limoges plates she inherited from her grandmother.

Ian doesn't get back from the San Juan market until half past twelve. He dumps a bag of sandy gray shrimp into the kitchen sink. "I bought a whole kilo of large shrimp at half the price the man was asking. And, surprise!" He holds up a lobster in a bag of water. I can see it moving its feelers.

"Oh Ian, I'm so glad you did that," Mummy says, "but I can't prepare anything else. I have to get ready."

"Your daughters can take care of the shrimp. They don't require any particular cooking skill. Cook them beforehand and we'll eat them cold. All you have to do," he addresses us, "is shell the shrimp and throw the lot into a big pot of boiling water."

"What about the lobster?"

"Same as the shrimp."

"We have to boil a lobster to death?" Anne asks.

"That's the way it's done," Ian says and walks out of the kitchen.

We ask Mummy. "There's a bit more to it," she says. "Why don't you phone Aunt Carlota and ask her how she would cook the lobster and shrimp?"

We phone Aunt Carlota and she says, "First you shell the shrimp, and remove the black veins. Make sure to clean out all the grit because food poisoning from shellfish can be fatal. How big are the shrimp?"

"Quite big."

"Cook them in boiling, salted water for five minutes, or until they turn pink."

"What about the lobster? Do we have to boil it—alive?"

"Yes, that's the way it's done, but be careful. Lobster," she enunciates the word, "is one of the great delicacies of the world, and you don't want to ruin it. First, fill a big pot halfway with water, add a couple of bay leaves, a few peppercorns, parsley, and an onion, then add two cups of French vermouth."

The water is boiling. Which one of us will do the dreadful

deed? We toss a coin and I lose. I cut the bag over the sink, trying not to see the lobster moving its feelers as I drain out the water, turn it upside down over the pot, and dump it in.

The lobster lets out a cry like a long s-s-s-s. Who said lobsters don't feel anything?

The Padíns arrive at two. Aunt Carmelita has soft green eyes, black hair pulled back in a bun like a Spanish lady's, and a lilting voice. Uncle Padín has a small, severe face and flinty dark eyes behind spectacles. I've been in awe of him ever since Mummy told us he's an atheist. I don't see how anyone can refuse to believe in God.

Mummy isn't ready, and I can tell the Padíns are not comfortable with Ian, who's trying to make conversation. He offers them Daiquiris he prepared himself, and they both say yes but don't look convinced. Anne and I have to see about lunch, and Aunt Carmelita talks with Mummy while she finishes dressing. Ian and Uncle Padín are discussing whatever men discuss together.

A black cloud slinks over the lunch. After boiling the shrimp for five minutes, they have shrunk, curled over, and look chewed on where we cut out the veins.

Mummy comes to check on the food and tells us not to worry about the shrimp. "The lobster looks delicious. Why don't you put it in the center of this platter with the shrimp around it and some tomato and avocado slices as garnish? Nobody will notice the shrimp size."

She's right. The way we arrange it, the lobster is a king surrounded by a little army of shrimp curls. You'd never know, unless you looked closely, what a bedraggled lot they are.

We serve the first course, and Ian brings out a bottle of German white wine. He jokes about this being the first time he serves a German product in his house, and it must mean the war is really over at last, ha-ha. Uncle Padín, who was in the Spanish Civil War, doesn't seem to find it funny, but the others laugh.

We bring out the platter with the lobster and the shrimp. Everyone, even Ian, says it looks sumptuous and congratulates us.

"Girls, get a move on with the rest of the food," Ian says, meaning where are the potatoes? The asparagus is already served in little glass dishes next to each plate.

Uncle Padín asks, "Why don't the girls sit down?" It's obvious neither he nor Aunt Carmelita will start serving themselves before we're seated.

We bring in the potatoes and a sauce for the lobster, and sit down. I expect Ian to do with the lobster what he did with the chicken and tear it into pieces; instead he asks the Padíns, "Is it all right with you if I divide this into four portions?"

"But we're six," Aunt Carmelita says.

"No, we're not," Ian answers. "This lobster is for grown-ups only."

Aunt Carmelita jerks back. "Oh," she says, staring at him in disbelief. Uncle Padín's eyes glint behind his glasses and his mouth narrows to a thin line.

"But Ian ..." Mummy says.

He frowns at her. "Why waste lobster on children who won't appreciate it?"

Aunt Carmelita says, "Then I don't think I'd appreciate it either," and "Nor will I," Uncle Padín adds.

Mummy asks, "Is this how you thank my daughters for all the trouble they went to?"

"I, personally," Ian blusters, "went downtown to the San Juan market to buy fresh lobster for this occasion."

Uncle Padín says, "That's not the point. If the girls are not allowed to have any, how can we enjoy it ourselves?"

Ian goes so red he almost bursts with anger. "If no one

wants this lobster, I might as well throw it away." He waits. The Padíns have nervous smiles as if they half believe Ian is joking. Mummy shakes her head, but for once she keeps quiet. Ian glares at her and then at the Padíns and when nobody says anything, he grabs the lobster off the platter, walks to the window, and throws it out into the parking lot.

We watch in astonished silence as he says, "You will have to continue without me. I am not well. Good day." He storms off.

Uncle Padín shakes his head. Mummy begins, "Please forgive Ian. He's not his usual self today…" when there's a ferocious crash in the bedroom.

"Dear God, Ian!" Mummy screams. She pushes her chair out so fast it falls over, and rushes off to see what's happened to him. We hear bangs and screams, "Ian, stop, please stop!" From the alarm on their faces, the Padíns must think he's hitting her.

"We should go and see what's going on." Aunt Carmelita stands up, and the rest of us follow her to the bedroom.

Ian has put his fist through the closet door and it's stuck there. He's struggling to free it, pushing and banging at the door with his other hand. It isn't clear whether Mummy is trying to help him or stop him because the way she's hanging onto him only makes it worse.

"Goddamit, Baby!" he shouts, "don't do that!" while banging away with his free hand.

He half turns, and seeing us in the doorway, yells, "Show's over. Get the hell out of here!"

We back down the passage and the bedroom door slams shut. We can hear Mummy shouting, "How can you behave like that in front of my family? Don't be surprised if they never come again."

Uncle Padín is waiting in the dining room. "We'd better leave."

"We can't leave the girls with Ian in that state," Aunt Carmelita says.

"Then we'll take them out to lunch." There's a gleam in his eyes as he nods at us. "And you can eat all the lobster you want."

We put away the forlorn shrimp that no one touched, along with the Hollandaise sauce, the asparagus, and the mutilated new potatoes. As usual, we didn't get past the first course.

The Padíns take us to Delmonico's, one of the best restaurants in Mexico City, and we order Lobster Thermidor, a tasty dish. Even better because I wasn't the one who boiled it to death.

24

WHEN IS MURDER NOT A MORTAL SIN?

Sometimes on Sunday, when Anne and I go to Granny and Grandpa's house, we get there early because we need a bath. I like to wash my hair, but there isn't always time for it to dry and set in rollers before lunch.

Aunt Carlota arrives at two o'clock. She's wearing the navy blue suit she wears every Sunday and hasn't sent to the cleaners in eight years because "why bother if it doesn't show the dirt?" I have to bend to kiss her as she seems to have gotten shorter and more roly-poly. I'm five feet, three inches, and she only reaches my chin. She smells of musky old French perfume.

She ignores Grandpa's frown of disapproval and serves two small glasses of *Tio Pepe* sherry for herself and Granny, and when he isn't looking, passes hers to me and serves herself another. It's her opinion that young people should learn to enjoy wine the way more civilized Europeans do, and truthfully, I do enjoy my weekly glass of sherry.

Her false teeth crackle as she dishes out the latest gossip about a high society wedding. "The bride looked terrified. I'd say they had to get married. I fear it is not a marriage made in heaven. At least they were not stingy with the Moët et Chandon."

Uncle Artie and his girlfriend Claudia sit on one side of

the table, Anne and I on the other, Granny at the head, and Aunt Carlota at the other end. Grandpa ate earlier, so he sits in his chair and listens to us talking.

"Carmelita told me about that man throwing the lobster out of the window," Aunt Carlota says, stretching her penciled eyebrows. "I can't imagine Tita married to such a person." Granny's maid, Nativitas, serves her a cup of chicken consommé.

Grandpa speaks up from his chair. "Never understood what she saw in him in the first place."

"He's worse every day," Granny says, a note of despair in her voice.

"It seems to me it would not be a mortal sin," and Aunt Carlota chews her words to make them sound important, "if someone mur-der-ed him." She pats the hairnet covering her roll, which she never un-pins, not even at night, until she has it done every fortnight at the beauty parlor.

Granny draws back in alarm. "God forbid, Carlota. You shouldn't say such things."

Aunt Carlota sticks up her nose and sniffs to show she doesn't give a hoot. "I haven't the slightest intention of committing murder. But it is not a sin to discuss it." She butters and salts a piece of warm *bolillo*-bread roll and pops it into her mouth.

"I can't agree with you," Granny says, with obvious annoyance.

"Well, I do." Grandpa speaks up again. "Someone should have got rid of the man long ago. They'd be doing the world a favor."

Aunt Carlota inclines her head towards him. "See, Amada, Connie agrees with me."

Granny's chin shakes with indignation. "If you go on like this, I'll leave the table."

"Doesn't the way the man treats your granddaughters

make you angry?"

Aunt Carlota might as well have stuck a toreador's lance in Granny's side. Her face twists with anger. "Of course, but I would never dream of murdering him."

Despite her words, I know she prays all the time to God to deliver Mummy's soul from Ian's clutches, in whatever manner He sees fit, and if He sees fit to take Ian, so be it. "Why don't we change the subject?"

"I'm trying to add spice to the conversation." Aunt Carlota shakes some salt onto her chicken consommé, and squeezes a lemon over it, then pepper and a little chili salsa. "This is as good a topic as any. Conversation is an art, and it needs some pepper and salt to make it palatable. Now how would you go about—shall we call it—Ian's demise?"

"If we planned it like an Agatha Christie novel," I say, "that wouldn't be a sin."

Aunt Carlota's beady eyes light up under clotted mascara. "That's a good idea, Pennie. Now, tell me, what is the most important part in an Agatha Christie novel?" She clacks her teeth for emphasis.

"Who dunnit?" Uncle Artie says at once.

"The deduction process," Grandpa adds.

"The motive?" I ask. "Or how the murder was solved?"

"The cover up," Aunt Carlota states triumphantly. "It confuses the issue and allows the killer to get away—or try to—with murder." She sits back, sipping her wine.

Uncle Artie jumps in. "The point is not to find out who's guilty until the end."

"Then we'll begin with the end," Aunt Carlota says. "And work backwards from there."

"Why don't we end this discussion before it begins?" Granny sounds like a goat bleating.

Anne asks, "Don't people ever read the end?"

"You're not supposed to," I tell her, "In Agatha Christie novels, the whole idea is to find out who the murderer is, and put them in jail."

Aunt Carlota shakes her head. "We live in Mexico and this would be a Mexican murder. Here, nice people don't go to jail."

"Depends on how much they cough up," Uncle Artie says. "Most times it's easier to put it down as food poisoning or a heart attack—less red tape for the police and more money in their pockets."

"Suppose they want to do an autopsy?" I ask.

Aunt Carlota curls her lips. "Who would permit a member of their own family to be cut up after they're dead?"

"Can't the doctors tell?"

"What doctor would want to be involved in an argument about a corpse?" Uncle Artie says.

Aunt Carlota agrees. "No doctor in his right mind would call the police. It would cause too many complications and compromise his reputation. Anyway, there's no time. In Mexico a body has to be buried within twenty-four hours."

Anne seems puzzled. "Why so fast? Can't they wait?"

She shudders. "In Mexico, a dead body decomposes fast because the gasses make it swell and stink to high heaven." Aunt Carlota makes it sound like she's describing a tasty dish. "Why, I remember when my dear sister Clara's first husband Pepe—may he rest in peace—passed away during the Religious Persecution, and we couldn't find a priest to bury him. The stench was horrible. Everyone in our house was sick to their stomachs. In desperation Clara and I went to the jail and bribed the guards to let us in to see our cousin the Pater who was detained there. We dressed him like a woman, and got him out so that poor Pepe was buried with the proper rites."

Uncle Artie grins. "At least you knew he was dead. Not like poor old Tío José."

"Oh yes, we should have realized something was wrong when he didn't stink." Aunt Carlota's bosom jiggles with emotion. "Years later, we wanted to move his bones in the crypt to make room for my brother Manuel, but they were gone." She crosses herself. "What a shock that was. We never found out what happened to them."

"Please, Carlota, why do you insist on talking about such things at the table?" Granny sounds like she's at her wit's end.

Uncle Artie asks, "What makes cremation the neatest way to dispose of a body?"

Granny shakes her head at him, but there's no stopping him and his jokes.

"You accelerate the process, ha-ha-ha."

I laugh weakly as does everyone else, except for Granny who says, "Cremation is against the laws of God."

"That can go wrong as well." How Aunt Carlota loves stirring up things. "Remember the story about the family who made Mrs. Schultz's grandmother's ashes into soup?"

"Were they cannibals?" Anne asks.

"Of course not," Aunt Carlota says. "They thought it was a soup package from Germany. Later they received the letter saying what it contained."

I start to laugh, but then I see the little gray shreds floating around in my pale yellow consommé.

"Think of all the ways you can get away with murder," Uncle Artie says. "How about some tacos-a-la-Ian? Like the woman in the Centro who cut up her husband and stuffed him into the tamales she sold in the Zócalo."

Aunt Carlota cuts him short. "We're not talking about what to do with his corpse, but how to turn him into a corpse."

Nativitas removes the empty cups and serves up the roast chicken that Uncle Artie brought, the kind with gold, crackly skin that you eat with your fingers. Aunt Carlota and Anne both ask for a wing and a drumstick; I want a thigh; Uncle Artie and Claudia share the breast, and Granny likes the back part, the Pope's Nose.

Nativitas comes in with fried potatoes, and Aunt Carlota directs her to bring a finger bowl with warm water, a slice of lemon, and a little napkin. I think Granny is hoping Aunt Carlota has forgotten what we were talking about, but she is relentless. "Now, where were we? Oh yes, the reason people are caught is because their motives give them away."

"Other people might have reasons to murder Ian," I say, "like revenge for what he did in the war."

Uncle Artie nods. "Nutcases like him had a ball."

Granny gives us a murderous look. "Let's talk about more pleasant things."

"What could be more pleasant than discussing the make-believe murder of someone you hate?" Aunt Carlota picks up her chicken wing and nibbles on it.

"Please, Carlota, change the subject," Granny begs her.

Aunt Carlota is merciless. "If it will make you happier, Amada, we'll call the victim Mr. X. Now, how would we commit the murder? Let's say Mr. X has a bad habit like drinking too much. Or he has high blood pressure, and the doctor has warned him to watch out or he'll have a heart attack, and he doesn't look after himself. Or he mixes medicines with dire results."

"What if he takes too many pills?" I ask.

Aunt Carlota scrunches up her face in delight. "He might take an overdose." She dips her manicured claws into her finger bowl. "The crux is that no one should suspect it was murder. A bad habit, like alcohol, drugs, staying out late, driving too fast, is very convenient. It means he could do it to himself, and no one else would be to blame. All you have to do would be drive him to it. He'd take care of the rest."

"How?"

"With a *manita*, of course. There are ways of pushing up blood pressure to the boiling point. Or using certain herbs or intoxicants. Too many drugs can cause an overdose. A mixture of alcohol and sleeping pills will do it every time."

"What about Seconals?"

She nods eagerly. "Oh yes! Or too many Equanils."

"Are there times when murder isn't a sin?" I ask.

Granny is pretending to be engrossed in her chicken. Aunt Carlota says, "If someone forces a person to sin, or is the cause of sin, or to save someone from committing a major sin."

"Like when?"

"If a man tries to do the unspeakable to a woman. Or in self-defense."

"Then murder isn't always a mortal sin?"

"Murderers go to hell," Granny says firmly, "unless they seek forgiveness."

"A priest is bound by his oath," Aunt Carlota adds, "to grant absolution for any sin." So that's why she could go see *And God Created Woman* with Brigitte Bardot despite it being on the Church's forbidden list.

"A person could murder someone and go to Confession and receive absolution?" I ask.

"You must truly repent your sins in order to be absolved," Granny says.

"You can be sorry for offending God," Aunt Carlota adds, "even though you are not sorry for what you did." The way she puts it, murder doesn't sound much worse than skipping Mass on Sunday.

"Carlota," Granny tells her, "please stop putting ideas into Pennie's and Anne's heads."

Grandpa says, "Why don't you look up poisons in the Encyclopedia Britannica?"

The chicken bones have piled up on the plates, and we've finished the salad made with Aunt Carlota's special dressing. Nativitas clears the table and brings dessert, fresh mangoes and the meringues we brought.

"What do you think," I ask, "would be the penance for committing murder?"

Aunt Carlota shrugs. "Perhaps a novena to the Blessed Mother," and she digs her false teeth into her soft mango.

*

In the afternoon Uncle Artie and Claudia take us to the movies. Then we go to Sanborns for supper where we have *molletes*—bread rolls with mashed frijoles and melted cheese and *salsa* on top. Uncle Artie warns, "Beans, beans, musical fruit, the more you eat the more you toot."

By the time we go home Mummy and Ian are already in bed. Good. It's my fault the conversation took that track. Is Ian's craziness a good enough reason to murder him?

The beans are beginning to toot, and Anne needs to use the bathroom. She doesn't want to do it in a chamber pot and stink up her room all night. She tiptoes down the passage and closes the bathroom door as quietly as possible, but Ian comes out of the bedroom and shouts, "Get out of my bathroom at once," with several loud bangs to show he means it. You'd think he was in a hurry to go himself.

Now when you're sitting on the toilet halfway through doing your business, it isn't easy to stop all at once. Even Mac is allowed ten minutes or more twice a day.

He bangs on the door again. "Finish whatever you're doing in there and get out."

He goes back into the bedroom.

Anne comes out making a face. "I'll have to finish in the morning."

I follow her into her room. "Remember Aunt Carlota

189

mentioned medicines. In one Agatha Christie book the murderer used a high blood pressure medicine, Trinitrin. Suppose I put that in Ian's soup?" She's doubtful. "Who knows if that really works."

"How about poison?

"Where would you find a poison? You don't even know where to start."

"Grandpa said to look it up in the Encyclopedia Britannica."

The next day I look up "poison" in the Encyclopedia and find everything from toxins to drugs, poisoned arrows, chemicals, venoms, food poisoning, metallic poisons, natural toxins, and cyanide. I make a list of forty-six poisonous plants including ones like *bella donna* or *mescal* or *amanita*. What is deadly nightshade or hemlock or wolfsbane in Spanish?

Of course I'm only toying with the idea of getting rid of Ian, but it's a relief to know I can always go to Confession afterwards.

25

TURNING THE TABLES

I decide to take my revenge after Ian causes a break-up with my first boyfriend. He comes around once to collect me, and for Mummy to meet him, and Ian gives him the scary glare he has after taking pills—the one that's straight out of a horror movie. My boyfriend looks like he wants to flee and he answers Mummy's questions with a stuttering "yes" or "not sure" and "Excuse me, we must leave," grabs my hand and pulls me out of the apartment. Whenever he phones, Ian answers. At first the *Farmacia Jesús* excuse works, but Ian catches on it's the same person, the same voice, and when he hears it again, he says, "This is not a *casa de putas*," —a whorehouse—and hangs up. This happens three times until my boyfriend stops calling. I hear he told a friend my situation was too complicated for him to continue seeing me.

Enough is enough. Time to put our plan to get rid of Ian—at least for a while—in action.

At lunch, I watch as Ian unfolds the silver wrapping on the Philadelphia cream cheese and loads a chunk onto his slice of bread. I can almost see the powdered Equanil on the cheese's pure white surface. He stuffs the whole slice into his mouth and munches away.

Anne did a beautiful job smoothing over the cheese and

making it look just right after adding the powdered Equanils. We didn't put in enough to kill Ian, only knock him out, but with all the other pills he takes, you never know.

He spreads another hefty dollop onto his bread. Anne snorts into her napkin, and I can't hold back anymore. I try to make my laugh sound like a cough.

"What's the matter with you two?" Mummy asks, and we both say, "Nothing," in the same innocent tone.

The new maid sets down a full soup bowl, sloshing a bit onto Ian's plate.

"Where do you find these idiots?" he asks Mummy after the maid leaves.

"You have no idea how hard it is to find a decent maid," she says. "As soon as I break them in, they leave."

Anne and I can't take our eyes off him. He has another slice of bread and cream cheese, followed by two spoonfuls of noodle soup. Uh-oh, he wrinkles his big nose and makes a noise of disgust. He's noticed the taste.

"Who prepared this muck?"

"Oh, I'm so glad you said that," I say without thinking.

Mummy darts me a puzzled look. "The new maid did the cooking," she says.

"Can't she do better than this? It's watered-down pasta."

"I'll have to teach her how you like your soup."

"Aha!" Invisible horns sprout from his forehead. "I will not tolerate pig swill." He picks up his bowl and flings it at the wall. Noodle soup splatters across the picture of Emperor Maximilian facing a Juarista firing squad.

"What kind of example do you think you're setting?" Mummy shouts. She's about to go into full swing when Ian jerks back and groans as if he's been hit over the head. He's starting to have one of his fake attacks, but no, he stands up, steadies himself, and with a dazed expression says, "I'm going to lie down," and totters off to their bedroom.

Mummy doesn't catch the smile that passes between Anne and me. The Equanils worked.

Mummy calls the maid to clean up the mess of noodles on the wall and the carpet. She looks in on Ian and comes back saying, "I don't know what came over him. He's fast asleep." We finish our lunch in peace. Even the dreadful soup tastes good.

How long will Ian stay conked out? Putting sedatives in his cheese is in the experimental stage. It could be too little or too much. But we're prepared. If anything goes wrong, we can always call the doctor. He won't be surprised that Ian took too many pills.

When we spike Ian's cream cheese, he sleeps the rest of the afternoon. We don't do it all the time, maybe once a week, or twice when he's nasty, especially when he didn't get much sleep the night before. So in a way, we're doing him a favor because he's able to make up lost sleep.

It's not easy to doctor his cheese and do it right; it takes time, and we can't do it to unopened packages because of the tight silver wrapping. We have to think of other ways to give him powdered Equanils, like putting them in his soup. The problem is that Equanils don't mix well with his favorite Campbell's cream soups, and he's not as fond of watery soups like vegetable where the pills would dissolve easily.

I shouldn't worry. The Equanils are a little shove; Ian's always taking pills and loves them even more than Mummy loves hers. He couldn't stay off them when he tried. He takes a Seconal after lunch to help him sleep all afternoon. Then, in the evening, he has two or three Scotches, and another Seconal around eleven to go to sleep. When he's slept all afternoon, he's too wide awake to sleep, especially since Mummy's out for the night after taking her pill. I dare say, most of the time, Ian is only half-awake when he gets up around two.

A bang on my door flings me out of a pleasant dream. "I'd like to have a word with you and your sister."

"At this hour, Ian?" My clock says ten past three in the morning.

"Both of you in the living room," he says in his colonel's voice.

We pull ourselves out of bed and with sleep clinging to us, stand before him like scolded children as he rants on about how we need to comprehend our position in the household. After half an hour of this, he mellows. Please, help him make Mummy happy.

I repeat for the umpteenth time, "You can't make her happy. I mean, things upset her."

He glares at me. "Then we must think of ways to make her happy."

Another time, it's four in the morning, and all he can talk about is his concern for us. "I'd have you know that I want only the best for you, and if I seem strict, it's because children need the right training." He reminds me of a torturer trying to persuade his victims that what he's doing to them is for their own good.

Why be content with making him sleep in the afternoon? He needs to sleep at night too. Suppose we increase the dosage? Or mix it with other stuff? Try something else? Put ant poison in the coffee percolator? He's the only one who drinks coffee.

How about ground-up apricot pits? That's real cyanide. A bit every day should do the trick. Ian introduced me to Agatha Christie with *Sparkling Cyanide*. It would be a kind of poetic justice if we gave him cyanide and he died. Still, I don't want to kill him—commit a mortal sin—but I can't help thinking of ways to do it.

This last bout with Ian leaves me with a headache and puffy eyes. Yet Anne, usually a crybaby, thrusts out her chin and stays dry-eyed throughout. She never gives in to him, nor pretends to.

The next morning I'm as nauseated as if last night's meal had been off. I ask to be excused from class and from work in the office and am about to leave when Mother Thomas calls me in for a talk. Is everything all right at home? She doesn't come out and say it, but I'm sure she suspects things are terribly wrong. I tell her I have insomnia, but don't mention that it's Ian's insomnia. She tells me to pray a rosary when I can't sleep. I try it, and she's right; a rosary is better than counting sheep. It's also good for my soul.

The night comes when I wish Ian was talkative or plain old angry. I don't know what devils he's seeing, but he eyes us as if we're the enemy, which makes me wonder if, in his mind, he's back in the trenches. The pills have got the better of him. He growls, "I've had enough. Just get out." At first, I don't believe him, and stand there shocked, and so does Anne until he yells, "GET OUT." Anne and I flee the apartment with his shouts in our ears. We spend the night on the sofas in the lobby.

Fausto finds us there when he comes in to work at six in the morning. We go upstairs, knock on the door, and the maid opens, and we creep back into the apartment hoping Ian won't hear us. We don't tell Mummy. She'll be mad at him, and he'll take it out on us. She finds out anyway when Don Enrique asks her why we had to sleep downstairs and she questions Anne.

"I will not condone child abuse," she tells Ian, "especially when it concerns my own daughters." She sounds very calm, which has more effect than when she shouts.

Ian cowers at one end of the sofa as if he'd like to disappear into it. "I don't remember doing any such thing," he says. "Why would I chase your daughters out of the house at that time?" He sits up and with an air of indignation says, "They're trying to turn you against me."

If I didn't know he was guilty, I'd believe him. Maybe he's forgotten like when someone drinks a lot and can't remember what he did the next morning.

"My daughters didn't tell me anything," she says. "It was Don Enrique."

He gapes at her as if understanding it's the truth. For a second his eyes meet mine and just as I realize he's up to something, he falls over onto the floor, writhing like a dying man.

Then it's the same old phony attack with Ian begging, "Don't ever leave me, Baby," and Mac barking his head off, and Mummy pleading, "Ian darling, please don't die."

In the end she's so worried he will die that she's ready to forgive what he did. "I don't think Ian was aware of what he was doing," she says.

I tell Anne, "The next time Ian gets us up, if he calls us lazy or useless or we sit on our fat fannies, let's walk out on him."

The next time Ian wakes us, two weeks later, he uses all those words at the start of his tirade. It's two in the morning.

"We refuse to listen to any more of your insults," I say and we march to the door. In his army officer's voice, Ian booms, "I order you to return," but we don't stop. I hope to God the elevator arrives before he comes after us, and it does, just in time. Ian comes charging out as the doors are closing.

Once we reach the lobby, we have no idea what to do, apart from staying there again. We can't go to Granny's because Grandpa's not well.

An hour later Ian comes downstairs, very annoyed but normal, looking for us. "It was most thoughtless of you to leave like that. Do you want the whole building to know about our personal life?"

Anne says, "Then stop waking us up."

For a while, he doesn't bother us. I'm itching for another

showdown.

It comes one night around ten when he stomps down the passage, throws open Anne's door and shouts, "Get out of my house. At once."

In my room, I hear him shouting. I shoot out to see Mummy right behind Ian, tugging at his arm, screaming, "You have no right. This is her home as well."

He hesitates. As if thinking it over. Then Anne tells him, "I'll be glad to. I hate living under your roof."

"Then go to the devil," he says.

"Ian, you can't do that to a minor." Mummy is like an annoying little terrier, scrabbling at his sleeve.

My bloodthirsty juices are boiling. "If that's what you want, Ian, I'm leaving as well."

He turns to me. "I have no quarrel with you, Pennie."

"Yes, you do. I won't let you throw my eleven-year-old sister out onto the street at night all by herself."

"I'm not throwing her out on the street. I'll pay the taxi to her grandmother's." He puts his hand in his pocket and pulls out a bill and offers it to Anne. "Here's five pesos."

"I don't want your money," she tells him.

"Here, Pennie, you take it."

I shake my head.

"Then so-be-it. You and your sister can go to hell."

"Then I'm leaving with my daughters," Mummy says.

Oh no, that means we'll never leave.

"Shut up, Baby." Ian gives her a dirty look. "Nothing will happen to them. They know how to take care of themselves." He grabs her arm and forces her into the bedroom, ignoring her shouts of "I'll see you in hell first."

"Quick, before she stops us," I say to Anne. We dress in record time and as we hurry out of the apartment, we can hear Mummy screaming at Ian.

The streets are dark and empty, but it's an adventure to be out this late. Intoxicating. Smells like forbidden pleasure. When I grow up, I'll live at night.

"Maria Bárbara?" I say. The restaurant where we sit at the soda fountain and read movie magazines. It stays open until twelve a.m. Chucho, the soda fountain attendant, looks surprised to see us come in. Girls our age aren't allowed out by themselves at this time of night. Anne asks for a banana split and I eat a hot fudge sundae. They cost nine pesos plus one peso tip. That leaves me twenty pesos. I have money because once a week I'm giving English lessons to two little girls, the granddaughters of Granny's best friend. They pay me fifty pesos a lesson.

I look through the new *Photoplay*, and Anne reads the latest Archie comic. Then I grab *True Confessions*, which is probably high up on the sinful list, but I don't know for sure.

An American boy, Bill, comes in for a hamburger, and we talk. He's twenty-one and he's studying at Mexico City College where Granny used to teach before it moved to the Toluca Highway. Do we need a lift somewhere? I'd ask him to put us up for the night, but he might think I'm after him. So I say we're waiting for my mother to pick us up. Anyway, I have twenty pesos on me. After Bill leaves, I ask Chucho how much does a room at the Motel Garage on Melchor Ocampo cost?

He looks horrified. "Nice young ladies like you shouldn't go to cheap hotels like that one."

"How about the *María Cristina*?" Anne asks.

It's a hotel on Rio Lerma owned by friends of Aunty Laura's. I use the public phone to call and ask how much for a room. Fifty pesos a night, and if I don't have a reservation I'll have to pay when I register. I ask Chucho if he'll lend me thirty pesos, but he says sorry, he doesn't have that amount.

I have an idea. "Why don't we walk to the British Embassy

and ask them to repatriate us to England? Tell them our step-father kicked us out. We're British subjects and minors. They will have to send us home to Daddy. Think how embarrassing that will be for Ian." He's spent months trying to get into the ambassador's good graces.

It sounds like a jolly good idea—if it works.

"Maybe we should call Mummy and tell her what we're planning to do," Anne says.

"No, Ian's sure to answer the phone."

"Then tell him. That's even better."

Ian answers. "Your poor mother is sick with worry. If you don't come right back here, I'll send the police after you."

"Why don't you do that?" I say, loving each moment. "Tell them to look for us at the British Embassy."

I hear his muffled exclamation.

"Do you think they will arrest us for taking refuge in our own embassy? What a scandal." I'm saying whatever comes into my head, but it sounds right. "We're going to ask for asylum because you threw us out at this time of night."

"Nobody will believe you," he says, "and I didn't throw you out. You left of your own accord. You're runaways." I hear Mummy's voice in the background. "Let me speak to my daughters."

"You told Anne to get out. Mummy heard you. You can't deny that."

His voice softens to the tone he uses when he's trying to be nice to us. "I want you to come home, both of you. Think of your mother. You don't want to hurt her." Mummy's screaming at him to pass the phone to her.

"We don't want to live where we're not wanted."

"Sometimes I may get a bit carried away. If so, I regret it." Hah, hah, he's never sorry about anything. "Please, Pennie, be good girls and come home."

"I'll let you know," and I hang up.

"Goody-goody." I hug myself with glee. "We have him where we want him."

We wait fifteen minutes. We'd let him stew longer, but it's ten to twelve and Chucho's ready to close.

I call again. This time Mummy answers. "Where are you? I'm so worried about you. What's this about the British Embassy?"

"I want to speak to Ian."

"He's not angry anymore. He promised to let bygones be bygones."

"We're fed up with being treated like unwelcome guests. We'll return on our own terms."

"What terms? Come home and we'll talk it over."

"No, Mummy, we don't want to talk it over. Put Ian on the phone."

"Please try to work things out with him, and come home."

Next I hear Ian's voice. "Please, Pennie, for your mother's sake, come back right now."

I try to sound grown up. "If we agree, there are some conditions."

"I don't like being blackmailed," he says.

Mummy, in the background, says, "For once in your life, Ian, listen?"

"What do you want?" he asks.

"Stop being rude to friends who call us, and insulting us, and waking us in the middle of the night. No, wait, I'm not finished." Anne is mouthing words and gesturing at me. "You get mad at us when we use the bathroom, we don't have a front door key, you barge into our rooms whenever you like, you won't let us use the telephone, and you treat us like dirt."

Silence, then he says, "I suppose I have been rather hard on you." The nearest to an apology we'll receive. "But you two

200

can be difficult, as well."

"If you'll behave with us, we'll behave with you."

"Will you promise to forget this ridiculous notion about going to the British Embassy?"

"If you give me your word of honor that you'll agree to our conditions." Anne is shaking her head. "Swear on your mother's grave that you'll keep your side of the bargain."

Sometimes I wonder if he didn't sell his soul in exchange for Mummy. I'm making a bargain with the devil.

"You don't need my word," he says pompously, "but if that's what it takes, I'll give it to you as a sign of my goodwill."

It's not so much that we believe him, but we're both tired and sleepy.

Ian keeps his word, but it won't last. It never does. I'm on my guard. Ready. The next time he's nasty, we won't put up with it.

We'll get rid of him.

26

GIVE HIM A SHOVE

Once the idea is in my head to get rid of Ian, it sticks there. The thought follows me around, reminding me we can do it and no one will know. I wrestle with my conscience. Anne says we don't have to go all the way, just start the ball rolling, so if something happens to Ian, we're not guilty.

Trinitrin is a possibility, but the man at the pharmacy says he's never heard of that poison. I suppose not. The Agatha Christie book was written in the 1920s. How about homemade cyanide? Put grated apricot pits in Ian's coffee? Doesn't sound hard. Worth trying.

*

Anne and I have tea with a friend of Mummy's, Diana, an English lady who used to be a lady-in-waiting at court when George VI was king. Back then, she was also beautiful, I'm sure. Her first husband died mountain climbing, and despite her remarriage, she carries an air of sadness about her.

"How are things at home?" she asks and then answers her own question. "I know Ian gives your mother a hard time, and he's a household tyrant. She told me he's not nice to you."

"He's not nice at all," Anne says. "He's out of his mind."

Diana looks like she'd hit Ian if she could. "I heard, from someone in the know, that he lost it after the war. So many men came back with mental problems from doing things they can't talk about. Do you have any idea what he did?"

"I don't." I'm not supposed to know anything about his wartime activities.

"I heard he was a Whitehall agent." She catches her breath and covers her mouth as though she's said too much. "Anyway, if there's anything I can do to help, you can count on me."

It crosses my mind to confide in her, but I stop before saying anything that might get back to Mummy.

"What a pity that a lovely woman like Tita should be married to that pompous old twit. People in the British community can't stand him."

"He thinks he's a pillar of society," I say.

"I don't know why your mother puts up with him. He does the oddest things. Last week your mother came to lunch, and he turned up before we had finished and insisted she leave at once. Another time we went out to a restaurant, and he was furious. He told your mother he didn't want her seeing me again. I managed to mollify him, but I know he doesn't like me."

"He's jealous of anyone who's a friend of Mummy's. He's already forced a separation between Mummy and her long-time friend Alva, who was her bridesmaid when she married Daddy. Mummy has to see Uncle Agustín's wife, Lucia, on the sly because Ian goes purple at the mention of his name."

"I fear for your mother. He has a violent streak. Most household tyrants are also wife-beaters. I hope he won't take it out on her—or on you."

"So far he's controlled himself," I say, but then I think of Mummy running out of their bedroom, screaming her head off, and Ian coming after her with that mad look in his eyes, and pulling her back into their room.

"He's crazy," Anne adds.

"I believe you're right. I hate to say it, but he's a walking menace and should be locked up. Or somebody should do your mother a favor and give him a shove."

"What do you mean by that?" Anne asks in her innocent voice.

"I mean, off him, or put arsenic in his coffee." She chuckles. "Something along those lines."

A stream of excitement runs through me.

"There must be another way," Anne says in the same sweet tone.

"If you think of one, let me know and I'll give you a hand." Her eyes fasten on me. "I'm very fond of Tita, and I hate to see her saddled with that bastard. Or him ruining your lives. If you ever need my help, call on me."

Is she saying she will help murder Ian? Or another kind of help? I don't dare tell her anything about what we've been up to because she might repeat it to Mummy. But it helps to know how she feels. And to know I'm on the right track.

I like what Diana called Ian. A household tyrant. I've been reading about tyrants in history, men like Henry VIII who kept getting rid of his wives or anyone whom he thought was against him. Sounds like he was also crazy. Maybe craziness and tyranny go hand in hand.

*

I read that cyanide comes from apricot pits so I'm guessing we can make poison. I buy some apricots and, after Mummy and Ian are in bed, Anne and I take turns grating the pits. It's hard work; we can only grate a small amount at a time, and the tips of our fingers are red and sore because they're grated as well. Tomorrow we'll put some in Ian's food and see if it works. One problem, I tasted it, and it's sort of bitter, so the food needs a strong flavor.

The next morning, Saturday, I convince Mummy to let me prepare curried chicken for lunch. The strong curry flavor should cover up the apricot-pit taste. I have to work out how to put the grated apricot pits into the curry on Ian's plate.

We sit down to lunch and the maid brings in platters of rice and curried chicken. Mummy serves herself and then Ian. As he lifts his fork, I say, "Stop, Ian. Mummy. I forgot an important ingredient." They both stare in surprise as I grab his plate and Anne takes Mummy's and we take them into the kitchen. Anne empties half a spoonful of grated apricot onto Ian's curry and mixes it in carefully so he won't know the difference. Then we take the plates back to the table.

"I want this to be just right," I say.

"Pennie made the curry herself," Mummy tells Ian.

He tastes it. "Uhmm, it's good." He gives me a smile. A nice smile. It makes me feel a bit guilty.

As usual, Mummy and Ian argue, this time about her going to see Grandpa today when she saw him two days ago.

"My father is dying," she says. "I'd see him every day if I could."

"I'm not stopping you. What's more, I'll drive you there and wait." He has a couple of mouthfuls. "Pennie, you're a good cook," he says. Anne almost falls out of her chair laughing.

Mummy is too intent on her own subject to notice. "Ian, do you have to honk your horn after half-an-hour?"

"You can't expect me to wait in my car all afternoon."

"I do expect you to wait," she flashes back. "If you can't, I'll take a taxi."

Ian doesn't say another word. He finishes his curry, stands, puts his hand in his pocket and takes out a bill that he gives to Mummy. "There's ten pesos, enough for your taxis," he says, and he stamps out of the apartment without taking his afternoon nap.

I have no idea if those grated apricot pits had any effect.

It's eight o'clock at night. Ian hasn't come home. Mummy's

forgotten what they fought about. "Whatever I said to him, it was in the heat of anger," she says. She sits on the sofa, pretending to read Time magazine, while she waits for Ian. "If anything has happened to him, I have myself to blame." She serves herself a whisky to calm her nerves.

By nine, she's in tears, nearly praying to his portrait. Ian is a wonderful man. Look how nice he is to us despite all he's gone through recently. Can't we get it through our heads that she needs our help to make her marriage work?

Ian comes back around ten. He throws a nasty look at Anne and me. "I'm not feeling well," he says. "I went for dinner with my sons." He serves himself a Scotch, and sits on the sofa, gazing at his medals.

I linger in the passage and listen to their conversation.

Mummy says, "Ian dear, I didn't mean to hurt your feelings."

"That's all right, Baby. I think I ate something that didn't agree with me. My whole body aches, and I'm dizzy."

I could faint. The ground apricot pits are working.

"I'll call the doctor," Mummy says.

Ian shakes his head. "It's just a stomach problem."

Then I hear, "Ian, what's the matter?" Silence. Mummy starts, "Ian, wake up. Open your eyes." I dash out to see him slumped over.

Mummy shakes him, and slaps his face, and he opens his eyes and says, "I'm cold. Very cold." She puts a shawl over him, but it's not enough. She yells for us to bring a blanket; even with that, his teeth are chattering, though she's hugging him to give him her body warmth, and he can't stop shivering. It goes on too long.

Is the cyanide working, and if so, how effective is it? Will he die?

An hour later, the doctor arrives.

Ian is shivering and his teeth are rattling, and he's having trouble breathing, and all the color has gone out of his face. I see dark shadows under his eyes.

I'm terrified he might, actually, die.

The doctor says Ian's blood pressure has dropped dramatically from his normal high blood pressure. He gives him something to make it rise and takes his blood pressure again every few minutes.

I watch, not knowing whether to pray that Ian kicks the bucket or leave it up to God. I don't know if I want him to die from our poison. I don't want to be a murderer.

A *murderer*? I've never thought of myself that way. What's more, I dragged Anne into it, made her an accomplice. Why did I ever think poison was a good idea?

It takes two hours before Ian's blood pressure returns to normal.

The doctor tells Mummy. "We caught him in time. It might have been fatal."

Almost, but not quite.

One side of me is thinking, what if we had grated more apricot pit, and the other is relieved I didn't have to see him taking his last gasps. I need to find a way to get rid of him without watching the end.

Anne says, "Better luck next time."

27

DO-IT-YOURSELF VOODOO

It starts as a game. Kind of.

I find a little book in the secondhand bookstore on Rio Nazas. They sell used Penguin paperbacks, back issues of movie magazines, and a few hardback books with loose or faded covers. I glance through a book about the magic of Haiti because I'm curious to find out if zombies exist. Oh, disappointment, the book's about an Englishman's travels there in the early part of this century. There is, however, one chapter about voodoo.

The writer says that voodoo in Haiti is a religion, but it can also be used as a weapon. He writes that "voodoo may work to demoralize or even cause death to the enemy," though this can be explained because "people can be influenced into thinking it is powerful." He includes a description of a voodoo ceremony that he witnessed. Interesting, but not enough to buy the book.

A few days later, Diana asks us to tea, and when we talk about Ian, she says, "Why don't you try a little voodoo on him? Find a wax doll and stick pins into it. Mellow him."

*

We might not have paid attention to Diana's suggestion if Ian hadn't told Anne, "This is the last time I remind you to remove your father's photograph from sight. If you refuse to do so, you must face the consequences."

"What consequences? What can he do to you? Throw you out?" I ask Anne.

"I want to live with Granny anyway," she says.

Anne used to be spunky and happy, but now she's angry a lot of the time. I wonder if I've also changed that way.

One Thursday evening, Mummy and Ian go out to a party.

"I want to have a bath," Anne says.

"I have a better idea. Why don't we try some voodoo? Hold a voodoo ritual."

"What do you know about voodoo rituals?" she asks, but there's a gleam in her eyes.

"I read about them in a book on Haiti." Whatever I scanned in half an hour.

The truth is, I don't know much at all about voodoo, though for Anne's sake, I pretend I do. "From what I remember, you stick pins into a little wax doll or effigy, but we don't have one."

"We could use a photograph." Anne glances at the one of Ian in his First World War army uniform when he was young and good-looking.

"He was a different person back then," I say. "Anyway, you can't stick pins into a framed photograph. We'll do it another time."

Anne shakes her head. "No, I want to do it now."

"We don't have anything we can stick pins into."

Anne points at Ian's portrait hanging there in all its glory. "How about that?"

I gaze at it—his hateful face and arrogant pose—and grin. "That might work," I say, licking my lips as if I were about to eat a delicious hot fudge sundae.

"But we also need the fresh blood of a young animal," I

tell Anne. "A chicken, or a rooster."

"What for?"

I'm darned if I know. "To symbolize a sacrifice," I say, making it up. "Like a pagan Mass."

"What will we do with it?"

"Cut its throat."

"Here?"

"In the kitchen."

"But where do we find a chicken at this time of night?"

"Don Enrique keeps chickens on the roof."

"But he lives next door to his pen," she says in her annoying, practical voice. "He'll catch us."

I imagine creeping up in the dark and grabbing one. The feathers, the claws. The squawking. She has a point.

"Why don't we look in the fridge and see if there's anything we can use?" I suggest.

We find some bloody chicken innards in a little plastic bag. "We need real blood, not things with blood on them," I say.

"We can put them in the mixer."

"It's not the fresh blood of a young animal." Stumped before we can start.

"There must be something we can do," Anne says.

Suddenly, I think of Mother Mary Louise and how upset she was when she saw that the Sixth Grade Spanish science book had *Darwin's Theory of Evolution* in it. "According to Darwin's theory, we're descended from monkeys. That makes us a kind of animal. Our blood should be enough."

"Our blood?" She looks scared.

"Yes. Young, fresh blood. Like yours."

"Why mine?"

"You're younger and fresher than me." At thirteen, I feel much older than Anne.

I try my best to convince her, but she won't budge until

I offer to sacrifice some of my blood as well. "We have to cut ourselves."

"With what?"

I look around. "The kitchen knife. We need a bowl to pour our blood into it."

"You're first."

I hold the knife trying to decide whether to slice my palm or stick in the point. As I'm about to plunge it in, Anne asks, "Shouldn't we disinfect it first?"

She brings the bottle of alcohol that Mummy keeps in the bathroom. That gives me an idea. "We can prick ourselves with a large needle." I get one from Mummy's sewing basket.

We light the candles on Mummy's candelabra and switch off the lights. Something is missing. "All voodoo ceremonies have a fire," I say, "and they burn things. Remember how the witch doctor cut a chicken's head off in the movie about zombies, and disemboweled it, and threw its innards in the fire?"

"We have the chicken gizzards," Anne says.

"What do we do for a fire?"

"We could use the fireplace."

"It would make a mess and leave a smell. They're bound to notice. We'll have to do it in the kitchen."

We make a little bonfire of paper in the sink and leave the gizzards sizzling over the flames. Then we sterilize a needle and prick our thumbs, and squeeze them until we have maybe one eighth of an inch of blood in a teacup. "We can smear this on Ian's portrait."

There's something missing. Sounds. No drums or chanting. "We need to be in the mood," I say. I rummage through the records and come up with *Scheherezade*.

This ritual isn't as easy as I thought it would be. "I have to call a spirit," I say and Anne asks, "What spirit?" I need to find a name fast, one like . . . like, "Beowulf."

211

"Where did you find that name?"

"From the book about Haiti," I say breezily, trying to remember where it came from. "Oh, mighty Beowulf, receive our sacrifice," I intone, and we lift the tea cup, stick our fingers into it, and rub blood onto Ian's image on the canvas. We take special care with his face, coating it as evenly as we can.

Then we stick pins into Ian's portrait. Or we try to, but they don't go in very far, and we have to slide them in sideways.

"I don't think this will work," Anne says. "We're not really sticking them into him."

"It's the symbolism that counts. We're offending him, if not in the flesh at least his image." If I say so myself, that was a first-class explanation. "Oh mighty Beowulf, hear our prayers," I intone again.

"Pennie, are you sure you know what you're doing?"

"Of course I know," I say, with indignation. I don't tell her I'm making it up as we go. Now I remember who Beowulf was—a mythical hero in Saxon times.

We dance around the living room to the strains of *A Thousand and One Nights*, chanting and waving candles in front of Ian's portrait.

Smoke is coming from the kitchen. The fire has burned out, but the gizzards are smoldering. We run cold water on them and fan the smoke out of the window.

The spell is broken. With the light on, we see that we will have to undo our work, wipe off the blood and take the pins out of Ian's portrait.

In a way, it's a relief to know we were playacting all the time.

*

Mummy and Ian come back and don't notice anything. They're too busy shouting at each other. They're so loud I can hear them in my room though my door is closed.

Ian accuses Mummy of flirting with a man, a concert

pianist, at the party. She says all they were doing was talking about Chopin and Lizst. They are still arguing when I fall asleep.

Next day, the pianist calls Mummy. I'm in the living room when she answers. She pretends he's a woman friend, but Ian runs over, grabs the phone, and hears the man's voice before hanging up. He gives Mummy a poisonous stare and asks, "Where can I find that man?"

He's so scary that Mummy tells him, "The Reforma Hotel."

"I'm paying that man a visit," Ian says, "and I'll break all his fingers. He will never play the piano again."

Ian pulls out the telephone cord so Mummy can't call the man and warn him that Ian is on his way over. As soon as he leaves, Mummy asks me to run across the road to the public phone in the pharmacy, instead of the one in the lobby, and call up the pianist to warn him. I do as she says, but the pianist isn't in his room, so I leave a message and pray he receives it.

He doesn't, and Ian finds him in the hotel bar. Since he can't break the man's fingers in front of everyone, he lands a couple of punches on the pianist's face before people stop him.

The next day, Mummy and Ian keep on arguing. At one point she rushes out of the bedroom as fast as her Bad Leg allows her to move, crying, "Children, we're leaving, right this minute. Call a taxi." Ian comes pounding after her, with Mac behind them barking his head off. They run in circles around the sofa, like Tom and Jerry, until Mummy lunges for the telephone.

Ian snatches it away from her and yanks out the cord that Teléfonos de Mexico just replaced. "Why can't we talk this over like reasonable human beings?" he asks and marches her back to their room.

Much later, she appears, screaming, "Ian's having an attack. Call the doctor."

"We can't," I say. "Remember, Ian pulled out the phone cord."

"Then use the public phone downstairs."

I'm surprised Ian's "attack" didn't happen sooner. Phony or real?

The doctor arrives within the hour, and by then, Ian has recovered. A man comes from the telephone company and reconnects the phone.

The next morning, Mummy has red eyes. She takes two Equanils to calm down, but since Ian stays angry, she has two more during the day. Ian won't talk to her; it's his way of punishing her, so she takes more Equanils in the evening because she's so upset.

Around nine Ian notices she's passed out, and he's worried she might have taken too many Equanils. We can hear him moving around and saying, "Baby dearest, wake up!" Then he bangs on my door and asks me to try to wake her up. When I can't, he calls the doctor, the same doctor who always attends to his attacks and overdoses, and the doctor gives her something. She throws up, but she's groggy. The doctor leaves with instructions for us to keep her awake, not let her go to sleep because she might never come out of it.

For once, Ian's scared—I can tell from his nervy look and hunched-over attitude as if someone had whacked him in his gut. Still, he orders us, "Put your mother under a shower of cold water and then walk her around." He goes off to the living room and serves himself a Scotch.

Mummy's half out of it, so it's not hard to get her in the shower, but when the cold water hits her, she screams as if we were stabbing her and doesn't stop until we turn it off. That does the trick. She's awake, though dazed.

Keeping her awake isn't easy. Anne and I make her drink black coffee and walk her around the apartment until we can't anymore. Anne goes to bed, but Mummy holds my hand and won't let me leave. She lies in her bed, wide awake, and talking non-stop while I try to listen, but my eyes are closing.

"I don't see how I can stay married to a man who won't let me out of his sight," Mummy says. "He won't be content until I'm all alone in the world except for him." And, "I can't understand why Ian made such a fuss. All I did was speak to another man, that concert pianist from Budapest. I never dreamed Ian would be violently jealous. Do you know that Ian throttled people with his bare hands during the war? If he's angry enough, he might strangle me. I hate to tell you this, but I live in fear for my life. One of these days, your mother might wake up dead." Which doesn't make sense but does, in a funny way.

When I go to bed at dawn, I lie shivering in the half-light, hearing Ian pace up and down the apartment until he comes to a halt outside my door. My heart jumps into my throat when he opens it. My eyes are closed tight and I can't see him, but I sense him there, watching me. The little hairs on the back of my neck stand up like a cat's.

Dear God, make him go away.

I take measured breaths and pretend to be fast asleep while praying he won't try to strangle me. Until, after long minutes, he leaves, and I can breathe normally.

The next day, Mummy is still weak. All is forgiven and Ian is at her side. It's Sunday, and Anne and I go to Granny's for lunch. We come home and Mummy's sleeping. Ian asks us to keep an eye on her while he goes to Maria Bárbara for a bite to eat.

Instead of taking the car, he walks. As he steps off the grass strip in the middle of the street, a car hits him.

*

The telephone rings and I take the call. A voice tells me

they're calling from the Green Cross to advise us that Mr. C. has been run over and is in the emergency room there.

The voodoo worked.

It's not possible. I made it up. But there's no other explanation. If Ian dies, it's because of what we did. I'm shaking when I tell Mummy. "Someone ran over Ian. He's in the emergency room at the Green Cross."

She stares at me as if not understanding and I have to repeat the words. Suddenly she sits up, "My poor Ian, I should be with him." She hops out of bed and for someone who could not move five minutes before, she's pretty agile. Not even her Bad Leg slows her down. "Is he badly hurt? Did they say anything?"

"Just that he was run over."

"It's my fault. I shouldn't have taken all those pills and said those awful things to him." Now it's her fault as well as well as ours. And, "Ian can't leave me. I don't want to be left a widow." And, "What shall I wear?"

"Black," I tell her and shrug. "Just in case."

The funny thing about Mummy, if it's a real crisis, she's calm. We take a taxi to the Green Cross that's nothing like the Red Cross. The Green Cross is all about people who have done things they shouldn't and may go to jail. In this case, not Ian, but the man who ran over him because he'd had a few drinks, and he was driving with his arm around his girlfriend.

Mummy argues about what should be done with Ian, who's been given a strong sedative. If he wants to press charges, he will have to remain there along with all the other Sunday night casualties. They will only let him out if Mummy signs a release that she won't press charges against the fat, sweaty man who ran him over.

The man shows Mummy his card—he has a German last name—and he promises to sign a witnessed agreement to pay all the hospital costs if she will sign the release. He says he doesn't want anyone suffering on his account. More likely, Mummy says, he doesn't want anyone to know he was with his girlfriend and "doing things they shouldn't do in a car."

Except for me, Mummy is alone as nobody she calls answers their phone. It's after midnight and people are asleep. She needs someone to tell her what to do, and at last, our family doctor arrives, cracking jokes that he might as well come live with us. He advises moving Ian to a proper hospital at once, rather than leaving him at the Green Cross for another day while legal matters are sorted out. So Mummy gives in and signs the release, and the man with the German last name signs a note promising to pay Ian's medical costs. To show his good faith, he gives her a check for five hundred pesos that she can cash tomorrow, but not too early so as to give him time to deposit funds in the bank.

Meanwhile, I sit in the lobby at the entrance to the hospital. Casualties keep coming in, some leaving trails of blood in their wake. A woman with a bucket pushes a filthy mop around the floor, leaving a faded red and black crisscross pattern. A man with blood gushing out of a hole in his head rushes in, supported by two men on either side, and the floor is covered with blood again.

What happened was our fault. Anne's and mine. Our slapdash voodoo ritual led to this. Even if it did, no one can blame us for his accident. So, in the end, the voodoo worked. Mummy comes to say Ian needs an operation on his leg.

"Is it bad?" I ask.

"Serious," she says. "Looks like his leg is broken in three places and he has other contusions."

That's all? What a letdown. Ian has two operations—one on his leg and the other to patch him up inside—and he's eight days in the ABC Hospital.

The man with the German last name does not keep his

word. Mummy is able to cash his first check, enough for Ian to go into the hospital, but that's all. Afterwards, the man sends word through his lawyer that the Green Cross release Mummy signed frees him from all responsibility. The paper he signed agreeing to pay for Ian's hospital costs wasn't valid because no lawyer was present. Ian's sons have to find the money to pay the rest of his medical bills.

*

I go to Confession.

"Bless me Father for I have sinned. I caused great harm to befall my stepfather."

The priest asks, "In what way?"

"Voodoo."

"What did you say?"

"Voodoo."

"Vudú?" His voice is disbelieving.

"Yes, Father."

"Where did you learn such a thing?"

"From a book, but mostly I made it up."

"It's a mortal sin to practice pagan rites." He sounds angry. "It goes against the teachings of our holy mother, the Church."

"Yes, father."

For a good ten minutes, he tells me off. How a good Catholic girl should not read books, or see movies, or have anything to do with pagan religions and rites that use the dark forces. How could I risk my eternal soul practicing witchcraft? Don't I know that is the most abominable sin because the devil is always on the lookout for young souls like mine?

At last, he gives me absolution and tells me to make a novena to the Blessed Virgin as penance for the voodoo.

He does not give me a penance for trying to kill Ian.

28

DEAR DADDY, HOPE YOU GET YOUR MONEY BACK

God punishes us for what we did.

Ian is at home all the time, lying on the living room sofa, a glowering presence. On doctor's orders he cuts back the Scotch, but he's taking pills for pain and to sleep and sedatives to stay calm. He sleeps a lot, but when he's awake, he's in an awful mood. His mind seems jumbled. Maybe when he was run over, he hit his head, but if he was not all there before, it's more obvious now. He wants to know where Mummy is going, how long she will be out, whom she sees and talks to, her every move. He blackmails her into canceling her plans. "Baby dearest, don't leave me here alone." He threatens to commit suicide, and since he's overdosed several times, that scares her. Or he puts on his act as if he's in his last throes, and she falls for it every time. He always finds excuses to detain her. If she stays out too long, he goes crazy.

Despite Ian asking Anne not to leave Daddy's photo on top of her dresser, she has insisted on keeping it there. So when it's not there and she can't find it anywhere, it's obvious to her who took it.

She comes charging out of her room and screams at Ian, who's lying like an invalid on the living room sofa, "Where's my daddy's picture?"

Ian glares at her, as though wanting to swat her out of the way.

"I know you took it. Where is it?"

Mummy puts a hand on her shoulder. "Anne, be reasonable. Why would Ian take your father's photo?"

Anne pulls away from her. "He's the only one who'd do that."

Ignoring Anne, Ian speaks to Mummy. "Why do I have to suffer aggravation at the hands of an insolent child?"

Mummy grabs Ian's arm. "Did you take it?"

"Did I not warn her on numerous occasions that if she left it out, I would remove it?"

"It's *my* room, and I can have what I like there."

"In my house, you abide by *my* rules."

"What did you do with Anne's photo, Ian?" Mummy asks.

"Threw it out of the window," he says on a note of triumph. "Into the trash, I hope."

Anne shrieks and advances on Ian, hand out ready to hit him, but Mummy is in the middle, so Anne grabs the photograph that Ian treasures most, the one of him in his Argyle and Sutherland Highlander uniform. "See how it feels when I throw your picture out."

Mummy screams, "Anne, I beg you, don't!"

Whirling around, Anne runs into her room and slams the door. We hear a crash outside. A faint sound of broken glass. Mummy stares at me with frightened eyes. Ian hauls himself up, grabs his crutch and hobbles over to Anne's door and pounds on it. "Return my photograph at once, or I'll break this door down."

Anne opens. "I threw it out of the window." She's shaking, but her voice is clear.

Mummy gasps. "Anne, how could you?"

"He threw Daddy's picture out first."

Ian says, "That child deserves a good whipping," but he's upset. I can see his anguished expression. That photo means a lot to him.

Mummy looks at him and then at Anne as if she doesn't know which one to believe.

Anne shouts, "I hate you! I hate you both!"

Ian bellows, "Get that brat out of my house before I call the police. She belongs in reform school."

"You belong in the loony bin!" Anne screams.

Mummy puts her hands over her ears. "Stop, stop, I can't bear any more of this!"

"From now on, her father or the devil can look after her," Ian says, and he hobbles off to their bedroom, shouting over his shoulder, "You'd better recover my picture."

Anne is crying. "I don't want to live here anymore."

"If you go, I'm leaving too," I say.

Mummy's shoulders sag. "Don't you care at all about your mother's feelings?"

"No," Anne says. "Not since you married Ian."

Mummy closes her eyes and lets out a sobbing sigh. "I wish to God I had died before you were born, rather than hear such words uttered by my child. You will dance on my grave." She turns, then stops and says, "From now on, forget I am your mother," before sweeping down the passage to their bedroom.

I can see what Mummy can't, a funny little smile hiding behind Anne's tears. She giggles. "Ian's photo is here, in my drawer."

"Then what did you throw out?"

"An empty Coca-Cola bottle."

We look around outside for Daddy's picture. In the dark, it's hard to find. Anne won't return Ian's photo until we find Daddy's, and only if it isn't ruined. She and I and the old caretaker, Don Matías, search in the dark for ten minutes, before something crunches under my foot. A piece of glass. The photo in its frame fell on the far side of the parking lot, near the trashcans. The silver frame is dented, but the photo isn't damaged.

Don Matías shakes his head and says, "*Que loco.*"

Anne holds it to her.

"You will give him back his picture," I say.

"I'd love to tear it up but …" she's calmed down, "two wrongs don't make a right. Then I'm leaving, and I hope I never come back."

*

We both stay with Granny and Grandpa in their small apartment. Anne sleeps on a daybed in Granny's room, and I'm on the lumpy, living room convertible sofa. We're crowded, and it's not very comfortable. But as long as we're proving a point, it will do.

A few days later Mummy comes over with Ian, who stays outside in his car. "He wants to have a word with you," she says to me.

"Why? There's nothing to say."

"The other day Ian wasn't himself. He had a bad reaction to his new medicine and had no idea what he was doing. The only things he remembers, unfortunately, are your sister's insults."

Is this the truth or more like a way to excuse Ian?

"Oh, how convenient. He did throw Daddy's picture out into the parking lot."

She concentrates on her cigarette. "Don't forget he has kept a roof over your heads for the last two years, as well as paid part of your tuition. Please, Pennie, help."

I rather like the idea of playing the peacemaker, so I decide to talk with Ian in his car.

He tells me I'm not a problem and never have been, and I should understand how the incident with the photo would not have occurred if my sister did as she was told, and how sometimes parents have to be firm no matter what. "Your mother is very upset that you left."

"I'll think about it," I say because I miss my own bedroom and my privacy, and I hate sleeping on Granny's sofa, and I need my typewriter, and there's nowhere I can write in peace here. For two days, I let Ian stew. Then I tell Mummy, "I'll go back, on one condition. Ian has to apologize to Anne."

Mummy shakes her head. "Ian has his pride. I can't ask a sixty-two year old man to apologize to an eleven-year-old. Try to make Anne understand he didn't know what he was doing because of his medicines."

Anne doesn't understand; nor does she want him to apologize. Not if it means living in his house.

He sends word with Mummy that he regrets throwing Daddy's photo out. "A grudging apology if I ever heard one," Grandpa says. "I can't see that he regrets anything he's done. Tita shouldn't hold her children hostage to that man's whims."

It's too crowded in Granny's house and I agree to go back there. Both Granny and Anne are furious about my giving in. Ian is pleased and says I'm always welcome in his house.

From my balcony, I can see the broken Coca-Cola bottle Anne threw onto the tin roof cover of the parking lot.

*

Ian writes to Daddy to tell him it's high time he took his responsibilities as a father seriously. Anne needs a strong hand. It would be best if she went to live with him in England.

"Jimmy won't do anything," Mummy says. "He never does."

Daddy does do something. He sends a telegram. "Agree. From now on will take full responsibility for both girls. Plane tickets on the way."

"Another of his promises," Mummy says.

The plane tickets arrive two weeks later. Four open-date plane tickets made out in our names: Mexico City to New York City and New York City to London.

Mummy sits heavily on the sofa and says, "Just like your father to make things difficult." You'd think Daddy had deliberately set out to ruin Mummy's life by doing precisely what she's spent years grumbling about his not doing.

I say, "Daddy came through. He did what Ian asked him to do."

Mummy goes on. "Ian asked him to take responsibility for you, not to take you away." Considering that Anne isn't living here, Daddy isn't taking her away. "Anne's not coming back," I say, wishing I hadn't agreed to try to patch things up.

"Your father doesn't do anything for years, then out of the blue he sends for you. Where will you live? With his mother? No, I can't let that woman bring up my daughters." I don't want to live with Granny-in-England but if it means returning there, I'll live with anyone, even as a boarder at the convent.

Mummy leaves the plane tickets on the desk in the living room. Our tickets away from Ian and back to Daddy. At last we're going home. If Mummy lets us.

Ian acts very nice to me, too nice. He has a smarmy, false smile and is nice in a how-fond-we-are-of-each-other way. He includes me in a dinner at Cardini's Restaurant when he and Mummy take out two "visiting firemen" from England. He tells everyone to order the Caesar salad. The owner, Alex Cardini's brother, Caesar, invented it some years ago, and it has become world famous. We watch as Mr. Cardini himself makes it for us right there beside our table. None of the old vinegar and oil mix. His dressing has olive oil, lemon juice and Worcester sauce—which surprises the two Englishmen because they never dreamed of using this sauce in a salad—beaten raw egg, anchovies, garlic bread, and Parmesan cheese on top.

Ian has a little chat with me. He wants Anne to go to England and for me to stay. "Your mother will be heartbroken if you leave," he says.

The battle lasts a week. Mummy says she can't lose the rest of our childhoods, and we'll be grown up before she sees us again. After all the sacrifices she's made to keep us fed and clothed and in school, is it fair for Daddy and his mother to take over?

"Are you so selfish that you're going to leave me and live with a father who abandoned you?" How I hate that word, abandoned. "And Miss Pennie, don't expect your grandmother to tolerate you wearing makeup or going out with boys. She'll expect you to toe the line and behave like a Victorian maiden. You'll end up like your Aunty Rena."

Her words scare me a bit. Anne's happy at Granny's. After three years in Mexico, I'd be happy too. If Ian wasn't around.

He gives his permission for Mummy to take me—Anne's still at Granny's—to see *The Swan*, the last film Grace Kelly made before she married Prince Rainier of Monaco. After the film ends we walk along Parque Sullivan looking for a taxi.

"Wasn't it nice of Ian to take you out to dinner at Cardini's?" Mummy says. "He wants you to stay."

I stick out my chin. "I want to go back to England."

"Don't I mean more to you than a father who abandoned you?" Her voice trembles like Grace Kelly's in the film. A sour little ball works its way up my throat. She goes on about all the sacrifices she has made for me, sounding a lot like Jessie Royce Landis, who played Grace Kelly's mother.

While Mummy jabbers away, I'm thinking why can't she understand we don't want to live with a madman, or with her, anymore? She's also crazy, always shouting and annoyed about everything. How can she stop us from wanting to be where we can be happy? But she won't listen or try to understand. She sees everything her way. Against my will, tears fall.

She says, "I can't drag a weeping child through the streets of Mexico. I'll have to call Ian to come for us."

"I'd rather throw myself off my balcony," I tell her, "than live one more day with you and Ian." What's more, when we're back at the apartment, I'll go straight to my balcony and throw myself off. Show her for once and for all how upset I am about not going home to England.

We stop at The British Bookstore. The manager, Toby Joysmith, has the same wavy gray hair and crinkly smile as Daddy. Mummy met Toby at *El Centro Mexicano de Escritores*, the Writers Center, when she went there. She tells him, "This child's playing up. She wants to return to England to live with her father, even though he doesn't have a home for her."

"I've wanted to go home for three years," I tell Toby, rubbing away my tears. I don't like anyone to see me crying and much less this man from the Centro.

"My daughter shows great promise as a writer," Mummy says. "She's already writing her second full-length book."

I don't like her showing off about me, but it draws his attention. He asks, "Second book? How long was your first?"

He must think it's like a long short story so when I say, "Two hundred and forty typewritten pages," I expect him to be surprised and he is.

"Good for you."

"She needs training. Do you think she's old enough for the Centro?"

Toby takes another look at me, and I see doubt. In his eyes I must be a child. "Perhaps in a few years."

Once Mummy wants something, though, she won't let go. "If she sat in the back and listened, she might learn a lot."

Toby says. "We had better wait a couple of years."

"You see, Pennie," Mummy tells me as if she hasn't heard him. "If you stay in Mexico, you can attend *El Centro Mexicano de Escritores*. It will help you more with your writing than if you return to England."

"A couple of years is a long time to wait," I say. "Nothing will make me change my mind."

Back in the apartment, I go straight to my balcony and look down. I imagine jumping off it, and big blobs of my blood and bones spattered all over the car park. I don't like the idea one bit. Suicide is the only sin you can't confess afterwards, which means a good chance I'll end up in hell. Unless I make a quick act of contrition on the way down. Would there be time before I hit the ground?

The plane tickets are sitting on the desk in the living room. Tickets back to life in Rustington with Daddy. He sent us a blurred photo of himself reading my manuscript. His hair is all white. It won't be easy after three and a half years, especially with no *Carlyon*, no home anymore. But we can go to the beach and have proper teas and eat Cadbury's milk chocolates and apples any time we like. Buy books in English that we can't find here.

Except, in Mexico I'm a young lady now. I wear stockings and high heels and makeup. I can attend *El Centro Mexicano de Escritores* and become a real writer.

Telegrams go back and forth between Mummy and Daddy.

Ian comes to talk to me. "Your mother can't allow both of you to return to England. It would make her very unhappy. But your father says it wouldn't be fair for one of you and not the other. So tell your sister that I promise, on my word as a gentleman, that all will be forgotten, and we'll try to get along."

Grandpa gives a loud snort of disgust when he hears me repeat Ian's message. "Don't be gulled by the man's promises. Believe me, he will not keep his word."

Anne is happier living with Granny, but she also wants to be Mummy's good daughter. She decides to come home, though not because she believes Ian will change.

*

June 5, 1957
Dear Daddy,
I'm sorry, we won't be coming home after all. I'd much rather go to school in England because the one here is not very good.
Uncle Artie is marrying his girlfriend Claudia, and I want to be here for the wedding. Grandpa isn't doing too well, Mummy says he may not have long to live.
Thank you very much for the tickets. I hope you get your money back. Maybe next year Mummy will give in.
Lots of love,
Pennie

29

ONE OF THE WRITERS

It's easy to convince Mummy to enroll me in *El Centro Mexicano de Escritores*. The summer before I turn fourteen, she agrees to give me a three-month course as a birthday present.

We walk to the Centro, eight blocks away, and into a two-floor house behind Paseo de la Reforma, the city's main street. We're on our way to see Toby Joysmith.

I hope he won't remember me as the crying child he met a few months ago, and he will see I've grown up since then. He and Mummy talk a few minutes about how the Centro is gaining importance and prestige and has writers endowed by the Rockefeller Foundation come here from the U.S. It sounds so important that when Mummy asks Toby to consider making an exception for me because I've written two full-length books, I hold my breath waiting for his answer.

Toby runs a hand through his wavy gray hair. "Pennie is rather young, and some of the writers might object."

Mummy persists. "She needs to learn her craft." In true form, she wears him down, as I knew she would, and he's such a nice man that it's hard for him to say no.

"I suppose we might allow her to audit classes and write pieces when asked. But this would be on a trial basis to see if she fits in and the other students accept her."

My first session is also the first of the summer. I'm as excited as an actress making her debut on stage. I wear my most grown-up outfit, a blue suit inherited from Aunt Carmelita, high heels, and makeup. Mummy accompanies me, but she can only stay for half an hour because Ian isn't well.

We are seven: George, in his twenties, is dressed like a beatnik in black trousers and a black top. Joan has glasses and dark hair pulled back in a messy bun. There's balding, pleasant John and his friend Marjorie, who looks like a sparrow. The other two are beginners like me; the difference is they are just starting to write.

George leads the session. He asks everyone about their writing. Why do we write? I must have several hundred butterflies in my stomach as I answer, "Because I have a tremendous urge."

"Have you written anything?"

"Two full-length books."

He makes a fainting movement. "How old are you?"

I meant to fib, say I'm fifteen, but I tell the truth—almost. "Fourteen." I don't say in two months.

He waves his hand, "Why don't you take over the class?" Everybody laughs. I'm in.

*

The room is full of smoke. I don't mind. After three sessions I'm used to it. Sometimes the small room is so clouded with smoke, I see everyone through a fog. Sometimes we're six and sometimes we're sixteen students. Toby gives the "Criticism" sessions on Tuesdays and "Observation and Description" on Thursdays, though quite often George fills in for him.

George is twenty-six and the best writer of all of us. He wants to be the next James Baldwin. I suspect that Joan, who dresses like a gypsy, is his girlfriend. He's here on a grant from the Rockefeller Foundation, and the others are working on novels. Good-natured John, who doesn't seem to write much, and Marjorie, his girlfriend from the Canadian prairie, who writes funny stories that make us laugh. These four, whom I think of as the inner circle, are a group. They're different from anyone I've met. They don't have normal jobs. They intend to become great writers, especially George, who is almost there.

Mummy says, "Don't be carried away, Pennie. Those people are bohemian. They come to this country because they think they will be free to do whatever they like. Don't forget that you live here and are part of this country's society."

"But they lead such interesting lives."

"That's exactly what I mean. By the way, I got the impression the colored man is a good writer."

"George. He's the best of all of them."

"Don't go getting a crush on him. Remember who you are."

*

My shadow walks before me in the rain-sodden street. No one liked my first stint. They said it was exaggerated, not a valid observation, and I used too many adjectives. I'm afraid they will ask me to leave the Centro.

It's Mummy's fault my piece wasn't right. If only she had let me go to the drawing at the Lottery building instead of telling me to make it up, and then she insisted on revising it herself. She said she knew the kind of work they expected. So I let her make revisions and add adjectives and adverbs. I will never forget the sarcasm in George's voice when he said, "I can't believe it. She gazed at him 'beseechingly.' And what's this about, a 'strange' expression crossed her face? Can't you find a better word to describe emotions?"

Mummy and Ian are sitting on the sofa in the living room having drinks. I want to slide by them without saying anything except hello, but Mummy stops me.

"How was the Centro?"

"We were only six."

"What did they think of your piece on the Lottery?"

"They didn't like it. They said it sounded made up."

"Well, it was made up. I can't allow my teenage daughter to go downtown at night to the Lottery building."

I'm thinking about what George told me, "Next time you have an observation stint, you need to do exactly what we said. Even if you have to observe all the dog shit in town."

"Did you tell them I corrected what you wrote?" she asks.

I shake my head. It would be the last thing I'd admit to. "They said it should be real, not make believe."

I don't tell them, not those two sitting over their drinks, this may be the end of my time at the Centro. It isn't, and from then on, I'm careful with my observation stints. I write descriptions of street crossings and supermarkets and church on Sunday. George says, "Yes, that's good, but you have to make it come to life. Give me action, feelings, use your senses. For example, Marjorie, describe a tight red dress without using any of those three words."

"Aw cummon, George. If I can't say it's red, or tight, or a dress, how do you expect me to describe it?"

"What does it remind you of? What did you feel like when you wore it?"

She thinks for a moment. "I might say something like, what I wore at Christmas made me feel like Marilyn Monroe with some colorful Santa influence."

"That works. Well done." He turns to me. "Pennie, what comes to mind if I mention a fancy party dress?"

I answer without hesitating, "I'm looking glamorous, everyone wants to dance with me, and we're drinking champagne."

George opens his arms wide as if to hug me. "Great. And how come you like champagne?"

In the autumn, George invites me to attend his Saturday

morning sessions on the short story. He has such a deep, expressive voice that when he reads *To Esmé With Love and Squalor*, the words embrace me. I decide to read the books and stories he talks about. *A Death in the Family* by James Agee, *Another Country* by James Baldwin, *On the Road* by Jack Kerouac, and anything by William Faulkner. I go out to coffee with the inner group after our sessions. Once they've accepted me, everyone else does. My insides churn and I sweat, sometimes, while pretending a coolness I don't possess. I wish I could push each day, each week along into the future, into a life where I'll be a real writer. Nothing will stop me.

Nothing, except Ian. If he can ruin my life, he will. He has four more years to do it, unless I can find a way to get rid of him. The idea is growing again like a bad seed inside me.

*

One October afternoon, we leave the Centro early, and George invites us to his new apartment for a drink.

Joan drives Marjorie and me to a place on Melchor Ocampo Street. We climb up some dark stairs, and the first thing I see in this writer's apartment is the fridge standing next to the front door. The tiny living-dining room is littered with manuscripts—on the floor, on a sofa and an easy chair, and crumpled in a fireplace. A rack holds *The Writer* and other magazines. The only thing in the bedroom is a big bed. Does Joan sleep there with George?

George, Joan, and John drink gin and tonics, and Marjorie has a Coca-Cola like me. George sits on some cushions on the floor and, in his deep, mellow voice, reads Faulkner's description of a writer. I'll never forget the silence of our hushed listening, or the dim lighting, or the pins and needles running up my right leg.

They move to another subject—a new book from the author of *The Blackboard Jungle* in which a young student gives up his studies to care for a dope addict. They don't agree with the way the author tries to make the boy seem noble by sacrificing himself for another.

Suddenly George asks, "What do you think, Pennie?"

I think of what the Church teaches, and of Mummy, who's always telling us how she's had to sacrifice herself for our sakes. "What if the person needs you, is very close to you, and you should make sacrifices for them?"

George frowns. "Why can't you be generous without having to make sacrifices? The other person usually knows how they affect you by bringing you into their problems."

"It's an imposition that you may come to resent," Joan says.

I don't let myself think before asking, "What if I said there's a person I want to get rid of? I'm not asking for advice. I have it all figured out."

No one gasps or looks alarmed.

"Do you have any idea of the implications?" Marjorie asks. She's always funny and we laugh a lot in class, but now she's serious. "If you mean murdering someone, it's a punishable offence."

George looks solemn as he says, "There are things you should consider before doing it. Do you want to kill this person or get him out of the way? And do you have to commit murder, if that's what you have in mind?"

I nod.

Silence. *Have I gone too far?*

"I can guess you don't have a great home life," George says at last, "but I don't recommend turning your own life into hell. And that's what murder would do to you."

"Sure, you might get away with it," Joan adds, "but don't expect to feel good about yourself ever again. Once you kill someone, you've crossed a bridge, and you will never be the same."

I'm annoyed because what they say makes sense. And I'm not sure I want to risk trying anything after what happened with the voodoo.

I'm usually home from the Centro at seven, but it's half past eight by the time Marjorie and Joan take me. As they drop me off, Joan says, "Pennie, maybe I shouldn't say this, though murder in some circumstances can be justified, stop thinking about it. It will ruin your life. That cold-blooded planning is wrong."

I'm hoping Mummy won't see me come in, but she always wants to know what happened at each session, and she's waiting. "Why are you so late?"

"Some of us went to George's apartment."

"You should have phoned me."

"I couldn't. George doesn't have a telephone."

"Then you should have come straight home. Who was there?"

"George, Joan, Marjorie, and John."

"We don't know anything about those people." Here it comes. The sermon about not trusting people we don't know, or who don't belong in our social class in Mexico.

"They happen to be my friends."

Her voice is sharp. "Don't give me a high-handed retort. I know what the Americans who go to the Centro are like, and they're not the kind of people I want my daughter associating with."

"Didn't you think I'd make friends?"

"There was a better caliber of people when I attended." She has that uppity sound in her voice. "I don't like the idea of my fourteen-year-old daughter consorting with who knows who, especially if you go out with them and come home at this hour."

At the Centro, I'm learning about writing and reading and life. At school, I'm wasting my time.

235

Mummy can't make me leave the Centro. What if she phones Toby? I won't let her. I just paid the next three months out of the money I made giving private English lessons. She can't stop me from going.

Later, as I'm about to switch off my light, Mummy comes in. "Penny, Ian wants to have a word with you."

Ian's lying in bed. His eyes have a crazy gleam in them.

"Your mother told me where you went," he says. "If I ever catch you with a Negro, I'll tan your bottom until it bleeds and kick you out of the house."

Anger explodes inside my head, but I can't say anything. His eyes won't let me.

"You have permission to attend sessions at the Centro as long as you come straight home after class. Do you understand?"

"Yes, Ian," I say, and his eyes half close, freeing me from their grasp. I run to my room and fling myself on my bed. My friends are the most wonderful people I've ever met, and George most of all. They've given me such a lot and now this monster is spitting on them. I wish to God Ian was dead. With a bit of luck I can arrange it.

I think of what we were talking about tonight in George's apartment. Why should I have to sacrifice myself because of what Mummy did for us? Nowadays, there's nothing lovable about her. Mrs. C., as I call her in my mind, is getting more like Ian, shouting and cursing and bullying us, except when she wants something—and then what honeyed words. I love only the memory of Mummy because she became another person when she married Ian.

Look at what she does to my writing. Wants to make it better, give it her flair. I glance at a page in my copy book. She's crossed out "a dreary day" and written "a somber day" and changed a "puzzled" to a "strange" expression.

I won't show her anything else I write, or anything that matters.

*

Just as we're starting the session at the Centro, a young man in a wheelchair enters the room.

Toby stops and says, "Hello, Miguel, where have you been?"

The man answers in accented English, "I was in New York for treatment." Except for a squint, he is quite handsome, rather like Prince Juan Carlos of Spain.

Someone reads a piece called *Witch Hunt on the Campus*. It isn't about real witches, but about hunting for Communists in the U.S. The piece goes all over the place and has too many adjectives, and so I'm indignant when George and Toby's criticisms aren't stronger. But I can't say anything because we're a big group today and I wasn't asked what I thought of it.

Miguel's criticism, in too correct English, is slow and painstaking. It's also honest to the point of disagreeable. I wonder if being in a wheelchair has made him cranky. But later, as he leans his cheek on his open hand, like a child, a kind of sweetness creeps into his face.

George reads Miguel's piece to us. Even in his melodious voice, the careful, precise writing is hard to follow. Toby tells him it needs more work and George says to lighten it up.

The sessions supposedly end at seven, but it's nearer eight when we get out. It's dark, and last week, a man followed me all the way home. I'm nervous because of stories I've heard of girls being pushed into doorways and violated.

"Can anyone give me a lift?" I ask.

Miguel offers. "My car and chauffeur are waiting outside," he says.

I get into the back of his sleek black Chevrolet and with his chauffeur's help, he pulls himself onto the front seat. Then he half-turns and asks why I'm at the Centro. I'm telling him when we reach the Edificio Nervión, and he doesn't seem inclined to end our conversation. "What did you think of the witch hunt piece?"

"Everyone was easy on her," I say, showing off a bit. "I was certain someone would criticize her piece, but you were the only one."

"Why didn't you say something?"

"I'm there to listen." I'm hoping he won't ask me what I thought of his piece, but he does.

I hesitate, and he says, "I don't want you to be kind to me. Kindness is useless. I'd prefer to hear the truth."

"Well, I think that maybe—you might be trying too hard to write correct English so it sounds a bit old-fashioned. And I agree with Toby—you explain too much."

He laughs and his laugh is like his smile. Bitter. "What would you advise me to do?"

"Forget you're writing in English, and as George said, lighten up and write from the heart."

Again, a bitter laugh. "I lost all feeling in my heart when I lost it in my legs ten years ago."

"Was it an accident?"

"I have multiple sclerosis."

What is that? I can't ask him.

He half-turns and says, "I enjoyed talking to you this evening." Then turns facing front. His way, I assume, of saying goodnight.

First thing tomorrow, I'll look up Multiple Sclerosis in the Encyclopedia. I have a feeling I might be the one who will help Miguel find his heart.

*

After the session, I dawdle on the street corner, waiting for Miguel to come out of the Centro. He's given me a lift home every week for four weeks, but today he stayed behind to talk to Toby. He's bound to see me here. I'll say I'm waiting for a taxi.

Dear God, give me a chance to talk to him. It's only once a week. I think I'm in love with him.

After twenty minutes, I see Salomón, his chauffeur, push him outside, help him into the car, and put the wheelchair in the trunk. They drive up the block. They have to see me; I'm practically jumping off the curb. Good luck, Salomón stops the car.

"Do you want a lift?" Miguel asks.

"I've been waiting for a taxi for half an hour," I lie. "They're all full."

"I'm glad to be of help." We make halting conversation until we reach the Edificio Nervión. I'm about to say thanks and goodbye when Miguel says, "Do you know how I learnt to speak English? Reading books." He tells me he was in hospital in New York for two years and he spent that time reading books in English. Even his nearsightedness did not hinder him. Then, back here in Mexico City, a friend at the British Bookstore suggested he try writing as well. "I have two limitations," he says. "My English and my writing ability. Toby is tutoring me, but my progress is slow. I fear I am not a natural writer like you."

After that, Miguel doesn't come back to the Centro for four weeks. When he does, he's very pale, his hands tremble, he squints more than ever, and he leaves early. If I hadn't said hello to him, he wouldn't have seen me. The next week, he behaves as if I'm a stranger. I don't dare ask him for a lift and he doesn't offer. What's wrong?

I ask Toby about Miguel.

"He isn't himself," Toby says. "He had some sort of attack and it affected his memory, and unfortunately, his writing. I don't think he'll be coming anymore."

*

I find out that Miguel lives right next door to the Santa Monica hospital on the corner of a gracious, tree-lined avenue with a grassy strip in the middle. It's a white house with a red-tiled roof and when I go to take a look, Miguel is seated on a raised terrace outside the front door. A wrought iron fence and a rose garden separate him from the street.

I'd love to walk up and say hello, but I hold back. He's been sort of distant the last two times I saw him and he may not like me intruding on his privacy. After that, several times I take the bus that goes by his house and most days, he sits on his terrace. So I know it's his habit. One of these days I'll get up the nerve to say hello and maybe he'll invite me to join him. We'll talk about writing for hours on end, and I can find out what the real Miguel is like.

30

SAVING MUMMY'S SOUL

It's Saturday afternoon in January, and Anne and I are on our way to the movies. The bus is moving slowly down the avenue when I catch sight of Miguel on his terrace.

"Anne, we have to get off the bus."

"What's got into you?"

"It's Miguel, he's there, sitting on his terrace. I have to see him." Drat, I have the inside seat and she's on the outside, blocking my way.

"You're crazy," she says. "We're going to the movies."

"He hasn't been to the Centro in two months." As if that makes any difference to her.

"I'll give you five pesos?" She shakes her head. "Ten?" Another no. In desperation, "Twenty pesos?" Again she shakes her head. Nothing in the world will make her miss this movie, *Funny Face* with Audrey Hepburn and Fred Astaire. Anne's twelve almost thirteen, and movies are the most important thing in her life.

There's a long line outside the movie house, and we don't reach the box office before the show is sold out. Now Anne has no excuse. Oh yes, she does. She wants to go to María Bárbara and read movie magazines.

"Please, I haven't seen him in ages, and I heard he's been ill."

"Why should I spend the afternoon listening to you two talk about writing?"

"I'll give you ten pesos."

She says. "Ten for two hours." She still wants to go to María Bárbara and spend her ill-gotten gains on comics.

As we walk up to Miguel's house, the winter afternoon sun is beaming on his terrace. He's reading, his face practically level with the book.

I call out to him from behind the wrought iron fence, but I'm shaking so hard that my voice catches in my throat. I try again and he glances up. He peers, and calls, "Come in," and beckons to the gate.

"Well, if it isn't Pennie?" He offers me a rare smile as I walk onto the terrace.

"We were passing by," I say, after I introduce Anne and we sit down. "We saw you here when we came out from visiting a friend in the hospital next door."

"If it hadn't been for the hospital I would have died two months ago."

I shudder. "What happened?"

"I had bronco-pneumonia. My left arm was completely paralyzed." He holds up his fingers, "I still have difficulty moving them. My tongue was also paralyzed."

"What's that like?" Anne asks, with sudden interest.

"You feel something is blocking out all taste and feeling. I couldn't eat or speak. They fed me intravenously." He looks at me. "Enough. Have you been writing?"

I should have expected this question, but I'm unprepared. "Not that much. It's not as important as before."

He smiles again. "Ah-hah, that means you're in love."

Oh dear, my face is going red. "There are other reasons." Anne can't hide her giggles.

"A romance? Ummmm."

"Oh no, not at all."

"Now I know," he says, folding his arms as if to show he is right. To my relief, I see that he's teasing me.

From then on, I see Miguel once a week. Sometimes, Anne comes with me and they become friends as well. I use him as a sounding board for the pieces I read at the Centro. Also, he needs my help with his writing. He tries so hard to get it right that I can't tell him the truth—his heavy-handed English makes his stories too dense and too dark.

He lends me a collection of short stories by Franz Kafka. Is that where he finds some of his weird ideas? Do I like Dickens and P.G. Wodehouse? Graham Greene?

He opens up to me, a little at a time and with prompting, about his multiple sclerosis and how it struck him down at twenty. "I was playing soccer when I fell down and couldn't get up. The doctor thought I'd damaged my spine. Then I couldn't see, and I was interned in the Sanatorio Español for two years. Finally, my mother took me to New York where I regained my sight."

"What do the doctors say?"

"I have made progress, but whenever I am ill, I have to return to the hospital for months."

Like most Spaniards he's very Catholic, and I hesitate to talk about Mummy and Ian. When I do, his expression is as grave as a priest's. "It must be difficult for you."

"It is." I tell him how I worry about her being married outside the Church, and the threat of hell hanging over her, and how this goes against everything the nuns have taught me.

"You can do something to remedy it," he says.

"Like what?"

"Like helping your mother realize that Ian is not a good man and he is hurting you and your sister."

"He isn't. Not physically."

"Up here." He taps the side of his head. "He is hurting you a lot. She must leave him to save you as well as her soul."

"But how?" I can't tell him about my plans to get rid of Ian.

He has a crafty smile. "You could—how do you say it in English—*deshacerte de ese hombre?*"

I shiver. "Get rid of that man."

"Exactly. We must think of a way to accomplish that."

I'm itching to say I've already tried several times, but I don't think he'd approve. Then his mother appears and nothing more is said.

Miguel's mother is a severe-looking woman who always wears black, her gray hair in a bun, and no makeup. She seems annoyed that I come to see her son. I'm never invited into Miguel's house. Does that mean I'm unacceptable? The Spanish society here is known to be closed and guarded against outsiders.

One afternoon I find him in a bad mood. "This is the only movement I can make and I can't control it," a sudden jerking of his left leg follows. Suddenly, he rallies. "I've been thinking about your stepfather and how to get rid of him. The best way to do that is to save your mother's soul."

This is a turn I didn't expect. "How would that help?"

"Your mother has turned her back on the grace of God and for what reason? Do you think she's happy?"

"No, not at all."

"To be estranged from God and in a state of sin is the saddest situation of all. Your mother must feel very lost and lonely. You need to help her return to the light of God."

"I tried that, years ago."

"You must try again, Pennie. I will help you."

"What about what you said—we had to get rid of Ian."

"When your mother sees the light, she'll get rid of him herself."

"Her problem is who will support us? What will we live off? Don't say God will provide because He doesn't."

His face loses its serious expression and looks eager and earnest. "She can find work as a teacher and you and your sister as well. You should have enough to live off. I will help you find English students."

He makes it sound easy, but then he's rich and he has no idea what it's like to wonder where he'll find the money to pay his bills. That's why Mummy puts up with Ian. She doesn't want to be insecure again. Maybe we shouldn't be so eager to get rid of him; at least not before I find out what will happen if he were to die. Would he leave Mummy enough money to support us?

"I'll try," I say, more because I want to keep Miguel smiling and feeling he's helping me than because I will actually do anything.

*

"Sit down, Pennie, I want to have a little chat with you," Mummy says. She puts on her special interested mother's voice. "I hear that you fancy yourself in love with an older man whom you met at the Centro, and he's in a wheelchair."

Wait until I get hold of that little sister of mine. I'll wring her neck.

"It's wonderful that you're friends with this crippled man, but Pennie, you can't save the world, and I fear there's no future in it for you."

I offer her one of my rebellious stares. "I don't care. Paralyzed men also get married. Look at Douglas Bader, the pilot, who lost both his legs in the war."

She sighs as if this is too much for her. "Pennie, you're only fourteen, much too young to be thinking of marriage. What does this man want from you?"

"He's a friend, that's all."

245

"That might be the excuse he needs. How old is he?"

"Thirty-one. I promise you, Mummy, he's a kind, decent man and a good Catholic." *And he wants to save your soul.*

"Pennie, because he's in a wheelchair may make it easier for him to take advantage of you." She has a grave expression meant to show me she's a wise and caring mother—but Mummy always thinks the worst. "I hope he hasn't behaved inappropriately."

I'm going to throw up on her. Ian must have given her that idea; he's such a dirty old man that he's made her think Miguel is too. "No, he's never tried anything, and he doesn't know how I feel about him. All we do is sit on his terrace and talk about writing and literature and the Centro." *And how to save you from Ian.*

"Let me ponder your friendship with this man."

"Please don't discuss it with Ian," I beg her. Of course she does. Next day she tells me, "I will allow you to continue seeing your friend. On one condition—I want to meet him."

I say yes, and then find excuses to delay a meeting: Miguel is in New York for a checkup; he's busy with his physical therapy; he's working at his father's office. She doesn't know when I see him. As far as she's concerned, I'm giving an English lesson. At the moment, saving Mummy's soul might end up in disaster. Instead, what I've been doing is putting the idea in her head that she needs to make sure she's the main beneficiary in case Ian kicks the bucket.

*

Miguel returns to the Centro in the spring and Toby puts him in charge of the library, which gives Miguel another reason to attend sessions.

Most of the old group have left. George is finishing his book and he doesn't come to the sessions as often as before. He's going back to the U.S. to have it published.

I have also changed. I used to attend the Centro to breathe in the writer's life, but now it's also because of Miguel. Every week when I turn the corner into Rio Volga and see his car, I'm filled with expectation. It's a letdown when he doesn't appear.

May is an enchanted month, the most confusing, yet the happiest of the year. The roses in front of Miguel's terrace have burst into bloom, it's the end of the hot, dry season, and the sun shines every day. Even life with Ian is bearable. Miguel is laughing again, and I believe I see fondness in his eyes.

He phones me and delights in inventing code names for when Ian answers the phone, ones like *Sanatorio Misericordia Eterna*—Eternal Mercy Hospital, or *Circo Maromas*—Somersault Circus. We go out together though you couldn't call them real dates: visiting his friends or the attractive, middle-aged divorcee who keeps inviting him to her home. On the way back, we stop in Chapultepec Park to talk in his car. He talks about saving Mummy's soul and I agree with him, but it is not the right time, I tell him, we have to think about who will pay the bills. We argue over that, a friendly tiff, because he does not, and will never, understand that side of life. He lives in a cocoon spun by his mother and it will be very hard for him to break loose.

We attend a performance of *Richard III* in the Anglo-Mexican Institute. It's more of a coincidence as we're both going the same night after a session at the Centro. We arrive together and sit together, but Mummy is also there, and she sees us.

"It's high time I met your friend," she says.

I dread asking Miguel over to the house. It will formalize our relationship and I'm sure Miguel is not ready for that. It will also open the door for Miguel to play the missionary with Mummy and broach the subject of saving her soul. Yet when I ask him if he will come over, he says, "Why not?" I light a candle to the Virgin and pray that Mummy won't stick her foot in it. Then I wonder if Miguel will try to save her soul and I light another candle.

Miguel arrives late and he's polite, but fidgeting, in a hurry. He declines the canapés Mummy has prepared or anything except, when she insists, a soda water that he barely touches. Ian stays in the bedroom. Mummy decides Miguel doesn't have evil intentions towards me, and she's nice to him and doesn't say anything she shouldn't. He doesn't say anything about God, the Church, or saving her soul. He stays less than an hour.

After he leaves, Mummy says, "How sad that a handsome young man like him should be in a wheelchair. I liked this Miguel, though I think he's too old for you."

"Age shouldn't matter. Ian's nineteen years older than you."

"That's different. I'm an adult and know my own mind. You're fourteen and know nothing of life. Also, Miguel is in delicate health. I hate to pour cold water on your hopes, but I doubt he has long to live."

The next morning my face is a strawberry blob from crying all night.

*

A week later, I'm walking home from the bus stop when I catch sight of George and Joan on the other side of the street. I don't want them to see me in my school uniform, so I lift my books to cover my face, but they see me anyway and call to me, and then cross the street to talk. "I'm glad we ran into you," George says. "We decided to start the class at five as some people can't make it earlier. It's not too late for you if we end at eight?"

"It's all right; Miguel always gives me a lift home."

"But Miguel's leaving for Spain and he'll be gone a year," he says.

I wobble as if he'd dealt me a vicious blow. Both my cheeks are stinging as blood rushes to my head. "Oh," is all I can say.

Joan asks, "Are you okay, Pennie?"

"I'm not very well." I don't want them to see me cry. "Until Tuesday. Bye." Who cares if I'm rude or abrupt? Why didn't Miguel tell me himself?

As soon as I'm home I phone him. "Yes," he says, in a cold tone. "We are leaving next week for Spain."

"Why didn't you tell me? How did George know?"

"We only decided yesterday when my mother received a letter from her family. I went to the Centro to tell Toby I could not attend to the library, and George was there."

"How long will you be away?"

"A year."

"That long?" I want to yowl, but I keep calm until we hang up.

I have no idea why Miguel doesn't sound friendly. Maybe having to come and be interviewed by Mummy. But she was nice to him. He fits me in for a swift goodbye in his car in front of our building. He doesn't have much time. There are many things to take care of before leaving. And I'm one of them, I think. Only once does he let down his guard when he says, "I'm sorry that I can't help you get rid of Ian. I wish you luck."

31

SALTING IAN

I need to see a witch about Ian before he completely goes off his rocker. Two weeks ago, he attacked a man in a restaurant because Ian thought he was making eyes at Mummy. He dragged her out of an event at the Hotel del Prado when he saw Uncle Agustín was also there with his wife, Lucia. Then Ian went after Diana and told her she was no longer welcome as Mummy's friend. Just a few of the many times he's behaved like that. Sometimes he follows her when she goes out. He likes to interrogate her as to where she's been and who she's seen.

You might say Ian is crazier by the day.

That's why I'm looking for a witch. It's not hard to find one in Mexico. A lot of people here believe in witchcraft. They go to witches for love potions or for a cure or when they want revenge. I often hear someone say, *"Estás salado"*—"You're salted" after a run of bad luck or *"Necesitas una limpia"*—"You need a cleansing," which means "Go see a witch to get rid of the salt."

Even so, I think long and hard about dabbling in witchcraft. It will probably count as a mortal sin. I don't wish for him to die anymore; just for something to happen to him. Like after the thrombosis when he wanted to become a monk. But this time it has to be for good—give him an irresistible urge to go back to Aunt Ethel. He'd have to pay Mummy alimony, so we'd have enough to live on. That would be a happy ending for everyone.

How about Gloria, the maid who left after she heard Ian call her a monkey jumped out of the trees? He said it in English at the table, never realizing Gloria would understand. She did because, three months before, she had asked me to help her learn to speak English. I used one of Granny's old teaching English books, and almost every night I gave Gloria a lesson. She was a fast learner, which is why she understood when Ian called her a monkey.

Gloria is working for another family in this building. In the evening I go downstairs to look for her. That's the hour when all the maids meet up with each other. Their excuse is always they have to buy bread for supper, and they do that at the *panaderia* next door, and then they linger outside talking among themselves or flirting with Fausto, or with the men who are constructing the new Teléfonos de México building down the road.

I take Gloria aside and ask if she knows a *bruja*—a witch— and how much to have her "throw the salt" on Ian.

Gloria offers to take me to the *bruja* herself. She wants to take revenge on Ian for what he called her. "No one has the right to call another person a monkey."

On Saturday, her day off, we go to a market downtown. To the dark, dirty, stinky miles of stands with swarms of flies buzzing around, and I'm sure there are hordes of rats under the boards. Everything smells of *fritanga*—food fried in oil used over and over—and of dust from the bare ground, and of garbage in corners, and of the soupy messes of rotten fruit and vegetables and other waste. We have to walk along planks placed over bumpy ground that's damp from the dirty water thrown out onto it.

At the end of what seems like a mile, Gloria takes me into a section where dozens of herbs are hanging on strings or are laid out in little bags on tables. She introduces me to the witch, who looks nothing like the Mexican version of Snow White's wicked witch that I expected to see. In her forties with a round, pretty face and a chubby figure, she could be a housewife. Behind a curtain, a pot of what the witch calls a calming tea is boiling, and she offers me some, but I say no, thank you. Gloria urges me to try it, and since she's drinking it, I take a small clay mug and sip a little. It's sort of sweet, a bit too thick for my liking, and after another sip, I put the mug down.

Gloria drinks all of hers. She says, "This tea makes you feel good," and so I have a bit more. All of a sudden, this place isn't dark anymore, as if a sun ray has found its way in. Gloria's eyes are bigger than usual, and you'd think she was floating. "It's so peaceful," she tells me. I'm dreamy myself, until I remember why we're here.

"I need something to get rid of someone," I tell the witch.

She frowns. "What do you mean by that?"

I fudge around. "My mother's husband—" I wish Gloria would help me say what I want, but the tea seems to have sent her into a trance. "Get him out of our lives. Go back to his family or somewhere else. It doesn't matter where."

The witch looks doubtful. "You want him to go away. That all?"

"For good."

She gives me an eager smile. "I have poisons, if you want."

"Just make him go away."

She nods and turns and searches among the herbs in the back, then shakes her head. "I don't have anything for that. I can prepare something to change his life. Or I have powders that will make him very tired and sleepy. Or, *Quieres echarle la sal?*"

Do I want her to throw the salt on him?

"Yes." Up to his neck.

"I have something you can use." She shows us a little clay doll about the length of my hand.

Gloria lets out a cry. "I know that one. Someone put it in my aunt's kitchen, and all the food went bad. Nobody wanted to eat at her table again."

"What would it do to my stepfather?"

Gloria says, "Bad things. It's like a curse."

The witch gives her a reproving look. "This is not like that. Think of it as a seed. You are planting a problem that will grow and make him go away. Or create a distance between him and your mother. He will leave, be out of your life, as you want. It may not happen at once. It takes time. You must have patience."

"How long does it last? Forever?"

"I cannot say. If that's your desire, you should consider a potion to finish him off." She waves her hand as if saying goodbye.

I'm not certain if it's the right curse, but I didn't come all this way for nothing.

"Yes, I'll take it," I tell her.

"Did you bring something personal belonging to this man?"

Gloria had warned me about this, so I pinched a pair of his drawers from the dirty linen basket, and a few hairs from his brush. The witch is pleased with the drawers because there are stains on them, which she says "will make the curse more effective." She rubs the doll with them and with a stinky mixture that turns the doll coffee-brown. Ian's hairs she winds around its neck and chest. She wraps it in *tela de angel*—cheesecloth— puts it in a cigar box, and hands it to me.

"Place it among his clothes," she says. "Hide it well so he won't find it soon, and it will be more effective."

I also buy a small bag of white powders to put in his drink to make him sleepy. They could come in handy.

I pay her fifty pesos for the curse and the powders, which

for me is a lot. I'm making a little money teaching English, but I need to find more students who can afford to pay me thirty-five pesos an hour.

Gloria is grinning as we leave the market. "You should have seen your face," she says. "You were scared."

"No, I wasn't," I answer indignantly. "Not at all. Except maybe at the beginning when she thought we wanted to kill him." Inside, I am scared. I don't know what the doll will do, but I've seen films where dolls were evil and caused terrible things to happen.

All the way home, in standing room only in the second-class bus, I'm wondering if I can undo what I'm about to do.

*

A week later, the first inkling Mummy and Ian have of the doll is an oniony smell, like under the arms when women don't use deodorant. At first Mummy thinks she's the one who's smelling, and she puts on more deodorant. Then she decides it must be the new maid, and buys her a deodorant, and then she checks both Anne and me under our arms.

After several days, the smell turns into a stink. Mummy realizes it's coming from their closet, but she's afraid to look.

"Some animal must have got in there and died. Maybe a rat from downstairs." Anne likes making Mummy shudder. "I heard they climbed up the walls from the garbage dump and got into apartments." Partly true, as the indoor yard with all the rubbish—wood, building materials, broken furniture—is a real dump, and someone on the first floor complained there were rats running around.

"Oh no," Mummy wails. "I'll have to send all our clothes to the cleaners."

The laundress, Leonor, tells her it can't be a rat or mouse as there'd be droppings. She and the maid help Mummy take everything out of the closet. They start with things on hangers and in clothes bags, and then the clothes on the shelves, and pile clothing on the beds and chairs. It isn't until the back of the very last drawer, the one with Ian's socks in it, that they find what I'd hidden in one of his Argyle Sutherland Highlander dress socks.

I hear Mummy's scream—probably the whole building hears it—as it goes on and on. I run to her bedroom, and she's fainted right on top of Ian's dress shirts on her bed. Leonor is trying to revive her, and the maid is just standing there looking like she will faint as well. Leonor asks for alcohol, and Anne brings it. Leonor holds it under Mummy's nose until she opens her eyes. "Get rid of that thing in the closet," Mummy cries. "Before it kills us!"

The stink from the closet is so strong, I can almost see it. Like raw onions, the kind that make your eyes water, that have rotted. I look into the closet and reel from the stench. I can see the doll, swollen like a large piece of poop oozing a syrupy brown liquid onto Ian's socks. I gag and retch, and Anne does too when she sees it. The maid scuttles out.

When I recover, I ask, "What is it?" as if I don't know.

"A token, a curse on *el señor*," Leonor says, and she shudders. "Someone wants to hurt him."

Mummy gasps. "God forbid! Poor Ian."

Leonor moves the clothes off the bed, so Mummy can lie down properly, and she holds cotton wool with alcohol to Mummy's nose.

"Who would do such a thing? It must have been that last maid, the one who left. I curse the day I hired her." Mummy glances at Leonor who nods, agreeing with her. "I'll have to throw away Ian's socks and order another pair, and they cost the earth. He needs them when he dresses up in his uniform."

One side of me wants to laugh and the other is full of guilt because it's Mummy and not Ian who's suffering. "Why would anyone do something like that?" I ask, with an innocent expression.

They both look at Leonor for an explanation. I do as well.

"It's a curse on el señor," Leonor says. "Whoever put it there hates him. That is meant to bring him very bad luck."

"Oh, dear God! If we burn that thing, will that end the curse?" Mummy asks.

Leonor gives a half nod. "It might."

"Then throw it down the incinerator," Mummy orders, but Leonor lifts her hands to show she's trembling too much.

"Don't ask me," Anne says.

Mummy turns to me. "Pennie, you will have to do it."

"Why me?"

"Because I'm in no condition to do it myself."

No choice. I agree. Anyway, I made the mess. What a waste of a good curse.

Mummy smiles and says, "You're such a good girl, Pennie."

Anne glowers at me.

I tie a scarf around my face and use rubber gloves to pick up the mushy ball, put it into the dust pan along with Ian's sock, and throw the whole lot down the incinerator chute.

Mummy douses the closet and bedroom with holy water that Leonor brings from the church, and hangs up several scapulars of saints for good measure. She sprays Chanel No. 5 to cover the smell, but it's too strong for Mummy and Ian to sleep in the bedroom, so they stay in Cuernavaca a couple of days.

Bad luck starts right away.

Although Ian's importation company closed two years ago, he's continued representing Crosse & Blackwell Worcester Sauce in Mexico, working from home. Shortly after my visit to the witch, Crosse & Blackwell decides to take their business somewhere else. Ian has fallen on hard times. He has nothing left to do except finish his book.

"Things will be all right again," he tells Mummy, "once my book is published and it starts selling."

Wasn't that what Daddy used to tell Mummy about his inventions?

32

THE NIGHT THE BUILDING ROCKED

A few minutes before three in the morning, I awake uneasy, perhaps because dogs are barking. They often bark at night, but not a whole lot at the same time. This continues a few minutes until suddenly they all shut up. Silence. The building shivers. Not enough to bother me, but it does it again, and again, each time harder than the last. The next I know, the building is rocking and rolling. I can hear the walls creaking and the floor is bumping so hard I'm sure it will break off in the middle, right on the floor where our apartment is located. Outside, a car horn is beeping.

I jump out of bed. The light doesn't turn on. I run out of my room into the passage where I collide with Anne. We're alone in the apartment except for the maid, Alicia, as Mummy and Ian went to Puebla.

"It's an earthquake," we both exclaim. Excited but not afraid.

This up-and-down jolting feels like the Edificio Nervión is tottering on stilts. Pictures dance on the walls. Anne runs to rescue Mummy's Limoges lamp that's about to waltz off the sideboard. We grab breakables and lay them on the sofa, even Ian's photo of when he was young. There's a terrifying crash down the road followed by more distant crashes.

The movement changes, stops bumping, and the building sways back and forth sideways, not as strong as at first, but it goes on and on. "The screen," Anne shouts. It's tilting over and we run to rescue it just before it topples on to the dining room table. We're holding onto it when the movement stops, though we can't be sure because the sensation remains, as if the building is resettling itself. Suddenly, everything is very quiet, except for a lone car horn.

"It went on for ages," Anne says.

"That was a really big one." We're used to earthquakes, but this was stronger and lasted longer than any other since we've been in Mexico.

We look out of the window. The lights are out and only vehicle lights shine here and there in the darkness. Another car starts beeping and another, and soon cars are blaring everywhere.

"I wonder if any buildings fell down," Anne says.

"That was an awful crash. It sounded nearby." Excitement gnaws at me.

We can't go back to bed. How did the rest of the building fare? We light two candles and, looking out of the kitchen window, see candles flickering in other apartments. We hear sirens. Lots of them. They must be all over the place and many nearby.

No sign of the maid. "Where's Alicia?"

"Hiding in her bedroom."

No answer when we bang on her door. "Maybe she slept through it," Anne says, "or went downstairs."

"Perhaps we should do that. Some buildings fall down after earthquakes."

We open the front door and join other tenants and maids walking down the stairs, holding candles like in a procession. No one says anything, as if speaking would hinder our progress. The sirens sound nearer, outside.

Don Enrique is very much in charge in the lobby. He's wearing a red satin dressing gown that makes him look like a big balloon. There's quite a crowd there, though I don't see Alicia.

"Please keep calm," Don Enrique tells everybody. "Don Matías and Fausto are checking the building for structural damage."

"What was that crash?" someone asks.

A man comes in to tell us to stay out of the street, and they are evacuating the Van Dorn on the corner as it's about to collapse. That ends my hopes of attending a party in the penthouse. Someone says it must be the worst earthquake in recent years, and who knows how many other buildings have fallen down. We'll have to wait until morning to find out as the phones aren't working. After a while Don Enrique says it's safe for us to return to our apartments, and we walk up the stairs to our floor. Our neighbors across the passage ask us if we'd like to come into their apartment. They're an elderly couple who managed to escape from Belgium before the Nazis invaded.

Just then we catch sight of Alicia creeping up the dark stairway. Her furtive attitude reminds me of a rat. "I went to visit my sick aunt," she says. At this time of night? It doesn't matter. We didn't need her. Anne and I took care of everything ourselves.

Our neighbors offer us brandy, and we accept because they're also drinking it. Weren't we scared? They're astonished when we tell them not at all. Perhaps a few seconds, at the beginning, when I thought the building would split in half, but we were too busy trying to save things from breaking.

Uncle Padín arrives early the next morning to ask how we're doing. He tells us this part of the city was the hardest hit. The Angel fell off the Independence monument and is lying on the ground, its head severed from its body. The swanky Edificio Americano on Reforma has fallen down. Tourists in the new

260

Hilton Hotel panicked and ran outside in their night clothes and many are still huddled in the park in front.

Not a window in our sturdy Edificio Nervión is broken.

The Van Dorn looks like the Tower of Pisa, and though it hasn't fallen yet, it will have to come down. We find out the earthquake measured 6.9 on the Richter scale, lasted almost three minutes, and was both oscillatory, meaning it swayed, and trepidatory, went up and down. Only three windows broke in the Torre Latino Americano, Mexico City's skyscraper, because it has a cushioned, anti-earthquake base. The Hilton Hotel will have to close temporarily for repairs, as will numerous other buildings along and around Reforma, including the Cine Roble where we go to the movies.

Everyone is joking about the Angel taking flight in the middle of Reforma, as well as the unfortunate tourists at the Hilton. The newspapers report five buildings fell down, but Uncle Padín went out and saw the damage early in the morning after the earthquake and he says it's far worse than five buildings. It appears the authorities want to keep quiet about the full extent of the damage. Many buildings have been declared unsafe, the Edificio Roble among them, though the movie house reopens two weeks later. Aunt Carlota says the owner of the building is staking his life that it's safe and has gone to live in the penthouse to prove he's right.

At the Centro, the writers are talking about the earthquake. Who cares about other stints when we can write about such an event? One of our group lived in the ill-fated Edificio Americano. She was in her bed when the whole floor collapsed, and she fell two flights down, in her bed, which cushioned the fall and saved her life.

I could never admit this in public, but I enjoyed the earthquake and what came afterwards. As Aunt Carlota puts it, "It added flavor to the everyday monotony."

33

A CHANGE FOR THE BETTER

"Shakespeare produced his plays at the Globe Theatre on the River Thames," my first-year high school English literature teacher tells the class. She has a Mexican accent, and she pronounces "Thames" the way it's written.

"It's the River Thames," I speak up, pronouncing it the correct way. *Tems.*

Her eyes alight on me. "Thames," she repeats it with the "th" and "a" sounds.

"Tems," I say again, and she gives me a vicious look. She knows I'm English, so why can't she realize I pronounce it correctly?

I'm on the verge of mutiny. This school year I have to put up with an English literature teacher who doesn't speak proper English, and cheaters who have high marks, and rich girls who pay other girls to do their homework, and with sub-standard English, and with religion and religion and more religion. As if that will get me anywhere in life. I'm not learning a thing. Maybe Latin, but what use is a dead language?

Anne is worse off. She's at a Mexican secondary school. Again, Mummy followed Granny's bad advice, this time that Anne should be given a Mexican secondary education, and chose what she thought was a bilingual school because of its

262

name. As Anne says, "The only Anglo thing about this school is me."

She comes home furious. She was removed from the classroom because she screamed at the teacher, a Mexican nun, for saying anyone who wasn't a Catholic went to hell.

"How ignorant of them," Mummy says. "Whatever happened to Christian kindness?"

It means Daddy is doomed and Grandpa-in-England, the sweetest, kindest man who died years ago, is already there. Not Grandpa-in-Mexico, because he was baptized even though it was against his will, nor Ian because he has a daughter who's a nun.

Granny explains to Anne that God, in His infinite wisdom, won't condemn non-Catholics who lead good lives, but Anne isn't convinced. She doesn't want to believe in God anymore. He's so unkind. She goes to Mass, but only to please Granny, because Anne's stopped believing in a religion that's so unfair.

I have a gripe with religion, as well, though for another reason. The high point of my last semester at this school was an oral quiz on the life of Pope Pius XII. I was certain I'd won first place until at the end I couldn't remember the name of his summer vacation home, Castelgondolfo. It was on the tip of my tongue, but for the longest thirty seconds, it slipped my mind. Another girl won even though she had missed one answer. We should have tied. Mother Thomas explained that some answers were more important and rated higher than others, which didn't convince me. I was upset until I got to thinking, why should it matter? It was a lot of useless information, like the movie star quizzes Anne and I used to ask each other. "What is Tony Curtis' real name?" "Where was Cary Grant born?"

So there we are, Anne and I, both of us unhappy at home and unhappy at school. Will anything in Mexico work out for us?

The only subject I like is Maths, one that I've never liked or been good at. The teacher is a young engineer who makes the subject interesting by giving examples and explanations. This way numbers become real to me, sort of like music notes, and for the first time ever, have meaning. When we step into algebra, I get ninety on my exam.

Sometimes, the Maths teacher comes to talk with the school secretary and me in the office where I work after classes. The secretary is pretty, and I'm sure the teacher is flirting with her. He's not bad looking, but he has greasy dark hair, and he wears cheap tweed jackets. He tells us he had wanted to become a priest, but he didn't have a vocation.

One afternoon, he comes in when I'm alone in the office and starts a conversation.

"My parents were divorced," he says, "so I know what you must be going through. Would you like to talk about it?"

I haven't told him anything, so how does he know?

"I'd rather not." I feel like ants are crawling up my leg.

He continues, "I attend a weekly gathering of people with divorced parents, where we play guitars and sing. Would you like to go with me on Thursday?"

It sounds like he's asking me on a date, but he is my teacher and I'm not interested in him. I say, "I don't think I can get permission to go out on a school evening."

"Then why don't we have coffee and talk?" he says. "I'm sure we have a lot in common."

Oh gosh, what can I say? I don't think we have anything in common, and I don't want to go out with him at all. Also, it seems odd that he's interested in a girl my age in a school uniform. He must be in his late twenties. He keeps asking me out, and I keep putting him off.

Then he's gone. Mother Thomas fired him. "I could hear her shouting at him through the glass doors," the school secretary informs me. "The mother of a girl in third year high school complained he made advances to her daughter."

I wasn't the only one. Were the other girl's parents also divorced, or was that a line he used on me? I didn't tell anyone about it. Perhaps I should have. If he was fired for asking out a student in third year high school, what about someone like me in first?

I tell Mummy and the first thing she asks is, "Did he try to touch you?"

"No, he was nice. He wanted to become a priest."

"Those are the worst ones. What on earth was Mother Thomas thinking when she hired that man to teach young girls? Look what happened to you."

"Nothing happened."

"Only because she fired him before he could get his hands on you. You're only fourteen, and you have no idea of the evil in this world. Men who like young flesh have one thing in their minds. You should have told me the minute he made overtures to you."

I learned long ago never to take her into my confidence. Why did I tell her now? To show off that older men find me attractive? I should have known better.

*

"That is the last straw!" Mummy cries. My high school is asking parents for donations towards the construction of their new building. "I can't afford to send you to a school that caters to the daughters of the rich," she says, though for the last two years she's paid only a nominal fee since I work in the office.

She's serious about changing our schools. Which school can we attend? The American High School and the English school Greengates cost too much. Mexican *secundarias*, after Anne's experience, are out of the question. Anne refuses to stay at her school because she's not getting any English there.

Where will we find affordable, high-level, English-speaking education in Mexico City?

Four blocks from where we live. The Maddox Academy, a *Secundaria* and secretarial school, also has a small but demanding high school with a part-British, part-American curriculum. The high school mistress, Miss Ethel Comstock, convinces Mummy to send us there. "Her appearance and no-nonsense manner remind me of Katherine Hepburn," Mummy says. "She's a latter-day suffragette. She believes education should open her students' minds to different prospects in life such as university and careers."

Miss Comstock interviews me before she accepts me. She's an older lady in her sixties with lively blue eyes and a forthright manner. "I try to prepare my students to take their rightful places in society. I tell them to think of themselves as little rocks on a hill. If they roll down, they can cause an avalanche." She grills me on my opinions about everything from literature to world events, and then regards me over the rims of her glasses, as if I were already in her classroom. "It will be a pleasure to have you as a student. I believe you can enter the Junior class. It depends on your French. Have you studied it at all?"

"A little." I taught myself, using Mummy's and Granny's old books, when I hoped to go back to England.

"Could you catch up with private tutoring?"

I'll do somersaults down Reforma if I can make up a lost school year. I'll have to take French lessons. It means a heavy load. I give English lessons four afternoons a week as well as attend sessions at the Centro. But I'll do whatever is necessary.

In its way, the Maddox high school is as exclusive as my former school. We're only thirty six students in the high school, thirteen nationalities, and some girls speak three or more languages. The girls are a mixed group with parents from Mexico, Spain, Germany, Holland, France, Romania, Lebanon,

Greece, Israel, Japan, Canada, the United States, and with me, from England. The entire high school shares the same schoolroom and we all take some classes, such as history and geography, together. Anne is in a separate classroom to study Eighth Grade, where she is happier not having to deal with nuns and religion. The girls in this school are not rich like the girls in my previous school. These ones work hard at getting good grades. The girl who always gets first place is the daughter of Spaniards. At the start of the school year, thinking she's not a native English speaker like me, I'm sure I'll beat her, but I never do. She always gets that coveted first place. Rumor has it she spends all her time studying because her parents insist she get only top grades in every subject.

I fall down on my first assignment, in English Literature, no less. Miss Comstock asks us to memorize a verse from *Hamlet*, which I do, only to discover I should have read and digested the entire section. I learn that if she leaves a history chapter to study, be prepared to comment on what came before and after, as well as the consequences and cultural impact of what is assigned.

It's important we know what is happening in the world, and she enforces this with questions she takes from sources such as *Time* and *Newsweek* magazines and *The New Yorker*. Sometimes she shakes with anger as she talks about the USSR. Nikita Khrushchev, whose last name she pronounces *Crookshov*, is her main target. When he bangs his shoe on the table at the United Nations, she's both horrified and delighted by her archenemy's display of bad manners. When Fidel Castro, who in Mexico is regarded as a hero, turns his back on the U.S. and allies Cuba with Russia, she places him on a par with Hitler and Josef Stalin.

"A woman's place is not necessarily in the home," Miss Comstock tells us. Sour grapes because she was never married?

Yet who says I can't go to university and then get married?

The school is not religious, but a priest comes in once a month to give the entire student body a sermon on good Catholic behavior. He stands on the second floor balcony above our high school and preaches for about an hour. A small, fiery, dark man wearing glasses, he threatens us with all the zeal of an inquisitional priest. "Beware of your feminine weakness for sinful men," he thunders. "You women who think you can redeem men forget that the only man who was ever redeemed died on the cross."

Most of the girls have been studying in this school since primary, so I'm a bit of an outsider. There's one other new girl in my class, an American girl, Judy Norton, whose mother teaches eighth grade. Judy has the whitest skin of anyone I've seen. So white I can see the blue veins in it. She has enormous blue eyes and would be pretty if she weren't so thin. One day I comment to a girl about this and she tells me, "Don't you know Judy is dying of cancer?"

I find out Judy has leukemia, cancer of the blood for which there is no cure. Even if there was, her mother refuses treatment of any kind. They are Christian Scientists, which means Judy cannot take any medicines or do anything to alleviate her pain. Sometimes she's fine, but there are days and entire weeks when she misses school.

One afternoon we're both seated in the main hall of the school and everyone who goes by says hello to her. "You're very popular," I say and she tells me, "That's because they know I'm going to die." It comes as a shock, her being so blunt, especially since I'd shoved that notion to the back of my mind. "You're not going to die," I say with the utmost conviction. I still believe in miracles and I'm sure God will save Judy. She's just sixteen.

Anne and I go to Puebla for a week to stay with the Pater. We get back to find out that Judy died during that week and was cremated according to Mexican law within twenty-four hours of death. Gone. Nothing left. No goodbye. Just the memory of a pretty young girl with her life ahead of her who never got to live it.

I seldom visit other girls' homes, and they don't come to mine. It's not a place I can share with friends. Ian is always there, sitting or lying on the sofa, often in his dressing gown, all pilled-up and vicious, or pilled-down, eyes half-closed, slurring words, making incoherent statements. Sometimes, when he's normal, we have an interesting conversation and talk about books. Anne accuses me of being taken in by him. I listen closely to what he and Mummy discuss at the dining table; when she's not complaining, they talk about contemporary issues the same as Miss Comstock at school. I can learn from them as well.

Then, without warning, Ian's mood changes, and we're caught, like in the aftermath of a bomb blast, trying to escape from the havoc he wreaks. Anne's right. I should never trust him or, for that matter, myself.

34

ENTER THE ZOMBIE

I awake because Ian is banging on my door. "I won't have lazy good-for-nothings living in my house," he shouts.

What right does he have to call me lazy? It's Saturday morning, and I wanted to sleep late. This week, I gave English lessons every afternoon. Yesterday I taught two classes of two hours each, until eight, and didn't get home until almost nine.

I haul myself out of bed, with the weight of lost sleep dragging me down. As soon as I open my door, Ian calls, "Pennie, Anne, I expect you to use your free time today to help out your mother. She has a lot on her mind." He's in a hurry because he's having breakfast with his sons.

Mummy is lying in bed, a mournful expression on her face. "I'm not well. Ian's constant demands are wearing me out. Doesn't he understand how frail I am? All the hardships of the war and postwar years in England." The misery of her life there has taken the place of her plane crash on her roster of woes.

She waves a list at us. "I need your help today because Leonor has no idea. You have to check to make sure she does what you tell her. It's a miracle these people have got to where they are; they never pay attention." Another of her pet gripes.

Mummy has a schedule of the mostly unnecessary things she wants us to do, such as count each item in the laundry. As if Leonor, who's been with us for years, is suddenly going to start stealing things.

My day brightens around noon. A letter arrives from a Mr. Alfred Martin, a literary agent in New York, in answer to a query letter I sent him for my second book, *Lady of the Mansion*. I let out a whoop and scream with joy.

Mummy calls, "Pennie, Pennie, what's the matter?" With the letter in my hand, I say, "Guess what I received?" I wave it at her. "From Mr. Martin. He wants me to send him my book."

She's sitting at her dressing table doing her face, and she turns with one eyebrow drawn on. "That's good news, Pennie. You see, I told you nothing ventured, nothing gained." Then she says, "I hope you've kept up with your writing."

"I'm trying to, but I don't have much time with all the lessons I'm giving."

"Then you make time. Instead of going out in the evening. Otherwise, you'll never get anywhere in life."

"I do write—whenever I can." Now that I'm fifteen, I'm dating more.

"Your problem is you're not willing to apply yourself to your writing. Your head is filled with romantic notions, so you go around in a daze. I expect more of you."

"Then it looks as if I was born to break your illusions," I say. "I have homework." I'd rather do that than listen to her.

*

For a year I've been giving English lessons in the afternoon. By now I'm earning enough to pay for all of my personal expenses, and my school fees, and have some left over to put into a savings account. My best customers are two sisters who are staunch Catholics and have lots of children; one has twelve and the other is about to have her sixteenth. They see English lessons as a way to keep their children occupied in the afternoon after they leave school. For me, the classes are endurance tests.

The children are spoiled, self-willed, and tired after six hours at school. They would much rather be playing than taking an English lesson. With this in mind, for the second hour of class, we play games that involve English conversation: Murder, Truths and Lies, Ask a Question. And they learn. I'm seeing results. A child who everyone thought backward becomes a star student. They win medals for English and get high grades at school. The mothers are happy and pay me well. I'm earning as much as Claudia used to as a bilingual secretary.

*

At midday, Ian arrives hot and bothered from the traffic. "Mexico City has grown beyond belief. That new freeway *el Periférico* isn't helping matters much."

Mummy agrees. "The city is becoming a nightmare. Look what they're doing to Reforma. Tearing down the old *Porfirian* houses to put up glass towers. Don't they realize this city is built on a lake, and those new buildings will come tumbling down in another big earthquake?"

"The traffic wore me out," Ian says, "and I didn't sleep much last night. I think I'll go and lie down. Wake me when lunch is ready."

Two hours later, when Mummy wakes him, he comes to the table in his dressing gown, and his eyes are fixed and blank as if there's nothing behind them. He lifts his soup spoon with a shaky hand, and halfway through the meal, he says, "I'm going back to bed. Will you join me, Baby?"

"I'd like to see my father."

Ian opens and closes his lids slowly in an odd kind of blink, as if struggling to understand. "Another time?"

"I can't, now that I'm working. You don't seem to understand how sick he is. He could die any day."

"If that's the way you want it," he says in a thick voice. He stands up heavily, punches the back of his chair like an angry child, turns and bumps into the screen, almost knocking it over, and walks off with stiff, jerky movements.

"He's walking like a zombie," Anne says, and we laugh. Anything is better than Ian on the warpath.

The Zombie becomes part of our lives. He's drugged, knowing only that he loves Mummy and wants her to himself. Everyone else is in his way, and of course we're the ones who must stay out of it. He sits or lies on the sofa, saying things that don't make sense, or insulting people who hurt him when he was Angry Ian, or ranting about nothing at all.

For us, Ian the Zombie is a relief. It's also sad. I may not like Ian, but seeing him turn into this soulless person means he's losing himself. The Zombie isn't someone who thinks. All he can do is drool over Mummy. He's a lost man.

We stay out of the Zombie's way. He glares at us and orders us to "Get out," and we get out. The Zombie can be scary. We never know how he will react.

*

We go with Mummy to see Grandpa. He's had another stroke and can't talk. He's not himself anymore, a withered old man with tubes stuck in him, who can only gesture and make blubbering sounds.

We return to find Leonor in the lobby, sitting on one of the sofas, but when she sees us, she stands, shaking as if she has St. Vitus' dance. Tears roll down her face as she flings herself at Mummy and gasps, "*Señora*, thank God you're here. *El Señor* attacked me!"

Mummy's mouth opens and she blinks several times, and I can see the same thought racing through her mind as in mine. Has the Zombie turned violent? She pulls herself together at once—she can be cool-headed when it isn't about her. The doorman Fausto is listening, and Don Enrique can hear us.

"Calm down, Leonor," Mummy says and, putting an arm

273

around her, leads her to a sofa, into which a terribly over-weight Leonor sinks so heavily that the springs groan. Mummy sits next to her and strokes her back. "Tell me what happened?"

"*Casi me muero de susto*—I almost died from fright." Leonor sobs, her big bosom heaving.

"Come on, Leonor, why did the Señor attack you?"

"*Señora*, I swear on the *Virgen de Guadalupe*," Leonor holds up her medal on a chain around her neck, "it's the truth."

"But why would the Señor do such a thing?" Mummy says in a soothing voice, though with a note of anxiety. "Perhaps he thought you were an intruder."

"No, *Señora*, I was ironing in the maid's room where I always iron when he came in. He had such big, angry eyes that he scared me. I told him, 'I'm Leonor, the laundress,' but he didn't know me. He was not himself." She clasps her hand to her breast. "That was when I saw he had the poker in his hand, and he raised it and I thought he would hit me with it. If I hadn't run out of the room, he would have split my head."

"He attacked you?"

"Well, no, but I'm sure he meant to. Forgive me, but *el demonio* is inside him."

I see doubt on Mummy's face. Who knows what to believe about the Zombie? She tells Leonor not to worry. We'll collect her things and bring them down to her with her money, and she should go home and rest. *But please, keep quiet about this, and don't gossip with anyone in the building.* That's asking the impossible of Leonor who talks to everyone who will listen, and both Fausto and Don Enrique have overheard.

We are quiet as we enter the apartment. Anne and I enter the back way to the maid's room. The iron is lying where it must have fallen on the floor. I pick it up; it's plugged in, but cold. Broken.

Mummy goes to Ian. We stay in the kitchen until she

comes back to tell us he's asleep in the bedroom. "He must have heard sounds and thought an intruder had got in. He couldn't have realized it was Leonor."

"Does this mean he will attack anyone he hears when he's all drugged up?" Anne asks.

"Leonor may have exaggerated that point," Mummy says. "I'd prefer you don't mention this to anyone."

"When Ian's like that, he's scary," I tell her. "If he came at me brandishing a poker, I'd run for my life."

Mummy rubs her forehead. "I'm so embarrassed. What is everyone in the building going to think? And what will I do if Leonor doesn't come back?"

"Assure her that someone else will always be here when she's ironing," I say.

Anne and I take Leonor's things down to her. "I hope the *Señora* believed me," she says, her face fearful. "Everything I said is true. Once I saw the same thing happen to a man in my pueblo. He was possessed by demons, and even the priest couldn't banish them. Sometimes they find a home in troubled minds and won't let go." She makes the sign of the cross with two fingers, then clutches her things to her chest and waddles off into the night.

Anne and I get into the elevator. "Do you think Ian is possessed?" she asks.

"It's possible. Think of his staring eyes. His odd behavior."

"But it's all the drugs he takes that make him act like that."

Agatha Christie springs to my mind. "I'm thinking it's what he didn't do that's important. He didn't recognize her. That's why he threatened her. Yet he knows who she is."

"He might have hurt her if she hadn't got away."

I say, "A zombie's like a dog you think is harmless until it bites you."

When he wakes up, Ian doesn't remember a thing. He's

275

furious that Mummy would listen to a servant's accusation against him. He tries to convince her Leonor had dropped the iron and it broke, and made up the story because she was afraid Mummy would be annoyed and take it out of her pay.

"Why would she invent a story like that?" I ask. "She was truly frightened. You know, Mummy, how Ian scares us when he's taken too many drugs."

"If it's my husband's word against a servant's, I have to believe him. I need to make sure to be here whenever she's doing the ironing. Unless—has Ian ever hit you or your sister?"

He's threatened us many times. "No, he's never hit us."

"There, you see. The woman's exaggerating. He must have come upon her and frightened her, and she made up the rest to explain the broken iron."

Leonor's words about a demon inside him haunt me. I light a candle in church though I don't believe it will do much good. But what else is left except prayer? As soon as I'm eighteen, I'll move out and take Anne with me.

*

Grandpa lasts through Uncle Artie and Claudia's wedding in October, but afterwards, he's worse and on Easter Sunday, a week before his eightieth birthday, he dies. Or they let him die. I'm there when they unhook the wires that keep him breathing.

By then Grandpa is very small and doesn't look like Grandpa at all. The dark shadows under his eyes are black— that's what I'll remember most—and he's gone in five minutes. No more Parkinson's or arthritis or trembling fingers or legs too hard to move. No more coughing or spitting or trouble breathing. No more "Goddammit, Amada!" No more sarcastic comments or letters to *Time* or burnt fingers from lighting cigarettes. No more Grandpa, and I'm angry.

So is Mummy. She blames Ian for her father's death, even though Grandpa had been ill for a while. "If you had let me see my father when I wanted to, he might have rallied," she tells Ian. And, "There you were, outside my parents' house, honking on your damned horn. You couldn't even let me visit my dying father for an hour." When Ian turns up to pay his respects, Mummy asks him to leave. This is her father's funeral and, in consideration for her mother, he's not welcome.

So many people come that they spill out from the living room into the large garden behind Aunty's Laura's house. It's a sunny day in early April and despite all the people wearing black, it's more like a garden party than a funeral. Grandpa's friends, the ones from Sanborns that look like gangsters are there, hair slicked back and wearing shiny black suits. Also, two of the older waitresses who served Grandpa for years, have come.

Everyone keeps saying what a remarkable man he was and how bravely he battled Parkinson's. Did they ever come to visit him when he sat in his armchair, dressed in his gray suit and starched collar, every day for years? My anger includes almost anyone there, enjoying themselves on this nice day. People who have come because it's the correct thing to do in Mexico. A distant uncle, a smartly-dressed aunt, a pretty cousin, a business partner, none of them knew Grandpa at all. Only the people from Sanborns and his friend Bill Wattles really cared. I stand apart in judgment.

The cortège stretches a mile, all the way down Avenida Virreyes and along Reforma, holding up traffic. People must be asking, what important person has died?

One newspaper has a heading: "We mourn the father of American football in Mexico." Another says, "Mexico has lost a great American friend." There's a whole page in *The Mexico City News* about Grandpa's achievements. At least on this day he isn't forgotten.

35

RETURN OF THE MONSTER

The days are heavy with Ian. Ill-tempered and with nothing to do, he barks commands as if trying to make up for when he's not all there in his head. He sits on the sofa, watching everyone as if it's his only entertainment. He hasn't read a book in ages. He demands Mummy's constant attention, expecting her to drop whatever she is doing and join him on the sofa to talk about—what? What is left for them to talk about? Which is why they bicker. "How do you expect me to get anything done?" she asks him.

Except for Ian, we all work, including Anne, who's giving lessons to our cousin. Money is short, and one month, Anne and I start paying the maid's wages. We sit down to lunch, Ian in his place at the head of the table, in his dressing gown. He can't be bothered to dress. "I'm not going anywhere," he says. The white stubble on his face makes him look old and sick.

The maid brings two glasses of Coca-Cola, one for me and one for Anne.

Ian's face darkens the way it used to frighten us, and he says in his old controlling voice, "The maid does not work for you."

"Yes, she does, Ian," I tell him, my pride surging at his defeat. "We're paying her wages."

Ian's eyes turn icy cold, and he aims them as if to split me in two. In the old days that expression would have been enough to make me shiver, but I look straight back at him. His eyes remain on me as he places both hands on the table and hoists himself up, then turns and walks away down the passage.

Mummy calls after him, "Ian, what's the matter?" She throws a nervous glance in my direction. "Pennie, did you have to be so blunt? Ian has his pride." She follows him to their room but returns five minutes later to say he's very hurt at my attitude. "Couldn't you have phrased it in a nicer way?"

"All I did was tell him the truth."

Ian's odor lingers everywhere, mainly because he doesn't bathe. He spends most of the day sleeping off the effects of the pills he takes. By evening he's his usual mean self, having a drink with Mummy while they tear everyone they know to pieces, as if they think themselves superior to others. At times Ian turns into a tame Zombie, half out of his head, babbling idiocies. Other times he's wild-eyed, ranting about the people he hates or the ones Mummy loves—they are all the same to him—and how he would cut their throats or strangle them with his bare hands, if he could. Once he uses the word "eviscerate." I look up that word: To disembowel. Take out internal organs. Did Ian ever eviscerate someone?

We're glad when he's the Zombie, with his blank expression and heavy, aimless movements. Not as scary as Svengali-eyed Ian. Or marble-eyed Ian, who has no feelings at all.

*

I work hard and play hard. I'm not interested in boys my own age; I prefer dating older men who have better conversation. During the summer, when American boyfriends are in town, I juggle five in one week, see three the same day. Mummy says to watch out, *me voy a chotear*, which means word will go around that I'm seeing too many men.

Anne is no longer my fellow plotter. She is growing into a strong-willed, rather bossy person who is more likely to stand up to Mummy or argue with her than I am. Anne is very much her own person. In a way, this makes me sad, as if I've lost her. She still looks up to me, but not with the same blind faith as before. She's not as sophisticated as I was at her age, but she's wearing more grownup clothes and makeup. We share a desire to return to England as soon as we're old enough, but getting rid of Ian is not as important as it used to be. Maybe because the way he's behaving, he'll get rid of himself.

I buy a blue satin party dress with a cowl over the shoulders connecting far down its low back, and navy-blue suede shoes with the highest, thinnest heels to go with it. Mummy says my outfit is too sophisticated for a fifteen-year-old, but since I paid for it out of my own money, she can't stop me from wearing it.

At Uncle Agustin's New Year's party, I'm grown up and attractive in my new dress, talking to two good-looking brothers. I know the younger brother Jorge, who's eighteen and very handsome, is impressed by me, but the oldest, Francisco, who's twenty-two and more mature, makes fun of my put-on air of sophistication. He speaks English, and he's traveled and talks knowledgeably about the places he's been to. When I make an airy statement that I don't care for Scotsmen—mainly because Ian is Scottish—Francisco claims he's of Scottish descent, and he's quite convincing. The three of us talk until two a.m. when it turns out Francisco has been teasing me and he's not Scottish at all. When we say goodbye, neither one of the brothers asks for my phone number. This punches a hole in my self-esteem. I enjoyed our conversation and I'd have liked seeing them again.

*

The days may be heavy, but the nights are heaviest with Ian. His shadow spreads throughout the apartment, invading every corner. He roams it in the wee hours as if searching for something that isn't there. The Seconals and Noctec don't seem to work anymore, though probably his insomnia is more because he sleeps all afternoon.

Even in my sleep and through my closed door, I can sense his restless presence. I hear him typing his book or talking to Mac or to himself. His voice rises and falls, begging, angry, threatening, a monologue that continues until daybreak, when he ends his nightly rounds with his demons and goes to bed.

Before Mummy married Ian, I would stay awake at night, afraid a monster would crash through the window. The monster had no real form, but I pictured it a beast, an ogre, a gorilla that would tear me to pieces. Now that same fear is back.

What I'm not afraid of during the day, I am at night.

Sometimes Ian opens my door.

I sense him standing in the doorway, looking at me. I'm careful not to move a muscle. It's as bad as any monster crashing through the window because I don't know why he's there.

I pretend to be asleep. My breathing comes out short and ragged, and I try to make it longer, but it's too quivery. My body is rigid, the hair on the back of my neck is on end, and my heart thumps away, beating too fast to be able to count. I open my eyes to slits and see his shadow. He has come to spread his darkness around me. Or to kill me. It's what I've expected all along. He knows how to strangle a person, to tighten and push in the right place, and it's over in a matter of seconds.

Does he intend to take over my dreams, fill my sleeping mind with his madness? Whatever he's dragging around inside him has already infected Mummy. Am I next? I won't let that happen. I'll leap out of bed and catch him by surprise. I have the walking stick Grandpa never used, and I'll bash Ian's head in with it—if I can make my limbs move.

He does nothing. Nothing at all. Just watches me, then closes my door and goes away.

I should be relieved. But I'm not. He's left his monster-shadow behind to haunt me. Sleep is impossible. It's scary in the dark. I turn on my lamp. Three in the morning.

What will I do? My thoughts are killing me. I walk outside on my balcony and look over the sleeping city, at the many lights. The thick decayed air is like a heavy liqueur tainted with the promise of excitement.

Someday I'll become part of this city, of its nightlife and prowling darkness. I'll live in a building like the Van Dorn—tilted but standing—in a penthouse done up in silver and white satin, with windows instead of walls, and a panoramic view. The kind of building where famous people go to parties and drink champagne and make mad, passionate love.

There's a light in the apartment across the way. A woman there may think she is hidden by the night and her gossamer curtains, but I can see her, her elbow on a table, her head resting on her hand; she's drinking from a glass. That woman is the person I will become. Alone. I've always known I'm meant to be alone.

Somewhere no one can reach me or hurt me.

36

HIGH HOPES

It's a year since Miguel left. We've written letters to each other that, on his side, have improved from lukewarm to close friend. He writes that he loves reading my letters and how much he's looking forward to renewing our friendship on his return. I can't help imagining his reaction when he sees how I've changed. At fourteen, I played at being grown up, but now, I am. In his last letter, he said they were returning in June. I keep phoning his house, even though the servants have no idea when he and his mother are arriving, and after several calls, they're quite cross with me. I haunt the street outside his house.

The month ends with no sign or word that he's back.

I feel like I've been stood up at the altar. I go crazy, crying and swearing. Then I make up my mind. It's time to leave my illusion of Miguel and find someone else.

*

Mummy tells me, "You're burning the candle at both ends." She has some funny notions about how I should behave and who I should see. On one hand she allows me to go out alone with Americans, Europeans, or older men, but Anne has to chaperone me with Mexicans or younger men.

Mummy's dresses fit me, and she's always happy to let me wear one of hers, as long as Ian doesn't catch me wearing her things. When Anne and I went to an elegant wedding, Mummy lent Anne the hat she wore when she married Ian. Anne didn't put it on until she was in the lobby. We were there waiting to be picked up when Ian came down on some errand and caught sight of Anne in Mummy's hat. Ian marched over and yanked it off her head, as if he was scalping her, in front of everyone.

"I forbid you to ever wear anything that belongs to your mother," he said. He walked away leaving Anne in tears, with her hair messy and her head sore from where he'd pulled out pins. We made a quick phone call to Aunty Laura, who brought Anne one of her hats to wear, but Anne sat at the wedding reception with a long face, unable to enjoy herself. That's what Ian does—time after time—ruins things for us. Did he also ruin his daughters' lives? They both left home before they were eighteen. Ian is what they call an *agua-fiestas* in Mexico, meaning he rains on parties.

I'm at Uncle Agustin's again for the 1960 New Year's party. This time I'm wearing a new red, Italian-silk dress with a tight skirt. It's not that I'm overly vain, but I'm sixteen, and tonight, I'm glowing, glamorous, and gloriously come into my own.

Boys gather around me. Will I dance with them? Talk to them? Give some of my time to them? None is very interesting, but I love the attention.

A man is watching me. From across the room. He must be the most handsome man I've seen outside of the movies. In his mid-twenties, I guess, and quick glimpses show he looks like a young Henry Fonda. His blue eyes fasten on me, and what draws my attention is they stay on me. All the time. Disconcerting. He makes no move to come over and introduce himself, and I try not to let him see I've noticed. But I can't help glancing at him every so often.

There's a moment when I'm climbing the stairs to the restroom when Mr. Blue Eyes is coming down. All he says is, "*Buenas noches.*" Two little words, but they sound like he's daring me to run away with him.

I fling back my head, stare him in the face, and say "*Buenas noches*" with deliberate intent to show I understand the challenge behind his words and proceed up the stairs. He doesn't follow me, nor make a move towards me, not then nor the rest of the evening—but rarely taking his eyes off me. I can't help glancing his way. Our eyes meet. I turn away. What does he want?

One of the good-looking brothers, the younger one, from last New Year's party comes up, and we talk. Much more than last year. He asks me out to the horse races the next day. He doesn't mind that I have to take Anne along as chaperone.

We start dating and since Anne comes along as well, my boyfriend calls her *hermanita*—little sister. Once, when we go to Cuernavaca on a double date with his older brother—the one who teased me the previous New Year's—and his girlfriend, we take Anne along as well. One evening, my boyfriend insists on coming up to the apartment to collect me. He's a nice young man who doesn't like picking me up outside. He couldn't have come on a worse evening. Ian's lying on the sofa, half out.

Mummy puts on her hostess face but I can tell she's covering up. "Ian is not feeling well," she says.

My boyfriend is wary, glancing at Ian. My hands are clammy as I pray Mummy won't keep him long. Then he mentions we met at Uncle Agustín's, and suddenly Ian lets out a string of insults about Agustin and keeps on going until we hurry away.

A month after we started going out, I'm seated with my boyfriend and his friends in the new Sanborns in Reforma. I see the man who was staring at me at the New Year's party coming towards us. He and my boyfriend say hi to each other and introduce me.

I act as if it's the first time I've seen Mr. Blue Eyes. As he sits down, he turns and seems to be searching around the restaurant, and I ask, "Are you waiting for someone?"

His blue eyes look straight at me, and he says, in English, "Yes, for you," then continues, almost in the same breath, in Spanish to everyone, "I had an appointment here at seven, but the guy hasn't shown up." Thank God for the noise and the dim light and smoke. No one else caught those words in English.

I'm filled with giddy excitement. The way he looks as if he wants to grab me and run off with me.

His name is Richard, Rick for short. Speaking fluent Spanish, he dominates the conversation, probably because he's older, twenty-six, and a man of the world. They mention a penthouse on Insurgentes where he used to throw parties. Does he miss it?

He shrugs and though he's speaking to everyone, his eyes are on me. "The *Bhagavad Gita* changed the way I see things."

I've never heard of the *Bhagavad Gita*, but I raise an eyebrow Mummy style. "In what way have you changed?"

"I give less importance to material things," he answers. "They come and go."

"Then what do you do for a living?"

Someone laughs and Rick glares at whoever it was and the person stops. "I'm in the investment business."

"What kind of investments?"

Someone says, "Local produce."

"Agricultural," from another and everyone, except for Rick, laughs. Even I do though I don't get the joke. He gives them a dirty look and says, "I'm serious," and they shut up.

A lot of the conversation is over my head. Still, in my new black polo-neck sweater, I'm grown up and self-confident. Rick is also wearing a black polo-neck sweater under a sports jacket, and I remark on this, using the word coincidence.

"The word, coincidence, is overused and trivialized," he says. "Nothing is coincidental; everything is preordained and meant to be." I'm a bit squashed by his remark but ready to take him on. "What has that to do with wearing the same kind of clothes?"

"Because we were meant to meet here today." He's shifted to English again, and most of the others can't follow what he's saying. It's not long before we're having a separate conversation of our own that my boyfriend with his so-so English is struggling to follow. Rick and I talk about Gandhi and his role in the fall of the British Empire, and what I think of democracy versus monarchy, and Kahlil Gibran's *The Prophet*.

My boyfriend is none too pleased that Rick is paying attention to me, but I'm enjoying this intellectual flirtation too much to care. And it takes my mind off what is waiting for me back at the apartment, namely, the Zombie, who more and more inhabits the living room sofa, so there's no way to avoid him.

Whenever we go to Sanborns, Rick always turns up as if he somehow knows he will find us there. We have more talks like the first one though it's hard for the others to follow our swift back and forth in English. Rick never flirts or asks me out or does anything that might appear he's interested in me and I'd like to think it's just our mutual love of discussions, but I suspect he's biding his time because the flirtation is not obvious, but it's there nonetheless.

One afternoon I wander into Sanborns and five minutes later, he turns up. We talk for an hour before his court of friends arrives. Even then he behaves as if I'm the only one who matters. I can see they resent this, but he flicks off their feelings like ashes.

An inner voice warns me to be careful. Rick is too good-looking, too charming, too smart. One of the group cautions

me to watch out. He says Rick has been involved in some
funny business deals that got him in trouble and cost him his
penthouse, and his marriage to a Mexican girl was annulled.
I'd better stop flirting with danger. The next time we meet,
I'm curt, avoid speaking to Rick, and don't make eye contact.
He corners me outside the restroom. "Did I do something to
upset you?"

"No, nothing," I say, flustered.

"Someone told you something about me?"

I can't deny that, so I mention the lesser of two evils. His
marriage. His face twists in anger. "He shouldn't have told you.
It was a marriage of convenience to obtain my working papers,
and we kept it secret."

"Then why was it annulled?"

"Her father found out and threatened to have me deported
if it wasn't. I had to go into hiding. That's why I lost everything.
Please, Pennie, don't believe gossip about me."

It's hard not to. He disappears. Nobody knows his whereabouts; they think he must have gone back to the States. I'm
sad but relieved. I like my boyfriend, we get along well, and I
don't need complications.

Four weeks later, Rick walks into Sanborns. Seeing him
again, I turn into a scorching, purple, shaking mass.

His face is all sharp angles, with a haunted expression.
He's no longer the smart-looking person of before. His clothes
float on a scrawny frame and look like he's worn them every
day for a month. He says he's been in hospital with a brain
concussion due to a bad fall. All month long? Yes, and he's low
on cash, can anyone lend him some until he collects his stuff
and what is owed him? In the meantime, he's moved into a
hotel on Rio Lerma.

"Near where I live." The words come out innocently
enough as I'm not angling for a date, but it must seem that

way to my boyfriend. I hope he won't be upset, but he is. We have a nasty argument that culminates in my telling him I do not want to be his "novia" anymore.

My first date with Rick is on a Sunday morning. It's the beginning of spring and the hot season, and there's the bluest sky with no clouds. In the distance, the snow-capped Popocatépetl and Iztlaccihuatl volcanoes rise like ancient guardians of the city. The air is clear and has lost its winter staleness, and the shabby trees along the street are reviving with new growth. A day that gives me hope for a better future.

Rick comes walking towards me with the blue sky as a background. Nothing can be wrong in a world this lovely.

We walk to María Bárbara and over *chilaquiles* he tells me about himself. He grew up in Springfield, Illinois, and lived in Chicago, New York, and Miami before coming to Mexico. I tell him about Daddy and England. A little about Mummy and Ian. We stop because I have to be at Granny's for lunch. Can he pick me up there in the afternoon?

"I have to hear evening Mass."

"I'll go with you," he offers.

"You're a Catholic?"

"It's been ten years since I last went to Mass, but I'd go every day if it meant seeing more of you."

What joy! I have a lot to thank God for today. When Rick makes the sign-of-the-cross, it doesn't matter that the church is stuffy, and all the incense in the world can't hide the lingering odor of the thousands who attended Mass today. Does that mean I will help him return to the Church?

Can we see each other that evening? Reluctantly, I say, "I'll have to ask my mother, and she'll want to meet you first."

"Great, I'd like to meet her as well."

I'm worried. You never know with Mummy. It depends on her mood, and since it's Sunday, whether she's had a fight with

Ian, or is presentable, or doesn't want to give me permission because I have school tomorrow.

Rick turns on the charm and, within minutes, she's as smitten as I am. Although, to show him who is in charge, she insists I be home by ten o'clock because it's a school night.

We go to *El Acuario*, a place where customers have to knock on a door to enter because, although they serve drinks, they don't have a license. We sit on a small couch at a table that is private, separated by gauzy screens, so we can't see who's at the next table, or who is necking and doing things they shouldn't. All we do is hold hands. We drink rum and Coke and talk about Frank Sinatra's latest film, *A Hole in the Head*. Rick says it makes him nostalgic for the time he lived in Miami. "Right where it was filmed, at the Fontainbleu Hotel," and how he'd like to adopt the song, *High Hopes*, as his motto.

It's past ten when we rush out and grab a taxi. The driver's radio is playing a love song and we sing along, "*Amor, amor, amor.*"

I know I'm late, and flushed, and a bit high, but this is the happiest day of my life, and Mummy had better not ruin it for me. She greets me, concerned rather than annoyed. "Sit down, Pennie, I have some news for you. I want you to take it calmly." Oh dear, she's decided I can't see Rick anymore. I'll see him in secret if I have to.

"Miguel called. I answered. He's back."

My glow evaporates. I stand up and scream, "Why? Why, just when I've found someone else."

I don't want her trying to offer me advice, so I rush into my room and fling myself on the bed. She follows me in anyway. "Go away, leave me alone," I say, but she sits down on the bed, puts her hand on my shoulder, and strokes my back. "I understand what you are feeling, Pennie. Caught between two men you like."

"How can you say that?"

"A mother can tell. You should be flattered. Two good-looking men courting you."

"Miguel isn't courting me."

"Whatever you want to call it. Do me a favor. Don't go too far with either of them. You don't want to lose their respect." She puts her arm around me. "You can confide in your mother."

She'd be the last person I'd tell. "It was a shock, that's all."

If Miguel had called yesterday it might have made a difference, but not today.

"Well, goodnight, Pennie." She gives me a kiss. "Promise you won't do anything rash. And remember, if you need me, I'm here to help you." How can she think she can help me when she can't help herself?

*

I never know when I'll see Rick or what mood he'll be in. We'll spend a lovely day together, and then I won't hear from him all week long. He has an urgent business deal to attend to, or his partner, who's named Hal, wants him to go somewhere. I don't like Hal. He's skinny, with a pinched, sallow face with pockmarks on his cheeks. He's always hopping around, in a hurry for them to take off and close a deal.

Rick phones, agitated. Something has come up; he has to leave for Cuernavaca and Acapulco, and can he see me for a quick goodbye in our lobby? He uses the phone there to call Hal and speaks in pure bop-talk. It's not easy to understand, but enough to know he is giving someone the slip, and he has three thousand pesos and a .38 on him, and he's asking Hal to fix things for him here.

He hangs up, and seeing the question on my face, he explains that someone's after him, but it's all a misunderstanding and will be cleared up in a day or two. "People here try to take advantage of foreigners, especially ones without papers." I am left with the impression that he came over to use the telephone rather than to say goodbye to me.

I don't see him for ten days. Unanswered questions gnaw at me. His business, his marriage, his absences.

The next time we meet, I tell him we need to talk. We walk to the park and sit on a bench. Before I can say anything he takes my hand and says, "I thought about this the whole time I was away, and I want to be completely honest with you. First, about my marriage. As I told you, it started as a marriage of convenience, but then we decided to make a go of it. We never actually lived together, but she got pregnant and had to tell her father about us. There was a big scene, and she had a miscarriage. Then he forced her to get an annulment, and you know the rest. The other thing I have to tell you is a lot worse."

I see anguish in his eyes before he looks down at our entwined hands and then at the other people in the park. "I love kids, and I want to have some of my own. Hope to be a better father than mine ever was to me."

He's playing for time before breaking the news. "It can wait," I say, desperate for him not to tell me, to allow me to know him better, and for my love to grow stronger before learning the worst.

"It's something I have to tell you. I'll understand if you don't want to see me again. I did time in jail."

"What did you do?" I whisper the words. As if anyone would be listening.

"I was seventeen and hanging out with some older boys when they decided to hold up a liquor store. I didn't know what they were doing. I was in the car the whole time, but we were caught, and given two years for armed robbery. I swear, Pennie, I was innocent, but in the wrong place at the wrong moment."

Poor Rick. "How dreadful going to prison when you're innocent," I say. "Of course it doesn't make any difference in my love for you." I hold out my arms to him, and he leans against me like a sad child.

"I had to tell you the truth, even though it would kill me to lose you. I love you, and I want to marry you and settle down with you at my side."

His proposal catches me by surprise, but I don't hesitate one second. "Yes," I say with total conviction, and "Yes!" again.

"You're sure?" he asks, a tease in his voice.

"Yes, I'm sure," I tell him. "I've never been so sure of anything in my life." He's the man I love, and I want to spend the rest of my life with him. Finally, I'll get away from Ian.

"Then we'll be married as soon as I return from the U.S."

"I think Mummy will insist we wait until I finish high school," I say. "End of this year."

"How about a December wedding?"

Seven months away. It seems a long time.

"Why do you have to go to the U.S?"

"I need a new re-entry permit, and Hal offered to cut me in on a deal in New York. I'll be back in six weeks."

I feel a choking in my throat. A premonition that he won't come back. And I'll be stuck living with Ian for another two years. "Why don't we elope?" I ask.

His expression shifts, he looks uncertain. "That's not a good idea."

"Why not?"

"What's the big rush? I'd think you'd want a white wedding."

"I do, but I can do without it. Who will pay for it, anyway? We can save ourselves and Mummy the trouble of scrounging for the reception." I keep trying to convince him; it takes a while but he comes around.

"Okay. We can be married in one of those border towns where they don't ask questions."

I confide in Anne because I need her to help cover up for me. Anne's shocked. "You're crazy, Pennie, you're carried away, as usual."

"No, this is serious, really it is."

"Then why can't you wait and have a proper wedding when he comes back? What's the hurry?"

"I don't want to lose him. What will I do if he decides to stay in the States? I'll go out of my mind."

"I don't know," she says. "Mummy will blame me because you ran away."

"You won't have to do anything except keep your mouth shut and give her a letter. I'll leave at the usual time for school and say I've been invited out to lunch and won't be home until late, which should give us at least a twelve-hour head start. Wait until midnight or you see she's worried and hand her the letter. It explains everything."

"I don't think you should elope," she says. "I want to be at your wedding."

"It's my one chance to get away from Ian and this life."

She's trying to hold back tears. "What about me?"

"I can't take you along."

"If you leave, it will be impossible to live here."

"You can live with Granny."

"Mummy won't let me. Not once you're gone. Suppose they send the police after you?"

"By then, we'll be married and far away."

Rick and I tell Hal our plans. He doesn't look at all pleased. "We're in a hurry to close a deal," he says, "and I will not transport a minor across the border in my truck." He glares at me. "I don't want problems with the authorities. Your mother will kick up a fuss when she discovers you're missing."

I'm furious at him for ruining my chance to run away, but Rick says, "Hal's got a point. We should wait until I come back, and we can get married with your mother's approval."

*

294

Rick leaves in early May. My premonition proves correct. Months pass without a word from him. I have an awful suspicion that I've been dumped in the worst possible way, even while assuring myself he will come back.

In late summer, there's a call from a friend of Rick's. He received a letter. Rick wants me to know he loves me and hasn't forgotten me.

"Why can't he write to me himself?" I ask. His friend can't or won't give me an answer. Whatever the reason for Rick's absence, I'm committed to him until I learn otherwise. It's like in the film, *An Affair to Remember*, where Deborah Kerr tells Cary Grant that if one of them doesn't show up for their rendezvous, the other should know it was for a "darn good reason". Well, Rick must have a darn good reason for not coming back. I bury my suspicion he might be in jail.

One September evening, the phone rings around ten. Late for a Sunday evening. Who knows why but I sense it's Rick and pray Ian won't hang up on him. I hear a scuffle in the living room, Mummy saying, "For once in your life, Ian, give …" I can't hear the rest but I don't wait. I open my door and Mummy says, "Pennie, it's Rick," and I let out a whoop and run to the phone. Ian walks off to the bedroom, disgust on his face. Tears pour down my face as I hear Rick's voice.

"I want you to know I love you," he says. "Will you still have me?"

"Of course," I say. "I've been waiting all summer to hear from you."

"I couldn't call or write." He pauses. "Are you alone? Anyone listening?"

Mummy followed Ian into the bedroom and I'm sure they're arguing. "No one."

"I was in jail in New Orleans." So I was right.

"A case of mistaken identity. The police came looking for

Hal, who was selling drugs, and found me in the hotel room. They said I was his partner and took me into custody after he skipped town. They needed a scapegoat, and they found me. Threatened me with a twenty-five year sentence. How could I write and tell you that?"

"I would have stuck by you."

"You think your mother would've let you? I contacted my parents. Hadn't seen them in ten years. They put up their house for my bail. Now I'm here with them in Illinois."

He goes on. Romantic words I've been longing to hear. "All these months I thought about you the whole time. Still want to marry me?" Of course. I never gave up on him.

Halfway through, Mummy comes and sits on the sofa, listening to what I say. When I hang up, after half an hour, she's excited for me, but says, "Pennie, hold your horses." She wants me to wait until I'm eighteen.

Ian is the one who convinces her to let us get married. He says Mummy had better give her approval before we jump the gun. The truth is, with Anne and me out of the way, he will have Mummy all to himself. She's on the verge of agreeing when she hears a rumor that Rick was mixed up in some shady business. She intends to inquire in Gobernación and the American Embassy about him. Oh dear.

Perhaps I should have my doubts about Rick, but I have to believe in the man I'm going to marry. There's a song from *Carrousel: "What's the use of wonderin'?"* The heroine asks herself if he's good or bad and decides it doesn't matter since he's "her feller" and she loves him. That's what matters.

The way I feel about Rick.

37

THE BEAR BAITING

One Sunday afternoon, we're at Granny's as usual when there's an urgent call on her neighbor's phone. I go to take it.

"Ian just threw all your sister's things down the incinerator," Mummy tells me.

"Why didn't you stop him?" I'm shouting into the receiver, furious at her.

"Don't get angry at me!" she shouts back. "I was in the bedroom. I had no idea until I went out and saw what he'd done."

"Everything?"

"Her bed clothes, and her school books, and her pictures, and her toys. I was able to stop him from taking her clothes. I don't know what possessed him."

"Something set him off. What did you say to him? That Anne had a messy room?"

"We had an argument." I hear the excuse in her voice. "But I never dreamed he'd take leave of his senses."

My voice rises again, this time on purpose. "Did you try to save her things?"

"Don Matias doesn't light the incinerator on Sundays. I beg you, please explain to Anne that I had no idea what he was up to."

Anne stares at me with a dazed expression. "What did I

do to deserve that?"

"I think he's mad at Mummy and took it out on you."

Granny shakes with rage. She stands up and grabs her cane. "This time, that man has gone too far. God forgive me, but I pray he ends up burning in hell." She phones Uncle Artie and Aunty Laura to tell them it's high time they rescue us from Ian, and Mummy as well, if she will let them.

Except—I don't want to be rescued. Ian is my excuse to go away and marry Rick. If they convince Mummy to leave him, she'll say I can't desert her in her time of need. I'll be stuck, bearing the brunt of her problems, for years to come.

Uncle Artie and Claudia, who have an apartment a few blocks away, arrive within fifteen minutes.

"He's nutty as a fruitcake," Uncle Artie says. "Although Tita probably drove him out of the few wits he had left."

Granny, who has sworn never to set foot in our apartment, is now itching to do battle on our account. "It's high time Tita made up her mind between that man or her children." We pile into Uncle Artie's car. Anne is stony-faced and hugging herself as if she's very cold. "Maybe Mummy was exaggerating," I say to her.

"It makes no difference," she says. "He took my things and destroyed them."

"How has Ian been behaving?" Uncle Artie asks.

"We're used to him doing crazy things," I say. "Mummy's the one who's scared stiff." He enjoys scaring her, making her miserable and afraid of him. Several times, Mummy's come running out of their bedroom, screaming he's trying to kill her and wanting to hide in mine, which makes him very angry, especially since I got a new lock for my door and won't let him in. He's banged on it so hard that it has several dents in it.

Anne and I aren't afraid of him anymore. Except when he has those marble eyes. They're what I think of as his spy eyes, the way he must have looked at people he was interrogating before he killed them. Well, I don't know for sure if he killed them, but knowing him, he did and enjoyed doing it. He's manageable. Except at night.

"He kicked Mac the other day," Anne says. Not like Ian at all. He's always gentle with his dog.

"Has he ever been violent with you?"

"Not with us." I've seen bruises on Mummy's arms where he grabbed her too tightly. She says he's violent by nature because of his savage Highland blood.

As we enter our building, Fausto tells us Mummy has already come down and pulled things out of the incinerator. We go look to see what we can recover. The incinerator hasn't been lit since yesterday noon, but it's smoldering inside.

Our eyes water from the smoky stench as Anne and I use tongs and a poker to rummage through the smutty, slimy, soiled, squishy, sick-smelling spoils from forty apartments. Vomit circles my throat. I take two steps back and draw a couple of breaths, pull myself together—after all, Anne must be feeling the same way or worse—and we keep on grimly sorting through the rubbish.

We find her pajamas and dressing gown tangled in the soot and slop of the building. At first glance, they need a wash, but then she spies little black burn holes in them. Her pink, heart-shaped cushions are stained with brown oil. The white lace bedcover Aunty Laura gave her for her fifteenth birthday is charred beyond repair, though the ratty stuffed spaniel she sleeps with is all right. Her blankets and sheets are scorched. We rescue her ornaments and photos, but not the unframed photos and postcards. Where's Daddy's picture? Her pretty bed slippers that Granny gave her are badly singed, as are two sweaters and a dress left on her bed after she decided not to wear them today. Her jewelry box is empty, and all her jewelry, except for one necklace, has disappeared, into the rubbish, we assume. We can't find her radio. Her bottle of cologne water is gone, as is the perfume she received on her birthday, and her clock is nowhere to be found; her night lamp is in pieces, the same as most of her ornaments. Her make-up bag escaped damage, but it's empty and the contents missing. Looks like someone took them.

Anne doesn't break down until we pull out her school bag. Nothing in it. "Where's everything? My books and copybooks? My homework?" She's sobbing as she jabs the poker into the pile, trying to unearth her books, then she uses her hands to rifle wildly through the rubbish, even though it's hot and fiery in places. After a moment's hesitation, I follow suit. We pull out the covers of her English literature and history books, the pages black or missing, and two scorched notebooks. Where are her Science, Geography, Spanish literature, and Latin books, as well as the rest of her notebooks?

"Even if we go through this with a fine tooth comb," I say after overturning the top half of the mound of rubbish, "we won't find them. They're probably in ashes."

Anne gazes at the pile of things we managed to recover. "What about my homework?" she says as if it's all that matters. "I can't tell Miss Comstock the truth, and she never accepts excuses."

"We'll ask Mummy to call her."

"What do you expect her to say? That her crazy husband threw my school things down the incinerator? What about the missing books and my notes for the whole year?" She stabs the trash viciously. The books are almost irreplaceable: ordered from England months in advance, and they cost the earth plus postage. Anne was fortunate enough to buy them from a former student. Her copybooks, containing all her notes, are as valuable because it's almost the end of the school year.

I'm both relieved and guilty that Ian threw only Anne's things down the incinerator. Not mine.

"If I see him again," Anne says, "I'll kill him."

"You'll be a lot better off with Granny," I tell her, at the same time hoping I won't have to stay there, as well. We wash off our hands under the spigot next to the trash and walk into the lobby, carrying Anne's things in supermarket bags that Fausto gave us. Mummy is there, hanging onto Uncle Artie's arm like a crutch. "Thank the good Lord. You were able to save your things."

"Only a few," Anne says through gritted teeth.

"A lot of her schoolbooks are missing," I add.

"Oh dear, how will we replace them? I recovered your daddy's photo and your radio," she says, "though the glass will have to be replaced on the photograph. I'm afraid your radio is broken."

"Don't worry, Anne, we'll buy you a new one," Aunty Laura says quickly. She and her husband, Uncle Bob, who looks annoyed—he had to leave his Sunday card game—have arrived.

"Thank God, you've come to the rescue," Mummy says, and her voice has a tremble in it. Her eyes are red with pouches underneath, her hair's a mess, and she hasn't put on any makeup.

"He should be taken away in a straightjacket," Aunty Laura says.

Granny's voice is stern. "Tita, now will you come to your senses?"

Mummy lifts her head and gives Granny a defiant look. "Believe me, I know what I have to do, Mother."

The eight of us troop up to the apartment and wait while Mummy goes to tell Ian her family is here and wants to have a word with him. We are all silent for several minutes, until she returns to say Ian doesn't see any reason why he should hear them out. She's not as certain as she was before, I can see.

Aunty Laura gives a hoot of disgust. "I'm not leaving until I have the pleasure of telling him—to his face—that he's *un hijo de la chingada.*"

Uncle Bob adds, "Tita, please ask your husband to behave like a man and come out and talk to us."

"I'm tell him that," Mummy says. "But I beg you, be careful what you say to him. Remember he has a weak heart."

Uncle Artie guffaws. "Wouldn't that be great? Nothing like a fatal heart attack to solve the problem."

Ian takes his time coming out. Ten minutes. When he does appear, he looks old and rundown. Crumpled clothes, white stubble on his chin, ruffled hair, and his face so red you'd think he'd broken a blood vessel. All the same, he sticks out his chest and says in his officer's voice, "I resent this invasion of my privacy. Please state the purpose of your visit and be on your way."

Granny stands, wobbling a little and clutching her white cane like a weapon. She confronts him, though her blind eyes are directed at the air behind him. "I can accuse you of many sins, but I will never forgive," and her voice becomes a snarl, "your abusing my granddaughters."

Ian recoils as if she has hit him. He bellows, "I refuse to be insulted in my own home. Please leave before I kick you out."

Granny brandishes her cane at him. "You're an evil man. May you burn in hell!"

He raises a fist. Mummy screeches, "Don't touch my mother!" and grabs his arm. Aunty Laura leaps up and lunges at him. Just as fast, Uncle Artie pulls her away.

Ian stares at them with hatred in his eyes. He asks Mummy, "What the hell are they doing here?" He turns and shouts, "All of you, get out of my house. At once."

"We've come here," Uncle Artie says in a reasonable voice, "to discuss your treatment of Pennie and Anne."

Ian puffs up with indignation. "I swear I never laid a hand on either of the girls, nor have I mistreated them. If I'm a disciplinarian, well, that is for their own good."

"Do you call throwing all of Anne's belongings down the incinerator discipline?" Uncle Artie asks in a stronger tone.

"I did no such thing," Ian replies.

Anne charges at him, arm raised, but Uncle Artie stops her from hitting Ian. She screams, "I hate you! I hate you! Why did you do that? Even my school books."

Ian turns cold eyes on her. "I told you, I have no idea what you're talking about."

"You know exactly what we're talking about," Uncle Artie says.

"You knew Tita had two daughters when you married her," Uncle Bob adds.

Ian sticks out his chin. "I have fulfilled my obligations to the best of my ability. Wasn't I the only one who took them on when their father deserted them?"

Aunty Laura's lips curl like the smoke from her cigarette. "You were the one who broke up their home, alienated their father, and made their lives a misery."

And so on, back and forth, they spit words of hate at each other. Everyone goes at Ian like angry terriers attacking a bear. I can almost see the rivulets of blood running off him onto the floor. Anne and I remain in the background. Our struggle is over.

Suddenly, Ian falls on his knees and walks on them over to Mummy where he pleads, "Baby dearest, I beg you, please forgive me." Everyone becomes quiet; his behavior is embarrassing to watch.

Mummy gives him a disdainful look. "Why beg my forgiveness? My daughter, Anne, is the one you should beg to forgive you."

Ian struggles to his feet and reverts to his usual haughty tone. "Anne, please accept my sincere apologies. Believe me, I did not intentionally destroy any property of yours."

Anne's expression is fierce, unrelenting. "I do not believe you, Ian, nor do I forgive you. Not now or ever." She turns her back on him.

Mummy says, "Anne, please be reasonable."

"No, Mummy, you be reasonable. It's time you recognize the truth. Ian isn't going to own up to anything and he's worse every day."

"You can't stay with this man after what he did to Anne," Aunty Laura says.

Mummy holds up her hands. "Please, stop. I can't take any more of this."

"I thought you asked us to come and support you," Aunty Laura tells her.

"Don't leave me, Baby," Ian begs her. "Don't pay attention to them."

Mummy's voice trembles. "You can't stop me. My duty is to my daughters."

This confrontation may save the day for Anne, and she's much happier living with Granny, but what about me? I've been Mummy's support and ally since I was ten, and I can't do it anymore. She's on the verge of giving in and leaving Ian. If that happens, my worst fears will come true. She will want me, no, she will insist I stay at her side, and I'll lose my chance of marrying Rick.

I tell him, "Ian, let me talk to you in private," and Ian, eager to flee the scene, follows me into the kitchen. This tyrant, bully, evil stepfather, decorated colonel, former spy, sometime diplomat, is now at my mercy.

He makes a last ditch attempt to get the upper hand. "Pennie, will you tell that bunch of idiots to go home before

I lose my patience?"

I feel a bit Machiavellian, "Wait. I have a proposition for you. If I persuade Mummy to stay, will you help me with what I want?"

His eyes recover their old shrewd expression. "What is it that you want, Pennie?"

"To travel to the States—and be married. I need a passport, a visa, and Mummy's consent."

He gestures to the living room. "How do you plan to handle them?"

"We'll have to stay at Granny's."

"Not your mother. I won't let her."

"I'll convince her to stay here."

"If you leave, she'll be upset."

We have reached the bargaining stage. "I have to stay there for now, to keep them happy, but I'll come back and stay until I graduate."

He gives me a nasty smile. "Then I want you back here soon. This is your home. When you return, I will help you, with pleasure. Despite our differences, I've always liked you, Pennie."

I draw Mummy away from the family into the maid's room instead of the kitchen where Ian is waiting, because she looks mad enough to spit on him. I tell her he's willing to make amends. Why drag the whole family into their problems? They've had their say and it's up to her to work things out with Ian.

"If you leave, I go with you," she says, but not with the same surety as earlier.

"There isn't room for all of us at Granny's. Think how uncomfortable it will be with the three of us in the cramped space there."

"I can put up with discomfort if I have to. All I want is a divorce and to live in peace with my two daughters."

That idea makes me cringe. "First, you must be earning enough to live off. Why don't you stay with Ian and get what you can out of him before you walk away? Don't you deserve something after all these years?"

She shudders. "I deserve half of everything he has, that is, what he has left." She strokes her chin and says slowly, "I might stay a bit longer. But I can't bear him to touch me anymore."

I can't let my mind go there. We already know more than enough about Mummy's love life. For now, I have to persuade her to stay with Ian at least until after I leave.

What helps convince Mummy is the money aspect. I add coals to the flame by telling her she should be recompensed for her years with Ian. Look at all Aunt Ethel got after their divorce. Mummy gives in, and informs everyone it has been decided Anne and I will live at Granny's, but she will remain with her husband for the time being.

"Tita, why waste our time trying to help you if you refuse to be helped?" Aunty Laura asks angrily. Even so, they are satisfied with their showdown with Ian. As Uncle Artie says, it had been brewing for a long time.

*

Things have worked out well. Anne will live at Granny's for good; which helps as Anne is happy there and Granny won't be on her own. Meanwhile, if Ian keeps his word, and I get what I want, he will get what he wants. Mummy. Though once Anne and I are both gone, she may not want to stay with a crazy man who has nothing to offer her.

So I made a pact with the devil. What else could I do? I have to fight for what I want in life. I'll pray God doesn't punish me. Though in the end, don't we always pay for what we do?

38

THE ZOMBIE ATTACKS

Two weeks at Granny's is enough for me. It's cramped, and there's no privacy with Anne and I sharing Grandpa's old room. We take turns sleeping on the bed and the pullout couch—neither are comfortable—and Anne is her usual messy self. At night I hear mice scratching under the floorboards. Poor Grandpa, he used to complain about them, and Granny would tell him they were all in his head.

I come home early. Granny is in her bedroom with Aunty Laura. They're talking and in this tiny apartment, I can hear everything. Granny's saying, "Pennie's difficult to control. Like her mother."

For one awful moment, I'm ten years old again, hearing Granny utter those same words. I relive the hurt, the feeling of being unwanted, and most of all, the implied judgment that I'm bound to make a mess of my life—like Mummy.

Granny goes on, "I'm sure Pennie is smoking. I smelled cigarettes in their room."

Anne's the one who smokes, not me.

I can't stay here any longer. Ian's been asking when I'm coming back. At least there I have my own room, and it's only for two months until I leave for the States. Also, I must make sure Ian keeps his side of our bargain.

Granny tries to talk me out of leaving. You'd think she really wants me to stay. So does Mummy. "You'd better wait," she says. "Ian's become quite unpredictable. The fight with my family unhinged him." *More than before?* "You should remain at your grandmother's."

"Didn't we agree I'd stay here until things calmed down, and then go back there?"

"Ian has the idea that you allied yourself with my family against him. He says you've forfeited your right to live here."

Oh God, does that mean I'm stuck? Or is Ian spouting off?

"Having both of us here is too much for Granny."

"Let me see what I can do. After all, this is your home. When do you think you'd be coming back? I need time to prepare him."

"Today."

"That soon? Make it tomorrow, and to be on the safe side, wait until Ian has gone to bed. He's easier to deal with in the morning. I'll leave the front door unbolted."

I have supper with Miguel and he does his best to talk me out of returning to the apartment. He's worried that Ian might become violent and try to hurt me.

"The worst he can do is throw me out," I say in a firm voice, rather than admit I'm apprehensive. "But I don't think he wants more trouble with Mummy or the family. And he does owe me a big favor."

Miguel has become my closest friend; I see as much of him as I can before I leave. He's resigned to the fact I grew up and met someone else while he was abroad, but sad that he will lose me.

It's late, after ten, when I get to the apartment. It's dark inside, with not a chink of light under Mummy and Ian's bedroom door. I undress and put on my nightgown, then tiptoe down the passage to the toilet, do what I have to in the

308

dark, listen in dismay to the loud whoosh, and wait while the tank refills.

Their bedroom door opens and I hear Ian come out. Oh no. He must have heard the flush. He doesn't try the bathroom door, just lumbers on down the passage, his bad leg making him slow and clumsy.

For at least a minute I wait, hoping he'll be in the living room, before I open the door.

Ian is standing, a shadow in the half-light, at the end of the passage.

He's waiting for me.

My short-lived bravado disintegrates into knock-kneed, trembling helplessness.

His words are foggy, a muffled echo, as if they come from deep inside him. "What are you doing in my house?"

I speak lightly, a little girl's tone, knowing this works with him. "I've come home, Ian."

"You have no right to be here. Don't think you can deceive me. You're a hypocrite like the rest of your family."

"But, Ian, we had an agreement."

"You've gone over to the enemy." He moves towards me, blocking my way. "I know what you're up to. You've come to take your mother away from me."

"No, Ian, that's not true," I say sweetly, hoping his misted mind will understand. I step back and the wall behind stops me. Cornered.

He reaches out his arms as if to hug me. "I won't let you threaten your mother's happiness."

His eyes are mad and bulging. His thick, grasping hands circle my throat. He's about to do what I always feared. His hands tighten.

A jigsaw puzzle of visions swamp my mind, of people and places that all merge into one—a lovely day on the beach in Rustington with Daddy.

Dear God, don't let this be the end, not before I go home.

I push against him and croak, "Stop, Ian! Stop!"

Something clicks in his befuddled mind. His grip loosens.

I let out a flustered squawk. "Ian, you're hurting me!" in Mummy's pained tone.

He hesitates, and the madness seeps out of his eyes. Very slowly, much too slowly, he removes his hands from my throat. He stares at me as if realizing it's me.

Then, with an abrupt, "You may spend the night here," he turns and limps back to their room.

I run to my bedroom, lock my door, and collapse on my bed, panting like an old dog. My chest is thumping, and the sensation of his fingers is on my throat. I pant huh-huh-huh until I can breathe normally. Did he really mean to strangle me? If he'd wanted to I wouldn't be alive, and he'd be a murderer. But even locking him up for life wouldn't bring me back. I hope to marry Rick and have children, and live in England and see Daddy again, and get my books published. In one crazy moment Ian would have taken all that from me.

Suppose he tries again?

I place a chair under the doorknob and build a small barricade with my books and my night table with a lamp on top. Then I grab Grandpa's sturdy walking stick, and I'm ready—even eager—to jab, poke, or slam it into Ian if he gets into my room.

For a while, I wait for him, straining my ears for any sound outside my door, until I can't stand it any longer. I want to run into the street and scream for the whole world to hear and take heed. A monster is on the loose.

Instead, I go out onto my balcony and scream, venting my fear and frustration into the night, shouting at darkened windows and empty streets, and to one lone man walking below.

*

October 11, 1960

Dearest Rick,

I'm back at the apartment. Last night, Ian cornered me in the passage and tried to strangle me. He was quite scary, with those staring eyes when he has had too many drugs. I can't go back to my grandmother's because she was furious at me for leaving. I suppose it was foolish, but I thought I could withstand the difficulties here a few months more. Now I admit I'm a bit scared as to how Ian will behave.

The nice old washerwoman Leonor will spend the night and will help if Ian attacks me again. It seems he's been hurting Mummy lately. The other day he left her black and blue from "affectionate" blows, and as he's rather strong, it took the combined efforts of the maid and Leonor to get him off her. I suppose it's her business if she wants to stick by him after all that.

Have to stop. He's coming.

I'd barely written those words when Ian came down the passage to tell me to "Get out!" He's phoned his lawyer or the police to come and oust me. Can you imagine a whole bunch of policemen coming here to force out one seventeen-year-old girl? As you may see, I'm not worried. Just annoyed. God knows I never liked him much, but two weeks ago, I was the one who stopped my family from making a big scandal out of it. I'm not sorry, but I can't say my actions help my present state of mind. Can't wait to get out of here.

I was rather worried about what Mummy did concerning you. She heard this rumor about your situation, which was exaggerated, and went straight to Gobernación (Ministry of the Interior) to one of the top dogs who's her good friend, as well as to the American Consul to ask if they have anything on you. They had nothing at Gobernación and "nothing positive" at the Consulate. I don't think we have anything more to worry about from that direction.

I'm worn out and dying of hunger, but I don't dare go for something to eat because of Ian. Perhaps I should adopt your creed and stop believing in the good in people, but I wasn't made that way, or I'm too much of an idiot.

I can't wait to escape all this madness and marry you.

All my love, Pennie

39

ONE LAST TIME AT THE CIRCUS

"I can't live with Ian anymore," Mummy announces.

Since going to work as an English teacher, she's changed her tune. Now she says, "Why should I have to nurse Ian in his old age? That task should fall to his first wife, Ethel. She had him in his best years, and she kept the homes. Let her put up with him in his old age."

She's finally coming to her senses.

She intends to look for an apartment where she, Anne, and I can all live "happily" together. I'd better hurry up and leave before she does that.

*

I want to take a look inside the Van Dorn building. It's been empty for three years since the '57 earthquake. Everyone expected it to be torn down, and it has "Condenado" pasted on some walls, though most of those signs have been scraped off. The brother of an old friend is looking after the building, making sure vandals don't get in. It's not coming down after all. The owner presented a project to construct another building next door to, as he puts it, stabilize this one, or in other words, to prop it up. They intend to fix it up and have luxury apartments again. I ask my friend, as a favor, to let me go up to the tenth-floor penthouse and take a look.

It's every bit as grand as I dreamed it to be, with a spectacular view from its picture windows. The silver and blue satin and brocade decoration, and the ivory-shade furniture, and luscious carpets are exactly as I imagined.

I have a bright idea. Will the caretaker rent it for an evening? My class is looking for a place to hold our own, informal high school graduation party.

He hems and haws a bit, but he's tempted, I can see, because he'll keep the money we pay him. He says yes, as long as he can come to the party and make sure no damage is done. And not too much noise, please. I assure him it will not be noisy. Miss Comstock lives on the next block and we don't want her finding out.

At last, my dream of attending a gathering in the Van Dorn comes true, though not exactly the way I hoped. The party should feel like high life on the tenth floor, but there aren't the right ingredients. On second sight, the penthouse reminds me of beautiful, outdated clothes, with a hint of shabbiness from years of use. Instead of champagne cocktails or dry martinis, there's fruit punch, rum and Cokes, or gin with orange juice. The buffet on the marble table looks out of place. Instead of caviar and smoked salmon canapés, there are ham and cheese sandwiches, hot dogs, potato salad, tostadas and tamales. The centerpiece is a large cake from Sanborns, with white frosting and flowery pink and blue decorations, that looks like a *quinceañera's* birthday cake.

All the girls are dressed to the nines, but no one is wearing the elegant, flowing evening dresses of my dreams. The boys' black and navy blue suits are nowhere near the tuxedos of my imagination. I'm wearing a white silk suit Aunty Laura gave me that she wore to Uncle Artie and Claudia's wedding three years ago, which I'll probably wear to my own wedding as well. I feel elegant and attractive and sad. I'm the only girl without an escort. Nor am I likely to meet anyone rich and famous here.

My dream has come true backwards. It's another party with school friends in glamorous surroundings. Will anything ever live up to my expectations?

A classmate's boyfriend, an older, more sophisticated European, asks, what are we doing partying in a condemned building? I assure him the owner believes it's worth rescuing, and he hoots with laughter. "*A la Mexicana!*" he says. It's too quiet for a party and without my knowing, he calls some mariachis to come and warm things up. Music rents the night silence, mariachis going full force, singing at the top of their lungs, and their trumpets blaring. The caretaker, horrified, asks me to tone it down or we'll have to leave, but the European boyfriend asks how much for the mariachis to stay, and hands him a week's salary or the equivalent, and the caretaker gives in. I suppose he figures if he's fired, at least he got paid.

Monday, Miss Comstock goes on about the dreadful noise the other night and how some people show no courtesy for other people, and hold big parties in condemned buildings, which she has reported to the authorities. I don't think she suspects it was us, but if she finds out, I'm the one who will pay for that din.

It's ten days since I received a letter from Rick, saying he can't come to Mexico until the case against him is settled. I'm terrified he might change his mind about us. Or that Mummy will leave Ian, and I'll be sucked into staying here with her. If that happens, who knows when I'd ever get away?

One sleepless night, around four in the morning, I decide what to do. I'll buy a ticket on a Greyhound Bus and go to Milwaukee where Rick is living. Once I'm there, we can be married; nothing can stop us.

The next morning I announce my decision. Mummy says, "You know that you need my consent to travel?"

I say yes and glance at Ian. He dips his head slightly. I hope he keeps his word and convinces her. I'm going ahead with my plans. When I tell Anne, she asks, "Are you sure, Pennie?" And why don't I give it a bit more time, wait until after Christmas? "If you leave," she warns, "I'm keeping all your books."

"You're welcome to them. I won't need them anymore." Why stop and think things over, or talk about it or have anyone tell me I'm too young, or impulsive, or ask what happens if things don't work out, or offer me a job as a way to keep me from leaving? I want to start a new life in a new country. Far away from Ian.

At the bank, I ask to withdraw my savings—about seven hundred pesos or fifty U.S. dollars. The teller, a young man whose face brightens whenever he sees me, goes off to find out how much I have and comes back to say I have one thousand, seven hundred pesos or about one hundred and fifty U.S. dollars. He insists that's the correct amount. I tell him I'll come back the next day and for him to check in the meantime. My accounts can't be a thousand pesos off—unless some guardian angel deposited in my account. Sure enough, the next day he says he's checked and the money is all mine. The thousand must have come from God—no other explanation.

I buy a Greyhound ticket, Mexico City to Milwaukee, Wisconsin. Then I send Rick a telegram, "Arriving December 6th."

He telegraphs back, "Received your great news this morning. Don't let anything stop you. I need you with me."

That's all it takes. He wants to be with me as much as I want to be with him. I squash a feeling that I'm being too hasty. Or questions about Rick. I don't know him that well. There were all those times when he disappeared for a week or more. Who cares? I'm in love with a handsome, witty, fun man, and life with him is sure to be exciting.

One awful thought crops up: could it be that I want to get away from Ian and Rick is my way out?

*

Ian keeps his word. He accompanies me to the British Embassy for a new passport. What usually takes two weeks, he has done in two days. Then he steers me through the Christmas crowds outside the American Embassy and, using his diplomatic status as honorary Norwegian consul, gains entry to contacts to speed up my visa.

The Americans see Ian as a distinguished British colonel and almost snap to attention. As his stepdaughter, I'm granted a visa in no time.

I do worry if it's fair to leave Mummy, with her thinking I'll be back in a few weeks. She keeps reminding me I can't be married without her consent. She doesn't know that once I'm there, nothing on earth will make me return. I doubt my wedding will be the kind I always hoped for, but I have to sacrifice some dreams to get what I desire.

Anne is not at all happy. "Mummy will want me to go back home, and I want to stay with Granny."

"Tell her you will never go back to live with a man who destroyed all your belongings. Sorry, but I'm not changing my plans for anyone. I have to leave, or I never will."

I'm ripe for my departure from this underworld.

It's my last day in the Edificio Nervión. The last day I wake up in my room. The wall paint has faded to a dirty yellow, the white gauze curtains are gray and frowzy, but there's the little desk and the Olivetti Mummy gave me when I wrote my first book, and her hand-painted mirror in which I watched myself grow up, and my bookcase crammed with books that Anne will appropriate, and of course, my handcrafted bed that, like the mirror and bookcase, belonged to Mummy when she was young, and where I did most of my reading and a lot of my

317

crying. All are a part of me that I'm leaving. I spent some of the worst moments of my life in this room, yet I'm sad to leave it. How can I not miss a place where I felt so much emotion, good as well as bad?

I'm not sorry to leave Ian. But he was also a part of my growing up. All those years were overshadowed by his presence. All our efforts to do away with him. Scraping away at apricot pits. Anne smoothing his cream cheese with the Equanils in it. Sticking pins into his portrait and leaving a curse in his sock. He almost died because of the grated apricot pit. He could have died from the overdoses when we put Equanils in his food. Who would have suspected us? We were such nice little girls.

Anne comes to lunch, reluctantly. Ian has "graciously" agreed for her to enter "his" house. As far as he's concerned, it's fine with him if she prefers to live with Granny.

My bus departs at five, so Granny will be coming in a taxi to collect me and Mummy and Anne, at four-fifteen. By then Ian should be taking his afternoon nap.

Or so we think, but he's having a bad day. He stayed in the bedroom most of the morning and kept Mummy in there with him. Still in his dressing gown and pajamas, he lies on the sofa and gives Anne a curt hello when she arrives.

She makes a beeline for my room. "I see I'm not welcome. If it weren't your last day, I'd never have come."

"I'm sorry; I wish he hadn't chosen today to be difficult."

"I had an idea this might happen," she says, "so look what I brought as a going away present." A package of Equanils. "Just in case."

I feel a grin spread across my face. "We haven't tampered with his food for a while."

She has a mischievous smile. "Why not?"

We find a leftover cream cheese. How deftly Anne stuffs

it and smooths over the white surface so that it looks the same as before.

Usually the first thing Ian eats is his cheese, but today he says, "I'm not hungry," and when Mummy reminds him I'm leaving this afternoon, he snarls back at her, "I'm well aware that Pennie is leaving today. Are you forgetting that you have me to thank for making it possible?"

"Of course, Ian, and she's very grateful."

He bangs his fist so hard on the table the salt cellar overturns.

"Oh, Ian, that brings bad luck." Mummy grabs a pinch and throws it over her left shoulder. "Please don't make a scene on Pennie's last day."

"Can't you see I'm making an effort?" He sticks a spoonful of soup into his mouth. "You know I'm not well." His face twists and he goes, *aaargh*. "This is disgusting. The maid didn't heat it properly," and he throws down his spoon, spattering the table around him.

There's a remedy to that problem. "Let me fix your soup, Ian," and I grab his bowl, gesturing at Anne to follow me into the kitchen.

I reheat the soup while Anne grinds two Equanils into powder, and we stir them into the soup, along with a tablespoon of Worcester sauce.

"Here you are," I tell Ian.

He tries a little and nods. "This is more like it." Only now do I see he's finished off the cream cheese.

The phone rings. No one moves. Mummy yowls, "Someone answer it!"

I answer. It's Aunty Laura wishing me bon voyage. We're two minutes on the phone.

"Who was it?" Ian asks as I sit down.

Why not tell him? It's my last day. "Aunty Laura."

The veins on his face seem to stand out as he turns on Mummy. "How many times do I have to tell you I won't allow calls from that bitch in my home?"

"Don't you dare call my sister a bitch."

"I don't care if she's the Queen of England."

"It's my phone as well, and you have no right to dictate who can call me."

"I'll do whatever I want to in my own house," he sputters. "I'm master here."

"You are not my master," Mummy shouts, and they continue, with the usual exchange of inanities leading up to his clutching his throat, making gurgling sounds, and almost, though not quite, falling off his chair.

As he teeters on the brink of another fake attack, Mummy screams, "Ian, Ian!" and Mac starts barking. Leaning heavily on her, Ian staggers to the safety of the sofa.

"The same old act," Anne says under her breath.

Mummy entreats him not to die, her words and gestures an oft repeated performance. Why has she has never caught on? She screeches, "Children, get his pills; they're on his night table."

As we leave the room, I glance at my watch. Twenty-past-three. "He should be groggy by now," Anne says.

"Perhaps the Equanils weren't strong enough. Or he's become immune."

We take Mummy the pills and wait until half past three to remind her it's almost time to leave.

All at once Ian has an agonized expression. I can't tell if it's real or put on. "I'm not feeling well. Please, Baby, don't leave me alone."

Mummy tells him she really wants to see me off, and how can she let her daughter leave without a proper goodbye?

"Perhaps I will be the one you should say goodbye to," he says.

"Dear God, grant me the wisdom to know what to do," she says, in her usual flap, torn between his hold over her and her duty to us. There isn't a doubt in my mind what she will decide.

She puts on her expression of despair. "Will you forgive me, Pennie, if I don't see you off at the bus station? After all your grandmother and your sister will be there, and you are coming back in two weeks, aren't you?"

"Of course, Mummy, you saw my return ticket." Which I intend to cash in as soon as I arrive.

"You do understand why I can't see you off?"

I understand only too well. She will regret not seeing me off. She'll blame him for it, and they'll have a frightful row which, thank God, I won't be around to hear. I suppose in the end, I'm escaping from her inability to face facts as much as from his madness.

I tell her, "Don't worry, Mummy, I'll be all right." I should add, "Without you." But I don't. Ian's eyes are glazed, and he'll probably conk out shortly, though not before I'm out of the house. He won't do that because he's afraid Mummy might leave him alone, and he can't stand the thought. He's capable of killing himself just to spite her. Maybe he will when she walks out on him.

Mummy reminds me to take the chicken sandwiches and potato salad she made for me to eat during my trip. It's eighteen hours from here to the border, with a stop in Monterrey. A friend of hers, the district attorney in Laredo, will meet me there, and I'll spend tomorrow night with another friend in San Antonio. Then two more days to Milwaukee.

Goodbye to sweet, fat, noble Mac, the one good thing about Ian. Whoever said a dog was like its master? Or was there a side to Ian we didn't know?

A last look at Ian. I will remember him this way—aged, defeated, loony, drugged, crying "wolf, wolf"—so often that no one will care when it comes true—clinging to Mummy for all he's worth, and lying next to his one memory of greater times contained in the ostentatious, coffee-table display of his medals.

I kiss Mummy goodbye, and she insists on making the sign-of-the-cross over me. Downstairs, I say my farewell to the Edificio Nervión. I will not come here again.

The world beckons to me. Mummy is always saying I want to grasp life with both hands.

She's right.

I do.

EPILOGUE

Ten days after I left Mexico City, Mummy flew to Milwaukee. She was present when Rick and I were married a week later. We lasted two months together before I walked out. I moved to New York City and got a job in an ad agency, thus starting a thirty-year career in advertising. I went to live in England, became part of the Swinging London scene, and enjoyed a close relationship with my father. After five years, I returned to Mexico City, remarried, had two children, divorced, and lived there for thirty years until moving to San Diego, California in 2000. Over the years I have written eight books, including this one. Another memoir, *Don't Hang Up! On the Border of a New Start*, and a historical novel, *Coronada*, are set for publication in 2016.

Anne stayed in Mexico and married the handsome older brother Francisco, whom I met at Uncle Agustin's New Year's party when I was fifteen. They were married until his death on their fiftieth wedding anniversary. They had two children and six grandchildren. She went back to England for a visit when she was nineteen—eleven years after she left—and many times since then. Author of *In the Shadow of the Amates*, she divides her time between Mexico City and San Diego, California.

Two months after I left, Mummy filed for a divorce from Ian. She got her own place, and Anne, reluctantly, left Granny's and went to live with her. Mummy continued her teaching career. In her fifties, she got her teacher's degree at the University of Essex in the U.K. and became a professor of Applied Linguistics at the University of Mexico. She died at 82 from a stroke.

Ian continued to go see Mummy after their divorce and to

beg, plead, and threaten her to remarry him. She refused, and he remarried Aunt Ethel. Ten days later, he was found dead in bed. Long after his death, a friend confirmed that Ian had played a vital wartime role as a spymaster. Ian never talked or wrote about this in his autobiography.

Daddy gave up his inventions. Within ten years, catamarans—not his—were all the rage on the south coast of England. After losing Carlyon, he lived with Granny and Aunty Rena, and acquired an interest in metaphysics and out-of-body travel. Years later, I discovered his ship in WWII had been torpedoed and he spent several hours in the water singing nursery rhymes to bolster his spirits. The only war experience he talked about was being in the last great sea battle of Jutland in WWI when he was 18 years old. A psychiatrist said Daddy's apathy may well have been due to undiagnosed PTSD. He died of a massive heart attack at 80.

In retrospect, my Mexican grandmother was one of the toughest women I have known. Despite being almost blind, she worked as a professor at Mexico City College, ran the household, personally cared for her husband who had Parkinson's, and paid most of the bills. As a child, I took my mother's side against her, but I came to realize her true worth later in life. She lived to 93.

Aunt Carlota continued to be a great character. On her 80th birthday, she danced the Can-Can and she was still going strong into her nineties. She died at 94.

Aunty Laura had six children, five boys and a girl, and twelve grandchildren. She died at 76.

Uncle Artie and Claudia had a daughter and two grandsons. In later years, Uncle Artie, who had been in the D-Day landings with the 101st Airborne Division, dictated his WWII memoirs to me. He died at 87.

Grace Searle continued to be Mummy's one true friend in

Rustington and they corresponded until Grace's death in 1978.

Miguel remained a close friend for many years. He was a witness at Anne's civil wedding and, in 1963, he showed me around the north of Spain. He remained in a wheelchair until his death at 57.

Granny-in-England died in 1967. Aunty Rena lived to 95, and when she died, our Rustington link should have ended there. In 2010, Anne and I finally returned to our old home, the former Carlyon, 57 years after we left, when the current owners invited us to dinner on Anne's birthday. Thanks to Dee Carolin and Brian Wood.

ACKNOWLEDGMENTS

This book would never have happened without the support and encouragement from many friends and fellow writers who kept urging me on even when I had given up hope of seeing it in print.

My thanks to all of you who have helped me with *Getting Rid of Ian*:

Jennifer Clement and her writing group in Mexico City where this book took its first steps twenty-two years ago.

Marsh Cassady, friend and editor, who has accompanied me on my writing path almost from the start. Also, members of his writers group: Jim Kitchen (RIP), Barbara Sack, Anne Valadés, Nirmala Moorthy, Carl Nelson, Jill Limber, Ellen Snortland and Jo-Ann and Stan Middleman.

Members of my current writers group: Laurie Richards, Larry Edwards, Mike Irby, Kathy Foley, and Walter Karshat for their help with key chapters.

Katherine Porter, who edited and helped give shape to *Getting Rid of Ian*.

Special thanks to Laurie Richards who, as I have told her many times, is the best editor I know.

Barbara Sack, who catches those little mistakes that are so easy to overlook.

Larry Edwards, a fine editor, who gave this book a last go-over.

Maki Winkelmann and Julia Pitts for letting me stay in their lovely homes in Santa Fe, N.M. where I completed the first full draft of this book.

Marty Safir at Double M Graphics for his great cover design and for telling me that come hell or high water, he'd help me get this book published.

Lucia Gayon at *ComunicaSoluciones.com* for her help and unfailing good humor setting up the *Getting Rid of Ian* website for a very demanding client.

If you liked this book, please consider writing a short review and posting it on Amazon, Goodreads and/or other book sites. Reviews are very helpful to readers and are greatly appreciated by authors such as me. Whether or not you post a review, I'd be delighted to hear from you. Drop me an email and let me know what you thought. I may feature it or part of it on my blog or website.

gettingridofian.com

COMING IN 2016

What are the odds that a former top professional, 56, broke, homeless, and an invalid in Tijuana, Mexico can make a new start?

The medical treatment she sought in Tijuana is not working. She feels, as sung in a narco-corrido, "neither here nor there." She is a bird unable to fly. Out of place, separated from her life, mourning her affluent past, and unwilling to come to terms with her present.

A middle-aged has-been.

Who would bet on her?

After an operation restores her mobility, she crosses the border to San Diego and starts job hunting. Her background and experience count for nothing. As a last resort, she takes a job as an $8-an-hour phone room worker.

A newcomer in the U.S. and in the ranks of low-wage earners, she is out of her depth. In time, she will learn the ropes and become an expert.

She is, after all, a professional.

At 57, she feels young and vital. She finds unexpected happiness.

But this is not what she wants in life.

She is ready to face another challenge.

An entirely new career.

www.donthangupbook.com

Made in the USA
San Bernardino, CA
20 August 2019